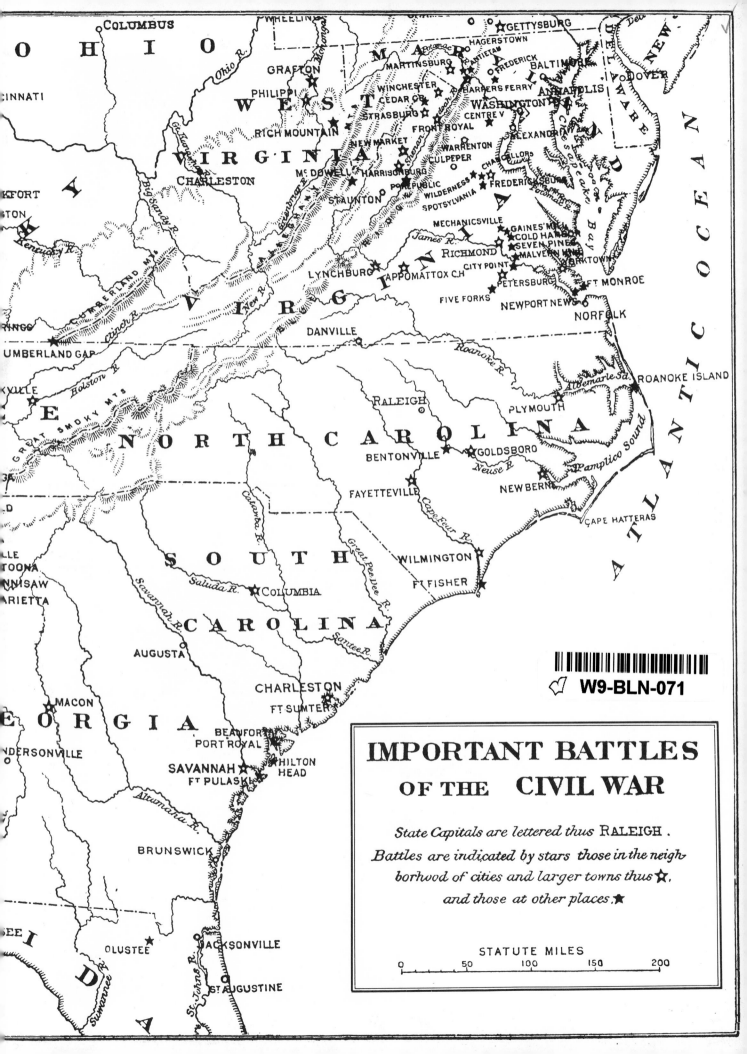

W9-BLN-071

IMPORTANT BATTLES
OF THE CIVIL WAR

State Capitals are lettered thus RALEIGH.

Battles are indicated by stars those in the neigh-
borhood of cities and larger towns thus ☆,
and those at other places ★

STATUTE MILES

0   50   100   150   200

BATTLE CHRONICLES
OF THE
CIVIL WAR

BATTLE CHRONICLES OF THE CIVIL WAR

SIX VOLUMES

BATTLE CHRONICLES
OF THE
CIVIL WAR
1861

JAMES M. McPHERSON, Editor

Princeton University

RICHARD GOTTLIEB, Managing Editor

Grey Castle Press

MACMILLAN PUBLISHING COMPANY
New York

COLLIER MACMILLAN PUBLISHERS
London

Text © 1989. *Civil War Times Illustrated*, a division of Cowles Magazines, Inc., Box 8200, Harrisburg, PA 17105.

Introduction, Transitions, Index and Format © 1989. Grey Castle Press, Inc., Lakeville, CT 06039.

Published by Macmillan Publishing Company
866 Third Avenue, New York, NY 10022

ILLUSTRATION CREDITS—Some sources are abbreviated as follows: B&L (*Battles and Leaders of the Civil War*), CWTI Collection (*Civil War Times Illustrated* Collection), HW (*Harper's Weekly*), LC (Library of Congress). Illustrations without credits are part of the *Civil War Times Illustrated* Collection.

Library of Congress Cataloging-in-Publication Data

Battle Chronicles of the Civil War.

    Includes bibliographies and indexes.
    Contents: 1. 1861—2.1862—3. 1863— [etc.]
    1. United States—History—Civil War, 1861–1865—Campaigns.   I. McPherson, James M.
E470.B29   1989   973.7'3   89-8316
ISBN 0-02-920661-8 (set)

Printed in the USA

EDITORIAL STAFF

Editor
James M. McPherson
Edwards Professor of American History
Princeton University

Managing Editor
Richard Gottlieb

Senior Editor
Jenny Elizabeth Tesar

Consulting Editors
John E. Stanchak
Jim Kushlan
Douglas C. Moul

Production
G&H Soho, Ltd.

Contents

Preface

One hundred and twenty-four years have passed since Appomattox and yet the Civil War is still with us. Thousands of Americans drill and march for reenactments of major battles which hundreds of thousands attend. Over a dozen magazines focus on this war, and each year hundreds of books about the war are published. While Jefferson Davis' birthday is still celebrated in some Southern states, millions of Northerners travel to visit Gettysburg each year.

BATTLE CHRONICLES OF THE CIVIL WAR makes available, for the first time in recent history, a multi-volume chronological history of the Civil War that focuses on the military campaigns. All significant battles of the war—from major events such as the Battle of Antietam to smaller but ultimately crucial encounters such as that at Mobile Bay—are described in detail.

The set is arranged chronologically for Volumes 1 through 5; Volume 6 contains biographies of the major leaders of the war as well as a comprehensive index.

BATTLE CHRONICLES OF THE CIVIL WAR contains approximately 100 articles written by 40 authors. Additionally, the set contains hundreds of extensive quotations and full text from original source material including letters, autobiographies, and court records. Much of the material included herein is drawn from the archives of *Civil War Times Illustrated*, which since 1962 has been the leading publication featuring original material on the Civil War.

James M. McPherson, Edwards Professor of American History at Princeton University, edited the work. He has written an introduction and transitional articles between chapters. The result is a comprehensive and coherent overview of the war.

Professor McPherson is the author of *Battle Cry of Freedom*, which won the 1988 Pulitzer Prize for History. It is part of the *Oxford History of The United States*, edited by C. Vann Woodward.

BATTLE CHRONICLES OF THE CIVIL WAR is a reference work aimed at a wide audience: Students in secondary schools, colleges, and graduate schools; teachers of history; and the general public. A bibliography prepared by Professor McPherson should aid the reader interested in continuing study of the Civil War.

An especial note of thanks is due Alan Humason and John Stanchak and their staffs at *Civil War Times Illustrated*.

Richard Gottlieb
Managing Editor

Contributors

Ambrose, Stephen E. Professor of History; Director, The Institute for the Comparative Study of Public Policy, University of New Orleans. Former associate editor, *Civil War Times Illustrated.* Author of numerous books on American history including *Crazy Horse & Custer; Duty, Honor, Country: A History of West Point; Eisenhower; Ike: Abilene to Berlin; Nixon: The Education of a Politician.*

Bearss, Edwin C. Historian, National Park Service. Author, *Decision in Mississippi; Steele's Retreat from Camden; Rebel Victory at Vicksburg; Hardluck Ironclad; Fort Smith: Little Gibralter on the Arkansas.* Editor, *A Southern Record; A Louisiana Confederate; Memoirs of a Confederate.*

Brown, Colonel Campbell H. Former Executive Director, Tennessee Civil War Centennial Commission.

Brown, D. (Dee) Alexander Librarian, University of Illinois. Author of numerous books including *Bury My Heart at Wounded Knee; Action at Beecher Island; The Galvanized Yankees; The Gentle Tamers: Women of the Old Wild West; Showdown at Little Big Horn;* and *Grierson's Raid.*

Castel, Albert Professor of History, Western Michigan University. Author, *General Sterling Price and the Civil War in the West; A Frontier State at War: Kansas, 1861-65; William Clarke Quantrill: His Life and Times; The Presidency of Andrew Johnson.*

Crewdson, Robert L. Contributor to *Civil War Times Illustrated* and other publications.

Cullen, Joseph P. Former Chairman, Publications Committee, Eastern National Park & Monument Association. Author of *The Peninsula Campaign* and numerous articles on the Civil War and general American history.

Davis, William C. Editor in Chief, National Historical Society. Former editor, *Civil War Times Illustrated.* Author or editor of over 20 books dealing with the Civil War and Southern history including *Breckinridge: Statesman, Soldier, Symbol; The Orphan Brigade; Duel Between the First Ironclads; Fighting Men of the Civil War; The Battle of New Market;* and the 6-volume photographic series *The Image of War 1861-1865.*

Fowler, Robert H. Founder and Chairman of the Board, Historical Times, Inc. Author of *Jim Mundy* and other historical novels.

Grimsley, Mark Doctoral student in military and diplomatic history, Ohio State University.

Horn, Stanley F. Former Chairman, Tennessee Civil War Centennial Commission. Author of numerous works on the Civil War including *The Army of Tennessee* and *The Decisive Battle of Nashville.*

Jones, Virgil C. Congressional Administrative Assistant. Author, *The Civil War at Sea* (3 volumes); *Eight Hours Before Richmond; Gray Ghosts and Rebel Raiders; Ranger Mosby; The Hatfields and the McCoys;* and *Birth of Liberty: The Story of the James River.*

Joynt, Robert H. Instructor of American History, Westminster Academy (FL).

Julian, Colonel Allen Phelps Former Director, Atlanta Historical Society. Author, *MacArthur, The Life of A General.*

Kelly, Dennis Ranger, Kennesaw Mountain National Battlefield.

Klein, Maury Former Associate Professor of History, University of Rhode Island. Author, biography of E.P. Alexander.

Kurtz, Wilbur G., Sr. Former artist and historian. Restorer, Cyclorama painting of the Battle of Atlanta. Technical advisor to the film "Gone With the Wind."

Luvaas, Jay Professor of Military History, United States Army War College. Author, *The Military Legacy of the Civil War.*

McDonough, James Lee Professor of History, Auburn University. Author, *Schofield: Union General in the Civil War and Reconstruction; Shiloh—In Hell Before Night; Stones River—Bloody Winter in Tennessee; Chattanooga—A Death Grip on the Confederacy.* Co-author, *Five Tragic Hours: The Battle of Franklin* and *Sky Riders—History of the 327/401 Glider Infantry.*

McMurry, Richard Adjunct Professor of History, North Carolina State University. Co-editor, *Rank and File: Civil War Essays in Honor of Bell Irvin Wiley.* Author, *John Bell Hood.*

McPherson, James M. Edwards Professor of American History, Princeton University. Author of many articles and six books on the Civil War era including *The Abolitionist Legacy: From Reconstruction to the NAACP; The Negro's Civil War: How American Negroes Felt and Acted During the*

War for the Union; Struggle for Equality: Abolitionists and the Negro in the Civil War and Reconstruction; and *Battle Cry of Freedom: The Civil War Era,* winner of the Pulitzer Prize for history.

Miller, Edward Special Projects Engineer, Propulsion Dynamics. Part of the team of scientists that identified the *Monitor* and actively involved with the state of North Carolina in several expeditions to the ship's site. Author, *USS Monitor, The Ship That Launched A Modern Navy.*

Morsberger, Robert E. Professor of English, California State Polytechnic University.

Nash, Howard P. Former Librarian, Old Dartmouth Historical Society and Whaling Museum.

Nye, Colonel Wilbur S. Former Managing Editor, *Civil War Times Illustrated* and *American History Illustrated.* Author, *Carbine and Lance: The Story of Old Fort Sill; Plains Indian Raiders: The Final Phases of Warfare from the Arkansas to the Red River.*

Oates, Stephen B. Paul Murray Kendall Professor of Biography and Professor of History, University of Massachusetts at Amherst. Author, *To Purge This Land With Blood: A Biography of John Brown; The Fires of Jubilee: Nat Turner's Fierce Rebellion; With Malice Toward None: The Life of Abraham Lincoln; Let the Trumpet Sound: The Life of Martin Luther King, Jr.;* and *William Faulkner: The Man and the Artist.*

Oder, Broech N. Chairman, Department of History, Santa Catalina School for Girls. Contributor, *The Historical Times Illustrated Encyclopedia of the Civil War.*

Robertson, James I., Jr. C.P. Miles Professor of History, Virginia Polytechnic Institute and State University. Editor, *The Civil War Letters of General Robert McAllister.* Author of numerous books on the Civil War including *The Stonewall Brigade; General A.P. Hill;* and *Soldiers Blue and Gray.*

Sears, Stephen Author, *Landscape Turned Red: The Battle of Antietam; George B. McClellan: The Young Napoleon;* and *The Century Collection of Civil War Art.*

Stackpole, General Edward J. Former Publisher, *Civil War Times Illustrated* and *American History Illustrated.* Author, *They Met at Gettysburg; Drama on the Rappahannock: The Fredericksburg Campaign; Chancellorsville: Lee's Greatest Battle; From Cedar Mountain to Antietam;* and *Sheridan in the Shenandoah.*

Stinson, Dwight E. District Ranger, Chesapeake & Ohio Canal National Historical Park. Former historian, Harper's Ferry National Historical Park.

Sword, Wiley Author, *Shiloh: Bloody April; President Washington's Indian War, Firepower from Abroad;* and *Sharpshooter: Hiram Berdan, His Famous Sharpshooters and Their Sharps Rifles.*

Thomas, Emory Professor of History, University of Georgia. Author, *The Confederacy as a Revolutionary Experience; The Confederate State of Richmond: A Biography of the Capital; The Confederate Nation, 1861-1865; Bold Dragon: The Life of J.E.B. Stuart;* and *The American War and Peace, 1869-1877.*

Tucker, Glenn Correspondent for the New York *World* at the White House during the Wilson, Harding, and Coolidge administrations. Author of numerous books on the Civil War and other phases of American history, particularly the early American Navy. His books include *Chickamauga: Bloody Battle in the West; High Tide at Gettysburg;* and *Tecumseh: Vision of Glory.*

Walker, Hugh F. Former Feature Editor, Nashville *Tennessean,* and official historian of Metro Nashville and Davidson County. Author, *Tennessee Tales.*

Wert, Jeffry History teacher, Penns Valley (PA) High School. Author, *From Winchester to Cedar Creek: The Shenandoah Campaign of 1864.* Regular contributor, *Civil War Times Illustrated.*

Westwood, Howard C. Contributor to *Civil War Times Illustrated* and other historical publications.

Wiley, Bell I. Former Professor of History, Emory University. Author or editor of more than 20 books, including *The Life of Johnny Reb; The Life of Billy Yank; Southern Negroes, 1861-1865; The Road to Appomattox; Confederate Women;* and *The Common Soldier of the Civil War.*

Williams, T. Harry Former Boyd Professor of American History, Louisiana State University. Author of numerous books and articles on American history including *Lincoln and His Generals; The History of American Wars; Huey Long; Lincoln and the Radicals;* and *P.G.T. Beauregard: Napoleon in Gray.*

Young, John Russell Newspaperman and president of the Board of Commissioners, Washington, D.C., during the late 1800s.

America's Bloodiest War

by James M. McPherson

The Civil War was the most dramatic, violent, and fateful experience in American history. At least 620,000 soldiers lost their lives in this war. An unknown number of civilians also died from disease or hunger or exposure brought on by the disruption and destruction of the war in the South. More Americans were killed in the Civil War than in all of the country's other wars combined. The number of casualties in a single day at the battle of Antietam (September 17, 1862) was four times the number of American casualties at the Normandy beaches on D-Day, June 6, 1944. Twice as many American soldiers were killed in action that day at Antietam as in all of the other wars fought by the United States in the nineteenth century *combined*.

How did this happen? Why did Americans go to war against each other with a ferocity unmatched in the Western world between the end of the Napoleonic Wars in 1815 and the beginning of World War I in 1914? The origins of the Civil War lay in the outcome of another war a dozen years earlier. The peace treaty with Mexico in 1848 transferred 700,000 square miles of Mexican territory to the United States and confirmed the Rio Grande as the border between Mexico and Texas. The spectacular victory of American forces in the Mexican War, however, fulfilled the prediction made by Yankee philosopher Ralph Waldo Emerson when the war began in 1846: "The

"The political hostilities of a generation were now face to face with weapons instead of words," said Confederate General Pierre G.T. Beauregard, neatly summarizing the evolution in the conflict between those who championed slavery and those who wanted to abolish the practice. (CWTI Collection)

United States will conquer Mexico, but it will be as the man swallows the arsenic, which brings him down in turn. Mexico will poison us."

The poison was slavery—not slavery in the territory conquered from Mexico, for that country had abolished the institution a generation earlier—but American slavery, which southern politicians desired to plant in the new territories. Anti-slavery northerners, however, wanted to keep slavery out. They had the votes to pass the Wilmot Proviso (a resolution introduced by Congressman David Wilmot of Pennsylvania) in the House of Representatives, stating that slavery should be excluded from all territories acquired from Mexico. Southern senators defeated this resolution when it came before them. Their leader, John C. Calhoun of South Carolina, offered instead a series of resolutions affirming that slaveholders had the constitutional right to take their slave property into any United States territory they wished.

These opposing views set the stage for a crisis when gold was discovered in 1848 in California, potentially the richest of the regions acquired from Mexico. One hundred thousand gold seekers poured into California in 1849. To achieve some degree of law and order, they organized a state government and petitioned Congress for admission as the thirty-first state. This petition met fierce resistance from southerners, for California's constitution prohibited slavery. The crisis intensified when President Zachary Taylor encouraged the huge territory of New Mexico (which included most of the present-day states of New Mexico, Arizona, Utah, Nevada, and Colorado) to apply for statehood without slavery, too.

Proslavery southerners vowed to secede from the Union rather than accept this violation of their professed right to have slavery in these territories. "If, by your legislation, you seek to drive us from the territories of California and New Mexico," thundered Robert Toombs of Georgia to northern congressmen, "*I am for disunion.*" Albert Gallatin Brown of Mississippi asked the North "*to give us our rights*" in California; "if you refuse, I am for taking them by armed occupation." The controversy in Congress became so heated that Senator Henry S. Foote drew a loaded revolver during a debate and his colleague Jefferson Davis challenged an Illinois congressman to a duel. The American nation seemed to hang together by a thread, with armed conflict between North and South a real possibility in 1850.

But calmer heads prevailed, and a showdown was averted by the Compromise of 1850. This series of laws admitted California as a free state but left it to the settlers themselves in the remainder of the Mexican cession, divided into the territories of New Mexico and Utah, whether they would have slavery. (Both territories did legalize slavery during the 1850's, but few slaves were taken there.) At the same time the slave trade in the District of Columbia was abolished, ending the shame (in northern eyes) of the buying and selling of human beings within sight of the White House and the Capitol. But the South was compensated with a tough new fugitive slave law that empowered federal marshals backed by the army to recover slaves who had escaped into free states and carry them back into slavery.

The Compromise of 1850 did not resolve the sectional crisis. It merely postponed the final break for a decade. During that decade the conflict escalated to larger proportions and a higher pitch of emotional intensity. The fugitive slave law did more to anger northerners, who watched helplessly as black people, some of whom had lived in their communities for years, were returned by force to slavery, than it did to reassure southerners that Yankees would respect their property rights. In an attempt to bring more slave states into the Union, southerners agitated for the purchase of Cuba from Spain and the acquisition of additional territory in Central America. Private armies of "filibusters," composed mainly of southerners, even tried to invade Cuba and Nicaragua to overthrow their governments and bring these regions into the United States. Disputes about these adventures exacerbated North-South tensions.

But nothing did more to polarize slave and free states than the Kansas-Nebraska

Act of 1854 and the subsequent guerrilla war between pro- and anti-slavery partisans in Kansas territory. The region that became the territories of Kansas and Nebraska was part of the Louisiana Purchase, acquired by the United States from France in 1803. Three slave states had come into the Union from the Louisiana Purchase— Louisiana, Arkansas, and Missouri—and one free state, Iowa. When Missouri had applied for statehood in 1819, northern congressmen tried to bar slavery there. This precipitated a controversy that was settled in 1820 by the Missouri Compromise, whereby Missouri came in as a slave state but slavery was banned in the remainder of the Louisiana Purchase north of the latitude of 36° 30′ (the southern border of Missouri). Regarded by northerners as an inviolable compact, the Missouri Compromise lasted for thirty-four years. But in 1854 southerners broke it by forcing Stephen A. Douglas of Illinois, chairman of the Senate Committee on Territories and leader of the northern Democrats, to agree to the repeal of the ban on slavery north of 36° 30′ as the price for southern support for the creation of Kansas and Nebraska territories.

Douglas caved in to southern pressure even though he knew it would "raise a hell of a storm" in the North. It certainly did. Indeed, the storm was so powerful that it swept away many northern Democrats and gave rise to the Republican party, which pledged to keep slavery out of Kansas and all other territories. One of the most eloquent spokesmen for this new party was an Illinois lawyer named Abraham Lincoln. Like many northern people, Lincoln had always considered slavery to be an institution "founded on both injustice and bad policy. . . . There CAN be no MORAL RIGHT in the enslaving of one man by another." But like most northerners, he recognized the constitutional right of slavery in the states where it already existed. Nevertheless, it should be restricted to those states and not allowed to take root in any territories. The great "moral wrong and injustice" of the Kansas-Nebraska Act, said Lincoln, was that it opened territory previously closed to slavery, thus putting the institution "on the high road to extension and perpetuity" instead of restricting it as the first step toward persuading the states where it existed gradually to abolish it.

"The monstrous injustice of slavery," said Lincoln in 1854, deprives our republican example of its just influence in the world—enables the enemies of free institutions, with plausibility, to taunt us as hypocrites." Lincoln and the other members of the new Republican party, which carried most of the northern states in the presidential election of 1856, were convinced that the growing polarization between the free and slave states was an "irrepressible conflict" between social systems based on free labor and slave labor. The United States, said Lincoln in 1858, at the beginning of his famous campaign against Douglas for election to the Senate, was a house divided between slavery and freedom. But "'a house divided against itself cannot stand.' I believe this government cannot endure, permanently half *slave* and half *free*. . . . Either the *opponents* of slavery, will arrest the further spread of it, and place it where the public mind shall rest in the belief that it is in the course of ultimate extinction; or its *advocates* will push it forward, til it shall become alike lawful in all the States, *old* as well as new—*North* as well as *South*."

Douglas won the senatorial election in 1858. But two years later, running against a Democratic party split into northern and southern halves, Lincoln won the presidency by carrying every northern state on a platform pledging to restrict the further expansion of slavery. This was the first time in more than a generation that the South had lost effective control of the national government. Southerners saw the handwriting on the wall. The North had a substantial and growing majority of the American population. So long as slavery remained a sore, festering issue—so long as the United States remained a house divided—the antislavery Republican party would control the national government. And most southerners feared that the "Black Republicans"—as they contemptuously labeled the party of Lincoln—would enact policies that would indeed place slavery on the road to "ultimate extinction."

So to preserve slavery as the basis of their "way of life," the seven lower-South states seceded one by one during the winter of 1860–1861. Before Lincoln took office on March 4, 1861, these seven states met in Montgomery, Alabama, adopted a Constitution for the Confederate States of America, and formed a provisional government with Jefferson Davis as president. As they seceded, these states seized the national arsenals, forts, and other property within their borders—with the significant exception of Fort Sumter in the harbor of Charleston, South Carolina. When Lincoln took his oath to "preserve, protect, and defend" the United States and its Constitution, the "united" states had ceased to exist.

Secession transformed the principal issue of the sectional conflict from the future of slavery to the survival of the Union itself. By 1862 Lincoln would become convinced that slavery must die so that the Union might live. But in March 1861 the problem was one of stemming further secessions by the eight slave states still in the Union (four of them went out after the firing on Fort Sumter). So Lincoln soft-pedaled the slavery issue for a time and concentrated on measures to suppress what he termed an "insurrection."

Lincoln was determined not to accept the legitimacy of secession. "The central idea pervading this struggle," he said in 1861, "is the necessity . . . of proving that popular government is not an absurdity. We must settle this question now, whether in a free government the minority have the right to break up the government whenever they choose." Four years later, looking back over the bloody chasm of war, Lincoln said in his second inaugural address that one side in the controversy of 1861 "would *make* war rather than let the nation survive; and the other would *accept* war rather than let it perish. And the war came."

It started at Fort Sumter, as described in this volume. And four years to the day after the American flag was lowered in surrender at Fort Sumter on April 14, 1861, it was raised again in triumph to celebrate Union victory in the Civil War—a victory that preserved the nation and purged it of slavery. No longer was the United States a house divided—at least not by slavery or secession.

The pages and volumes that follow narrate the history of America's bloodiest and most momentous war. The principal focus is on the military campaigns and battles of the war. But the political, economic, social, and diplomatic dimensions of the conflict are also treated, in order to provide a context to highlight the larger meaning of those fateful battles. This narrative will shed light on a question almost as controversial as those that sparked the war itself: Why did the North win?

This question has elicited many different answers during the century and a quarter since the shooting stopped. For a long time the most popular answer in the South was the one advanced by Robert E. Lee himself in the farewell address to his soldiers at Appomattox: "The Army of Northern Virginia has been compelled to yield to overwhelming numbers and resources." Or as another proud Virginian expressed it: "They never whipped us, Sir, unless they were four to one. If we had anything like a fair chance, or less disparity of numbers, we should have won our cause and established our independence!" This explanation enabled southerners to preserve pride in the courage and skill of Confederate soldiers, to reconcile defeat with their sense of honor, even to maintain faith in the righteousness of their cause while admitting that it had been lost. And many northerners, while believing in the righteousness of *their* cause, agreed with this "overwhelming numbers and resources" explanation for northern victory. They could cite Napoleon's maxim that in war God is always on the side of the heaviest battalions.

This interpretation has a superficial plausibility. The North had two and one-half times the South's population, three times its railroad capacity, nine times its industrial production, and so on. "Surely in view of the disparity of resources," one northern historian has written, "it would have taken a miracle to enable the South to win." But

Both armies had their share of brilliant leaders and valiant soldiers, their tales of brilliant heroics. And both suffered enormous tolls in numbers dead and injured. (CWTI Collection)

would it have? While the overwhelming-numbers-and-resources interpretation did credit to southern military skill and courage in holding out for so long against such great odds, it seemed to do little credit to their intelligence. After all, southern leaders in 1861 were well aware of their disadvantages in numbers and resources. Yet they went to war confident of victory. Were they simple-minded? Inexcusably arrogant? As they reflected on this, many southerners and historians concluded that overwhelming numbers and resources did not explain northern victory after all. History was full of examples of a country winning a war against greater odds than the Confederacy faced. The foremost example for Americans of the Civil War generation was of course the United States itself in its war of independence against mighty Britain. Other precedents came readily to southern minds in 1861: the Netherlands against Spain in the sixteenth century; Greece against Turkey in the 1820's. And Americans in the late twentieth century who remember Vietnam are well aware that victory does not always ride with the heaviest battalions.

In the Civil War the North had to invade and conquer the South and destroy its armies in order to win. The South, by contrast, fought on the strategic defensive to protect its territory from conquest and preserve its armies from annihilation. To "win" the war the Confederacy did not have to invade and conquer the North; it needed only to hold out long enough to force the other side to the conclusion that the price of conquering the South and annihilating its armies was too high, as Britain had concluded in 1781 and as the United States concluded with respect to Vietnam in 1972. Most southerners thought in 1861 that their resources were sufficient to win on these terms. Most outside observers agreed, including the leading military experts in Europe. A writer in the London *Times* declared early in the conflict that "no war of independence ever terminated unsuccessfully except where the disparity of force was far greater than it is in this case. . . . Just as England during the revolution had to give up conquering the colonies so the North will have to give up conquering the South."

The overwhelming-numbers-and-resources argument has lost favor among most historians. They recognize that northern superiority in manpower and resources was a *necessary* but not *sufficient* cause of victory—that is, the North could not have won without that superiority, but it alone does not explain Union victory. But then, what does? Many recent interpretations have focused on one variant or another of a "lack of will" interpretation of Confederate defeat. Most such interpretations have emphasized internal divisions of interest or opinion within the Confederacy between slaveowners and non-slaveowners, between upcountry and tidewater, between proponents of state's rights and of centralized power, between supporters and opponents of conscription, certain war taxes, suspensions of certain civil liberties, or personality conflicts between Jefferson Davis and prominent political and military leaders. Other interpretations have argued that the South had a weak commitment to Confederate nationalism, pointing out that many southerners opposed secession in 1861 and that some of them continued to harbor reservations about the Confederate cause through the war. Thus, in the words of several historians, "the Confederacy succumbed to internal rather than external causes." The South lost because "its people did not will hard enough and long enough to win. . . . Lack of will constituted the decisive deficiency in the Confederate arsenal."

There are three problems with these interrelated "internal divisions" and "lack of will" interpretations. First, the North was at least as badly divided over many of the same issues as was the South. And while northerners were not divided between slaveowners and non-slaveowners, they *were* divided between Republicans and Democrats over the issue whether the war ought to be fought to abolish slavery. This issue came close to causing the northern war effort to founder on more than one occasion. As for a lack of will stemming from weak nationalism, a reading of the letters and diaries of soldiers and civilians on both sides should convince anyone that on the average, southerners expressed a fiercer patriotism, a more passionate dedication to "the Cause," a greater determination to die in the last ditch, than northerners did. Despite facing fewer hardships and less suffering than southerners did, the northern people came closer to throwing in the towel several times. If the North had lost the war—which almost happened more than once—internal divisions and lack of will would provide a more plausible explanation for Union defeat than it does for Confederate defeat.

Second, southern nationalism and will to win were stronger and internal divisions less serious than they had been in the United States of 1776. Yet the Americans won their war of independence and the southerners did not. This suggests that we must look elsewhere for an answer. Third, when the *lack* of will thesis is closely analyzed it turns out to focus mainly on a *loss* of will. These are two different things. A people at war whose armies are destroyed or captured, whose railroads are wrecked, factories and cities burned, ports seized, countryside occupied, and crops laid waste quite naturally lose their will to continue the fight, in large part because they have lost the means to do so. This was what happened to the South under the continual pounding and destruction by Grant, Sherman, Sheridan, and Thomas in 1864–65. *Loss* of will was a consequence of defeat rather than *lack* of will being a cause of it.

Another category of explanations for northern victory focuses on military and political leadership. In this interpretaton the North had evolved a stronger set of military commanders by 1864 than the South, several of whose ablest generals (Albert Sidney Johnston, Stonewall Jackson, and J.E.B. Stuart) had been killed. This interpretation may be true, but legions of southern historians would challenge the notion that Grant was a better commander than Lee, Sheridan than Forrest, Sherman than Johnston. These northern generals appear to have been better because they won, but it remains unclear whether they won because they were better. And in any case, even if the Union did have better commanders in the last year or two of the war, it had also had its fainthearts and blunderers, its McClellan and Pope and Burnside and Hooker who nearly lost the war to superior Confederate generalship in 1862 and 1863.

Another focus on the leadership interpretation enjoys wider support. One historian, a southerner, put it this way: "If the Union and Confederacy had exchanged presidents with one another, the Confederacy might have won its independence." This puts the case a bit too strongly. But a fairly broad consensus does exist among historians that Lincoln was more eloquent than Davis in expressing war aims, more successful in communicating with the people, more skillful as a political leader in keeping factions working together for the war effort, better able to endure criticism and work with his critics to achieve a common goal. Lincoln was flexible, pragmatic, with a sense of humor to smooth relationships and help him survive the stress of his job; Davis was austere, rigid, humorless, with the type of personality that readily made enemies. Lincoln had a strong physical constitution; Davis suffered ill health and was frequently prostrated by sickness. Lincoln picked good administrative subordinates and knew how to delegate authority to them; Davis went through five secretaries of war in four years; he spent a great deal of time and energy on petty administrative details that he should have left to subordinates. A disputatious man, Davis sometimes seemed to prefer winning an argument to winning the war; Lincoln was happy to lose an argument if it would help win the war.

But even this may not explain northern victory. Lincoln made some mistakes as a war leader. He went through a half-dozen failures as commanders in the eastern theater before he found the right general. Some of his other military appointments and stategic decisions could justly be criticized. And as late as the summer of 1864, when the war seemed to be going badly for the North, Lincoln came under enormous pressure to negotiate peace with the Confederacy, which would have been tantamount to admitting northern defeat. He resisted this pressure, but at what appeared to be the cost of reelection to the presidency. If the election had been held in August 1864 instead of November, Lincoln would have lost. He would thus have gone down in history as an also-ran, a loser unequal to the challenge of the greatest crisis in the American experience. And Jefferson Davis might have gone down in history as the great leader of a war of independence, the architect of a new nation, the George Washington of the southern Confederacy.

That this did not happen was owing to events on the battlefield—Sherman's capture of Atlanta and Sheridan's victories in the Shenandoah Valley, which turned the war around from bloody stalemate to northern victory. This assured Lincoln's reelection, which in turn ensured that the government would fight on to unconditional victory. These events suggest the true explanation for Union triumph in the war: crucial military victories at critical times. Sweeping generalizations like superior numbers and resources, southern divisions or lack of will, or better northern leadership all overlook this dimension of *contingency*, this truth that events on the battlefield on several occasions might have gone the other way, and that if they had the course and outcome of the war might have been quite different. These generalizations imply the inevitability of Union victory. But a study of the campaigns and battles chronicled in these volumes will convince the reader that *there was nothing inevitable* about northern victory in the Civil War. At numerous points things could have gone altogether differently.

Once we recognize this dimension of contingency, we can identify four major turning points in the war. The first came in the summer of 1862 when the offensives of Jackson and Lee in Virginia and Bragg and Kirby Smith in Kentucky arrested the momentum of a seemingly imminent Union victory. This prolonged and intensified the war and created the potential for Confederate success, which appeared imminent before each of the next three turning points. The first of these occurred in the fall of 1862, when battles at Antietam and Perryville blunted Confederate invasions, forestalled European mediation and recognition of the South, perhaps prevented a Democratic victory in the northern congressional elections that might have inhibited Lincoln's ability to carry on the war, and set the stage for the Emancipation Proclamation which enlarged the scope and purpose of the war. The third critical point came in

The bloody Battle of Antietam in 1862 was one of four major turning points in the Civil War. (Library of Congress)

the summer and fall of 1863 when Gettysburg, Vicksburg, and Chattanooga turned the tide toward ultimate northern victory. But one more reversal of that tide seemed possible in the summer of 1864 when appalling Union casualties and apparent lack of progress, especially in Virginia, brought the North to the brink of peace negotiations and the election of a Democratic president. But Sherman and Sheridan turned the tide one last time. Only then did it become possible to speak of the inevitability of northern victory.

These battle chronicles will help the reader understand the numerous points of contingency, the turning points that determined the ultimate outcome of the war. The best way to understand why the North won (or the South lost) the Civil War is to learn how and why its campaigns and battles began, developed, and ended. The pages that follow tell this story.

1861—AN OVERVIEW

Federal thrusts at the perimeters of the Confederacy characterized the fighting during 1861. Only one major battle occurred because neither side was prepared for—nor convinced of—the necessity for a major confrontation.

Capitalizing on Union sentiment in the extreme western portions of Virginia, Federal forces moved into that region from Ohio. Small Federal victories at Philippi (June 3), Rich Mountain (July 11), and Carrick's Ford (July 13) against green Confederate troops paved the way for that area ultimately in 1863 to become the new state of West Virginia. While those Federal troops were enjoying success, another contingent met a sharp reverse. Early in June 1861, a Massachusetts politician-turned-general, Benjamin F. Butler, started from Fort Monroe up the Virginia peninsula toward Richmond. Butler's advance got as far as Big Bethel Church, west of Yorktown, where on June 6 a makeshift Confederate force launched an uncoordinated attack that nevertheless had enough velocity to send the Federals in flight back to Hampton Roads.

The loudest and most persistent of Union battle cries during the Civil War was: "On to Richmond!" During the four years of conflict, six major Federal offensives were undertaken for the sole purpose of capturing the Confederate (and Virginia) Capital. The first attempt began midway in July 1861. Bowing to demands for action from Washington authorities, Major General Irvin McDowell moved southward across the Potomac River with an army of 35,000 men, mostly three-month volunteers. To

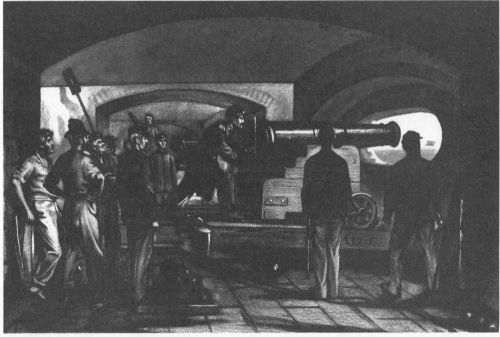

Fort Sumter: Captain Abner Doubleday prepares to fire the first Union shot of the war, aiming at the Iron Battery, from which the first Confederate shot was fired. (CWTI Collection)

Hampton Roads, Virginia, the channel through which the waters of the James River flow into Chesapeake Bay, with Fort Monroe in the foreground. (U.S. Army Military History Institute)

First Manassas (Bull Run), July 21, 1861, which many hoped would settle the dispute between North and South. Instead, it was but a preview of bitter fighting to come. (CWTI Collection)

General Nathaniel Lyon's charge at the Battle of Wilson's Creek on August 10, 1861. His death in the thick of the fighting demoralized his Union soldiers. (CWTI Collection)

protect his flank and rear during the advance on Richmond, McDowell had first to seize the vital railroad junction at Manassas.

Confederate General P. G. T. Beauregard learned of McDowell's intentions from Washington espionage agent Mrs. Rose Greenhow and others. He quickly positioned his equally untested 30,000 recruits north of the Junction. On a sultry Sunday, July 21, the Federals assaulted in force by attempting to overwhelm the Confederate left flank. The attacks were initially successful. The Confederate left crumbled in disorder back to the crest of Henry House Hill, where the Virginia brigade of Thomas J. Jackson withstood repeated attacks with the firmness of a stone wall. The arrival of fresh Confederate troops from the Shenandoah Valley turned the tide. The first "rebel yell" echoed across the fields as Southerners drove back McDowell's army in a disorganized retreat. Federal losses were 2,708 men; Confederate, 1,982.

While Southerners basked in the glory of the "great victory" won at First Manassas, and became more convinced that the Yankees could not and would not fight, the North resolutely girded itself for full-scale war. Lincoln named George B. McClellan, 35, as the new army commander and gave him free rein to raise an army of 100,000 or more soldiers. Such a host would be the largest fighting force ever seen in the Western Hemisphere.

Federal probes also occurred in the military theater west of the Appalachian Mountains. On August 10, a blueclad force attacked Confederates at Wilson's Creek, near Springfield, Missouri. The Federals suffered a defeat often termed the "Bull Run of the West." They also lost their commander, the promising Nathaniel Lyon, who was killed at the height of the fighting. On November 7, a small Federal army under an unknown general named Ulysses S. Grant managed to hold its own in a collision with Confederates at Belmont, Missouri.

One of the final actions in Virginia during 1861 was a small affair with far-reaching consequences. On October 21, Confederates ambushed a Federal reconnoitering force at Ball's Bluff, a Potomac landmark near Leesburg. The Federals lost over 921 men, including twenty-three officers captured. Numbered among the 234 Federals killed was Oregon Senator Edward D. Baker, commander of the expedition and a close

22

The fighting at Ball's Bluff, a 100-foot bank on the Virginia side of the Potomac River. The action of October 21, 1861, was a humiliating disaster for the North. (Library of Congress)

Bombardment of the forts at Port Royal on November 7, 1861. After only four hours of firing the Union navy secured this fine harbor on the south Atlantic coast. (CWTI Collection)

friend of Lincoln's. The "Ball's Bluff Disaster" sparked the creation of the Committee on the Conduct of the War, a watchdog Congressional agency that scrutinized closely all Federal military movements thereafter.

Largely overlooked in the big picture of war were inroads made in the South by Union naval forces. The fall of Port Royal, South Carolina, on November 7 gave the Federals their first toehold on the South Atlantic coast. Preparations were then undertaken for the seizure of Cape Hatteras, North Carolina, and the eventual recapture of the large naval base at Norfolk, Virginia. And with each month of the war, the Navy strengthened its blockade of the Southern coast.

—James I. Robertson, Jr.

THE BOMBARDMENT OF FORT SUMTER

by Albert Castel

In 1846 Congressman Jefferson Davis of Mississippi presented to the House of Representatives a resolution calling for the replacement of Federal troops in all coastal forts by state militia. The proposal died in committee, and shortly thereafter Davis resigned from Congress to lead the red-shirted 1st Mississippi Rifles to war and glory in Mexico.

Now it was the morning of April 10, 1861, and Davis was President of the newly proclaimed Confederate States of America. As he met with his cabinet in a Montgomery, Alabama, hotel room he had good reason to regret the failure of that resolution fifteen years earlier. For had it passed, he would not have had to make the decision he was about to make: Order Brigadier General P.G.T. Beauregard, commander of Confederate forces at Charleston, South Carolina, to demand the surrender of the Federal garrison on Fort Sumter in Charleston Harbor.

But before Davis made this decision, other men had made other decisions—a fateful trail of decisions leading to that Montgomery hotel room on the morning of April 10, 1861.

In a sense the first of those decisions went back to 1829 when the War Department dumped tons of granite rubble brought from New England on a sandspit at the mouth of Charleston Harbor. On the foundation so formed a fort named after the South Carolina Revolutionary War hero, Thomas Sumter, was built.

It was built very slowly, however, as Congress appropriated the needed money in driblets. Thirty-one years later it was over 80 percent complete, though without a garrison and with most of its cannons unmounted. Even so, potentially it was quite formidable. Surrounded by the sea, its five-sided brick walls stood 50 feet high and varied in thickness from 12 feet at the base to 8 1/2 feet at the top. Adequately manned, gunned, and supplied, it could—and in fact eventually would—resist the most powerful assaults.

Three and a third miles to the northwest across the harbor lay Charleston. Here on December 20, 1860, a state convention voted unanimously that "the union now subsisting between South Carolina and other States, under the name of 'The United States of America,' is hereby dissolved." During the rest of that day and all through the night jubilant crowds celebrated.

To South Carolinians the election of the "Black Republican" Abraham Lincoln to the presidency in November had been tantamount to a declaration of war by the North on the South. They had responded by secession, the doctrine so long advocated by their great leader John C. Calhoun, now lying in Charleston's St. Philip's churchyard beneath a marble monument. Soon, they were confident, the other slave states would join them in forming a glorious Southern Confederacy.

Meanwhile, South Carolina would be a nation among nations. For that reason the continued presence of "foreign" United States troops in the forts that controlled Charleston's harbor was more than irritating—it was intolerable. They must go!

Hopefully, the Federal Government would pull them out. To that end Governor Francis Pickens of South Carolina appointed three commissioners to go

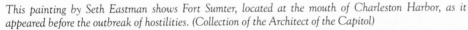

This painting by Seth Eastman shows Fort Sumter, located at the mouth of Charleston Harbor, as it appeared before the outbreak of hostilities. (Collection of the Architect of the Capitol)

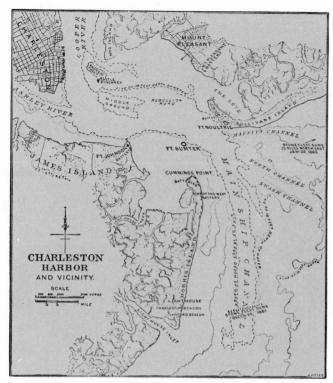

This map shows the strategic position of Fort Sumter at the mouth of the harbor. Charleston lies three and a third miles to the northwest. (Battles and Leaders of the Civil War)

the post in November 1860. Fifty-five, a West Pointer, and twice promoted for bravery in battle, he was an experienced and competent officer—exactly what was needed at Charleston. Moreover, his background should have been reassuring to the Carolinians. As a Kentuckian he qualified as a Southerner, he had owned slaves, and his wife came from an aristocratic Georgia family. Indeed, it is just possible that Floyd, a Virginian, hoped that the major would do what he himself was already doing: support secession.

If so, Floyd had picked the wrong man. Anderson may have been a Southerner but he was dedicated to "Duty, Honor, Country." Above all he was resolved to do everything in his power consistent with those principles to avoid a clash at Charleston that might plunge the nation into civil war.

That is why Fort Moultrie's vulnerability alarmed him. As early as November 23 he reported to the War Department that the Carolinians have "a settled determination . . . to obtain possession of this work." Since then they had made their determination even more evident. Should they attack, duty would compel him, despite the odds, to resist. And that meant war.

Hence he decided to transfer his troops to Fort Sumter. There they would be much more secure and so would peace. For on being confronted with a target less tempting than Moultrie, presumably the Carolinians would be less bellicose.

To be sure, Floyd had instructed him on December

to Washington and negotiate the evacuation of the forts. But if the troops did not leave voluntarily, they would have to be removed.

That did not appear difficult to accomplish. Hundreds of militia, Citadel cadets, and freelance volunteers were gathering in Charleston, spoiling for a fight. In contrast the United States soldiers numbered a scant eighty-five—nine officers and seventy-six enlisted men, of whom eight of the latter were musicians. Furthermore, nearly all of these troops were stationed in Fort Moultrie on Sullivan's Island. Designed to repel sea attack, this fort was practically defenseless on its land side: Overlooking it were high sand dunes from which riflemen could slaughter the garrison.

In 1780, Major Richard Anderson gallantly but unsuccessfully defended the original Fort Moultrie against British assault. Eighty years later his son, Major Robert Anderson of the 1st United States Artillery, arrived at the new Fort Moultrie and took command of the Federal troops stationed at Charleston.

Secretary of War John B. Floyd of the lame-duck Buchanan Administration personally selected him for

Major Robert Anderson (later Major General), the unhappy defender of Fort Sumter. (U.S. Army Military History Institute)

11 to "avoid every act which would needlessly tend to provoke" the Carolinians. But Floyd had also authorized him to move his command to either of the other two forts in Charleston Harbor should he have "tangible evidence of a design to proceed to a hostile act." He ignored a "confidential" letter from Floyd, received December 23, which in effect urged him to surrender the forts rather than "make a vain and useless sacrifice of your life and the lives of the men under your command, upon a mere point of honor." Also he was unaware that on December 10 President Buchanan had informally promised a group of South Carolina congressmen that no change would be made in the military status quo at Charleston.

The transfer to Fort Sumter took place December 26-27. Private John Thompson described how it was managed in a letter to his father in Ireland:

> Our Commander set about fortifying himself in Moultrie, with such unparalelled [sic] vigor that our opponents soon became thoroughly convinced that he intended to make a desperate stand in the position he then held, and the duty of watching us was performed with a laxity corresponding to the strength of their conviction. So completely did our Commander keep his own counsel, that none in the garrison[,] officer or soldier[,] even dreamed that he contemplated a move . . .

> On the night of the 26th Dec. shortly after sun down, we were formed in heavy marching order and quietly marched out of Moultrie leaving only a few men behind on Guard, and embarking on board a number of small boats . . . were safely landed in Sumter.

Several schooners carrying food, munitions, medical supplies, and forty-five army wives and children followed the soldiers. In the morning the rear guard also made the crossing after spiking Moultrie's cannons and setting fire to their carriages.

The column of smoke that rose from Moultrie merely confirmed what had been reported in Charleston by the crew of a harbor patrol boat: The Federals had slipped away to Sumter. The Carolinians fumed with anger and chagrin, and Governor Pickens promptly sent Colonel J. Johnston Pettigrew to the fort.

Pettigrew accused Anderson of breaking Buchanan's December 10 promise to maintain the existing military situation at Charleston. Anderson replied, truthfully enough, that he knew of no such promise, that he had every right to move to Sumter, and that he had done so to protect his men and prevent bloodshed. "In this controversy between the

Major Anderson and his men quietly evacuated Fort Moultrie (above) and transferred safely to Fort Sumter (below) on the night of December 26-27, 1860. (Above: The Soldier in Our Civil War. Below: Harper's Weekly, January 12, 1861)

North and South," he added, "my sympathies are entirely with the South"—but his duty came first.

"Well, sir," said Pettigrew with a bow, "however that may be, the Governor of the State directs me to say to you, courteously but peremptorily, to return to Fort Moultrie."

"I cannot and will not go back," answered Anderson.

Pettigrew left. Soon afterward, at noon, Anderson assembled his troops on Sumter's parade ground. Chaplain Matthias Harris delivered a prayer of thanksgiving; then to the accompaniment of the band playing "Hail Columbia" Anderson personally raised the United States flag that he had brought from Moultrie to the top of a pole, where it waved above the fort.

In Charleston Pickens, on learning that Anderson refused to return to Moultrie, ordered the state troops to seize that fort, Castle Pinckney, and the Federal arsenal, treasury, customhouse, and post office. He believed that he was carrying out justified retaliation against aggression. Instead he committed a bad blunder.

Buchanan would retain the constitutional powers of the presidency until March 4, 1861. However, he no longer possessed its moral and political authority,

he was old and tired, and his overriding desire was to finish out his term in peace—and with the nation still at peace.

To that end he sought to appease the South and thus prevent war. The North, he declared, was to blame for the sectional crisis. Secession, he announced, was unconstitutional—but so would be any attempt of the Federal Government to resist it by "coercion." He refused to reinforce the tiny garrison at Charleston and even ordered it to return muskets and ammunition it had drawn from its own arsenal. This was in keeping with his December 10 promise to the South Carolina congressmen which, along with the instructions sent Anderson, he hoped would keep the Charleston powder keg from exploding.

On December 26, the three commissioners appointed by Pickens to negotiate the evacuation of the Charleston forts arrived in Washington. William Trescot, a South Carolinian who was acting as an intermediary, informed Buchanan of their arrival and purpose. Buchanan replied that he would see them "as private gentlemen" and that he would submit to Congress their proposal that the forts and other Federal facilities in Charleston be turned over to

South Carolina in exchange for a fair monetary compensation.

The following morning the commissioners were discussing matters in the mansion Trescot had rented for them when a burly, bearded man came slamming through the door. He was Senator Louis T. Wigfall of Texas, a native South Carolinian and fanatical secessionist. A telegram, he announced, had just arrived from Charleston: Anderson had spiked his guns at Moultrie and moved his troops to Sumter.

The commissioners refused to believe it. So did Secretary of War Floyd, who also showed up. Then came another telegram from Charleston confirming the first.

Trescot, accompanied by two top Southern leaders, Senators Jefferson Davis of Mississippi and Robert M.T. Hunter of Virginia, hastened to the White House. Davis told the President the news from Charleston. Buchanan was dumbfounded. "I call God to witness," he exclaimed, "this is not only without but against my orders. It is against my policy."

The Southerners urged him to order Anderson back to Moultrie. Otherwise, they warned, South

Wartime Charleston, looking toward Fort Sumter. (Harper's Weekly, January 26, 1861)

Carolina almost surely would seize the other forts, attack Sumter, and begin civil war. But he refused to do so until he had consulted with his cabinet.

At the cabinet meeting Floyd charged that Anderson had disobeyed orders. Secretary of State Jeremiah S. Black, a Pennsylvanian, disagreed. To settle the issue, Buchanan and his secretaries examined a copy of Anderson's December 11 instructions. There it was, the authorization to leave Moultrie "whenever you have tangible evidence of a design to proceed to a hostile act." Obviously what constituted "tangible evidence" had to be determined by Anderson—and he had so determined.

Nevertheless, Floyd (who had been asked several days previously by Buchanan to resign for having misappropriated $870,000 of government funds) insisted that Anderson be ordered back to Moultrie. Unless this was done, he argued, Buchanan would be guilty of breaking his "pledge" to the South Carolina congressmen.

Attorney General Edwin Stanton, backed by the other Northern cabinet members, took a different view. "A President of the United States who would make such an order," he asserted, "would be guilty of treason."

"Oh, no! not so bad as that, my friend!" cried Buchanan in dismay. "Not so bad as that!"

The cabinet meeting ended without a decision. Several days later Floyd finally resigned. Eventually as commander of Confederate forces at Fort Donelson he would render great service—to the Union cause.

On December 28 the South Carolina commissioners visited the White House. They demanded that Anderson's troops be removed from Charleston Harbor, "as they are a standing menace which renders negotiations impossible and threatens a bloody issue." They also pressed for an immediate reply to this ultimatum.

Again Buchanan refused to commit himself: "You don't give me time to consider; you don't give me time to say my prayers. I always say my prayers when required to act upon any great State affair."

As Trescot shrewdly noted, Buchanan had "a fixed purpose to be undecided." Yet he could not avoid making a decision much longer. What would it be?

His impulse was to grant the Carolinians their demand: Anything to forestall war. But he felt countervailing pressures. The North cheered Anderson's action and hailed the pro-Southern major as a hero. To repudiate what he had done by ordering him to evacuate Sumter would raise a storm that might result in impeachment. Moreover, Black, a close friend, declared that he would resign if the Sumter garrison

was pulled out—and undoubtedly the other Northern cabinet members would follow suit.

What tipped the balance, however, was Pickens' seizure of Moultrie, Pinckney, and the other Federal installations in Charleston. This was, Black pointed out, an act of aggression that could not be justified. It was also something that could not be ignored by a President of the United States without violating his oath of office.

Hence on December 30 Buchanan sent a reply, drafted by Black, to the South Carolina commissioners. After referring to the "armed action" taken by South Carolina against Federal property in Charleston, Buchanan stated: "It is under . . . these circumstances that I am urged immediately to withdraw the troops from the harbor of Charleston, and am informed that without this, negotiation is impossible. This I cannot do: This I will not do." Instead, Sumter would be defended, and "I do not perceive how such a defense can be construed into a menace of the city of Charleston."

Having thus decided, Buchanan next gave the commanding general of the army, Winfield Scott, the go-ahead on a plan proposed by him earlier: To send the warship *Brooklyn* with supplies and 250 troops from Fort Monroe in Virginia to reinforce Sumter.

At Sumter Anderson's soldiers and a number of loyal civilian workers busily prepared to resist attack, which they expected at any time. They had a lot to do. Although the fort contained sixty-six cannons, only fifteen had been mounted prior to their arrival. Forty-one unfinished embrasures resulted in as many eight-foot square holes in the ramparts. There was plenty of powder and shot, but it lay scattered about the parade ground amidst piles of bricks and sand. Means for repelling a landing on the wharf, which lay outside the wooden gate on the south or gorge wall, were practically nonexistent.

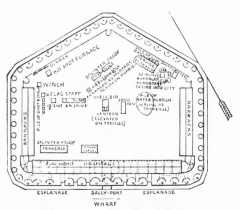

GROUND PLAN OF FORT SUMTER.
BASED ON AN OFFICIAL DRAWING.

Guns and gun carriages dismantled by Major Anderson's men at Fort Moultrie prior to their move to Fort Sumter. (Harper's Weekly, January 26, 1861)

Fortunately for the garrison, the Carolinians thought the fort impregnable. "Twenty-five well-drilled men could hold it against all Charleston," warned the Charleston *Courier* on December 31. "Its batteries could level Fort Moultrie with the ground in a few hours, and shell the city effectively. . . ." Besides, the South Carolinians were confident that Buchanan would evacuate the fort, thus making an attack unnecessary.

Hence they concentrated on building up their own defenses. They removed the soft iron nails with which the Federals, for lack of anything better, had spiked Moultrie's cannons, then remounted the big guns on new carriages. At the same time they constructed a battery on the east shore of Morris Island parallel to Charleston Harbor's main channel. Hundreds of black slaves and white volunteers did the work. Among the latter was 67-year-old Edmund Ruffin of

Battery at Fort Moultrie, its guns bearing on Fort Sumter. Raised on high: South Carolina's Palmetto Flag. (Harper's Weekly, January 26, 1861)

Virginia. For years he had dreamed and preached secession. Now he had come to Charleston to "commit a little treason."

While the Carolinians labored, so did the garrison. By early January Anderson was able to report to the War Department that he could "hold this fort against any force which can be brought against me," and that therefore the government could reinforce him "at its leisure."

This was exactly what the government was doing. First Buchanan postponed sending the *Brooklyn* to Sumter until the South Carolina commissioners replied to his rejection of their ultimatum. Then General Scott had some second thoughts—he feared that the deep-draft *Brooklyn* would have trouble crossing the bar of Charleston Harbor and that Virginia secessionists might seize Fort Monroe if its garrison was reduced. So with Buchanan's approval he arranged to charter the unarmed paddle wheeler *Star of the West* at New York, where several days were consumed loading her with supplies and 200 troops. He and Buchanan also hoped that a vessel of this type would be less provocative to the Carolinians than a warship.

Because of this shilly-shallying the relief expedition did not set forth until January 5. Worse, not until that date did the War Department get around to dispatching a letter to Anderson informing him that the *Star of the West* was on the way with reinforcements and instructing him to aid the ship if she was attacked. Furthermore, instead of sending this vital message by special courier, it entrusted it to the regular mail, apparently oblivious to the possibility that the South Carolina authorities might be intercepting all letters to Sumter—which in fact they had been doing for a week.

Consequently Anderson and his men remained unaware that a relief expedition was on the way. In fact, they were about the only ones in the Charleston area who did not know. Despite efforts by Buchanan and Scott to keep the *Star of the West*'s voyage secret, Southern sympathizers in Washington and New York provided ample advance warning. Panic gripped Charleston, and the South Carolina forces frantically prepared to beat back the Yankee ship when it appeared. However, their commander openly doubted that his ill-trained artillerists could hit a fast-moving steamer and predicted that Sumter's guns would blast Moultrie off the face of the earth.

The officers of Fort Sumter. Seated, from left: Abner Doubleday, Robert Anderson, Samuel Crawford, John Foster. Standing: G. Seymour, G.W. Snyder, Jefferson C. Davis, Richard Mead, and Theodore Talbot. (U.S. Army Military History Institute)

At dawn, January 9, the *Star of the West*, with 200 soldiers below deck, entered Charleston's main channel. When she was two miles from Sumter the Morris Island battery, which had been alerted by a patrol boat, opened fire. George Haynesworth, a Citadel cadet, touched off the first cannon. He missed. So did most of the other rounds from the battery's two cannons. Soon the *Star of the West* passed by, having suffered only minor damage.

From the ramparts of Sumter, Anderson watched the approaching ship through a spyglass. The normally calm major appeared "excited and uncertain what to do." He could see that the Carolinians were shooting at an unarmed vessel flying the United States flag, and only the day before he had read in the Charleston *Mercury* that the *Star of the West* was heading for Sumter with reinforcements. However, that rabidly secessionist paper was notoriously unreliable, and in any event he had no official information or instructions concerning the ship. Besides, the

The Star of the West, *with supplies for Fort Sumter, had to head back to sea after being fired on from Fort Moultrie and the Morris Island batteries. (The Soldier in Our Civil War)*

Confederates on Morris Island fire on Star of the West. *(Harper's Weekly, January 26, 1861)*

Morris Island battery was beyond the reach of Sumter's guns.

Then the *Star of the West* came within range of Fort Moultrie, which opened up on her. Anderson's gunners eagerly expected his order to return the fire. However, one of his officers, Lieutenant Richard K. Meade of Virginia, pleaded with him not to give the order: "It will bring civil war on us." In contrast, Captain Abner Doubleday, the New York-born "inventor of baseball," stamped his feet in frustration, and a soldier's wife attempted by herself to fire a cannon aimed at Moultrie!

Meanwhile, shot and shell rained about the *Star of the West* and an armed schooner approached her. Concluding that he could expect no assistance from Sumter, and fearful of sinking or capture, the *Star of the West*'s captain turned his ship about and headed back to sea.

On seeing the ship retreat, Anderson decided not to fire on Moultrie. Instinct and training urged him to do so, but while there remained the slightest chance of peace he would not strike the blow that could lead only to war.

By all precedents of law and history the Federal Government would have been justified in employing the full power of its armed forces against South Carolina for having fired on the *Star of the West*. It did nothing of the kind, nor did Buchanan even consider such action. First of all the armed forces of the United States were not very powerful. To be sure, the navy probably could have bombarded Charleston in retaliation, but the bulk of the army was scattered throughout the West, barely holding its own against the Indians.

More importantly, the free states were not ready for a showdown over secession. Most Northerners hoped for, even expected, another great sectional compromise like the ones in 1820, 1833, and 1850. Many of them believed that South Carolina was merely "throwing a tantrum," that the talk of a Southern Confederacy was simply a bluff designed to extract concessions. Others, mainly Democrats, sympathized with the Southerners, whom they viewed as defending themselves against Republican radicalism. Thus Democratic Congressman John Logan of Illinois compared the Dixie secessionists to the patriots of the Revolution. At the opposite ideological extreme, such prominent abolitionists as William Lloyd Garrison, Wendell Phillips, Charles Sumner, and Horace Greeley expressed a willingness to "let the erring sisters go in peace." That way the United States would rid itself of the sin of slavery!

Hence, as George T. Strong, a disgusted New Yorker who favored retaliation against South Carolina, wrote in his diary, "The nation pockets this insult to the national flag, a calm, dishonorable, vile submission."

The attempt to reinforce Sumter incensed the Southern secessionists, who saw it as coercion. At the same time the repulse of the *Star of the West* and the failure of the North to react to it made them all the more confident that the money-grubbing Yankees would not dare fight to keep the South in the Union. Senator Judah P. Benjamin of Louisiana sneered that the Federal Government in effect had relinquished all

Lieutenant Adam J. Slemmer, the aggressive defender of Fort Pickens. (Battles and Leaders of the Civil War)

Front view of Fort Pickens on Santa Rose Island in Pensacola Bay, Florida, showing the sally port (gate) and glacis (slope extending downward, at left). (Harper's Weekly, March 9, 1861)

Confederate "water battery" near Warrington Navy Yard, Pensacola, 1861. The Navy Yard was surrendered to Florida and Alabama troops on January 12, 1861. (National Archives)

Fort Moultrie, as it appeared from Fort Sumter. (Harper's Weekly, March 2, 1861)

claim to sovereignty. Jefferson Davis met with other Cotton State senators in Washington to plan a convention at Montgomery, Alabama, for the establishment of an independent confederacy. During January Georgia, Florida, Alabama, Mississippi, and Louisiana seceded and Texas prepared to do the same.

As these states pulled out, their militia took over Federal arsenals, forts, customhouses, and post offices. Nowhere did they encounter resistance. Thus on January 12 semi-senile Commodore James Armstrong surrendered the Pensacola Navy Yard to Florida and Alabama troops. Two days before, however, 1st Lieutenant Adam Slemmer, anticipating such an eventuality, had transferred forty-six soldiers and thirty sailors from nearby Fort Barrancas to powerful Fort Pickens on Santa Rosa Island in Pensacola Bay.

Following the seizure of the naval yard, representatives of the governors of Florida and Alabama demanded the surrender of Fort Pickens (named after the grandfather of the South Carolina governor). Slemmer replied, "I am here by authority of the President of the United States, and I do not recognize the authority of any governor to demand the surrender of United States property,—a governor is nobody here."

Thanks to Slemmer's initiative, the Federal Government now held another fort off the coast of a seceded state. Like Sumter it was too strong for the secessionists to seize immediately, but unlike the Charleston fort its location made reinforcement easy.

Anderson had refrained from blasting Fort Moultrie. Nevertheless, he was angered by the firing on the United States flag. As soon as the *Star of the West* steamed out of sight he dispatched a note to Governor Pickens. In it he threatened to close Charleston Harbor—which he could readily do—unless Pickens disavowed the attack on the ship as having been made without his "sanction or authority."

Pickens answered that the attempt to reinforce Sumter was a deliberate act of hostility, and that to close the harbor would be to impose on South Carolina "the condition of a conquered province"—something it would resist. In effect he countered Anderson's threat with a threat of his own: all-out war.

Since this is what Anderson hoped to avoid, he agreed in subsequent negotiations to a de facto truce while one of his officers, Lieutenant Theodore Talbot, went to Washington for instructions. For his part Pickens allowed mail to enter Sumter and the women and children to leave. Moreover, the garrison could purchase bread, meat, and vegetables (but not flour) in Charleston, and a South Carolina officer sent over several cases of claret.

Notwithstanding these friendly gestures, Pickens was anxious to attack Sumter. Two factors restrained him. First, a number of other Southern leaders cautioned him that precipitate action at Charleston might produce war before a confederacy could be organized. Thus Jefferson Davis wrote him on January 20 that the "little garrison" at Sumter "presses on

Fort Johnson, as seen from Fort Sumter. (Harper's Weekly, March 2, 1861)

nothing but a point of pride . . . you can well aford [sic] to stand still . . . and if things continue as they are for a month, we shall then be in a condition to speak with a voice that all must hear and heed. . . ."

The other and more basic factor was that Pickens lacked the means to assault Sumter successfully. Time was needed to furnish these means, the truce supplied the time, and the governor made the most of it. At his orders four hulks crammed with stones were sunk in the main channel in order to block future relief ships (though the tide soon swept the sunken hulks away). Working day and night, militiamen and slaves added more guns to Moultrie, strengthened the "Star of the West Battery," established an "Iron Battery" on Cumming's Point due south of Sumter, built batteries at Fort Johnson on James Island, implanted additional cannons at various other places, and constructed an ironclad "Floating Battery."

The garrison watched as the "enemy" surrounded Sumter with a circle of fire. Captain Doubleday, who was second in command, proposed to Anderson that he tell the Carolinians to cease work, and that if they refused, to level their still-vulnerable fortifications. But the major rejected his advice. Even had he been willing personally to accept it, he could not. His orders from the new Secretary of War, Joseph Holt, echoed those from Floyd: He was to "act strictly on the defensive."

Furthermore, the Carolinians represented no immediate or direct danger to the fort. By January 21 the garrison had fifty-one guns in position, among them two 10-inchers planted in the parade ground as mortars. Also the soldiers and the forty-three remaining civilian workers had closed the open embrasures and prepared a variety of devices calculated to inflict ghastly casualties on storming parties. Some can-

noneers, experimenting with one of the 10-inchers, discovered that Charleston itself could be bombarded: Using only a small powder charge, they splashed a cannonball near the city's waterfront.

What worried Anderson—and all of his men—was the long-range prospect. Despite purchases in Charleston, food stocks were dwindling steadily. At the same time the ever-increasing strength of the Carolina batteries, Anderson notified the War Department, "will make it impossible for any [relief expedition] other than a large and well-equipped one, to enter this harbor. . . ." In short, unless relieved or evacuated soon, the garrison would starve.

Buchanan realized Anderson's predicament. But after the *Star of the West* fiasco he returned to his basic policy of appeasing the South—which probably was for the best, given the fragmented and fluctuating state of public opinion in the North.

Hence when Lieutenant Talbot returned from Washington to Sumter on January 19, he brought instructions from Secretary of War Holt which boiled down to this: The government did not "at present" intend to reinforce or supply the fort. An "attempt to do so would, no doubt, be attended by a collision of arms and the effusion of blood—a national calamity which the President is most anxious, if possible, to avoid. . . ." But if Anderson decided he needed more troops and supplies, he was to inform the War Department at once, "and a prompt and vigorous effort will be made to forward them."

In other words, the peace-seeking major was asked to decide whether there would be war. It was a decision that he was not prepared to make.

At about the same time that Talbot reported back to Sumter, Buchanan agreed to let General Scott send the *Brooklyn* with a company of Regulars to Fort Pickens. As already noted, the Florida fort differed from Sumter in that there was no way the secessionists could block access to it, thus there was little risk of an armed clash. Meanwhile three other United States warships took stations in Pensacola Bay.

Former United States Senator Stephen R. Mallory of Florida, soon to be the highly competent Confederate Secretary of the Navy, assessed the situation at Pensacola and found it inauspicious. Therefore, through Washington intermediaries, he proposed a deal: If the Federal Government promised not to reinforce Fort Pickens or try to retake the naval yard, he pledged that no attack would be made on Slemmer's garrison. Buchanan agreed to this de facto truce, even though it meant that the government was refraining from doing what it could do easily, whereas

Confederate mortar battery on Morris Island commanded by Lieutenant C.R. Holmes. (Battles and Leaders of the Civil War)

Ships of the Union fleet stationed off Fort Pickens, Florida. Prominent, from left: Wyandotte, Sabine, Brooklyn, Crusader. *(Harper's Pictorial History Of The Great Rebellion)*

the secessionists merely promised not to do what they were incapable of doing successfully. When the *Brooklyn* arrived February 9, it landed supplies but not troops at Fort Pickens, then joined the other Federal ships nearby. As for the secessionists, they stepped up their preparations for an attack on the fort.

On February 18, 1861, the sun shone brightly over Montgomery, Alabama. Jefferson Davis, standing on the portico of the state capitol, took the oath of office as the first President of the Confederate States of America.

So far, however, the Confederacy consisted of only seven states, all from the Lower South. The Upper South (Virginia, North Carolina, Tennessee, and Arkansas) and the slaveholding Border States (Delaware, Maryland, Kentucky, and Missouri) remained outside the fold. Even worse, a foreign flag, that of the United States, waved over forts in two of the Confederacy's main ports, flouting its claim to independence.

Davis pondered the situation, decided what had to be done, then did it. Late in February he dispatched three commissioners—Martin J. Crawford, John Forsyth, and A.B. Roman—to Washington. He instructed them to seek recognition of the Confederate States by the United States and to settle "all questions of disagreement between the two governments"—that is, induce the Federal Government to evacuate Sumter and Pickens.

Next, early in March he sent Brigadier General P.G.T. Beauregard to Charleston and Brigadier General Braxton Bragg to Pensacola. Both had the same orders: As rapidly as possible make all preparations necessary to take, respectively, Fort Sumter and Fort Pickens.

Davis hoped that Crawford, Forsyth, and Roman would succeed in persuading Washington to let the South and the two forts go in peace. But if they failed, time would have been gained for the Confederacy to acquire the means to assert its independence and take the forts by war. Either way, peace or war, the result would be the same: the establishment of a great new nation embracing all of the slave states.

March 4, 1861, was dreary and chilly in Washington, D.C. Standing on a wooden platform in front of the domeless Capitol, Abraham Lincoln donned his steel-rimmed spectacles and began reading his inaugural address. The crowd listened intently. Since his election nearly five months earlier he had not given the slightest public clue as to what he proposed to do about secession in general and Forts Sumter and Pickens in particular. Now, surely, he would announce his decision on these matters.

He did so. Secession, he said in essence, was unconstitutional and unjustifiable. The seceded states remained in the Union. He would not send troops into any state nor interfere with slavery. But he would "hold, occupy, and possess" those places in the South still under Federal control—e.g., Sumter and Pickens. Should they be attacked, they would be defended.

"In your hands, my dissatisfied fellow countrymen, and not in mine, is the momentous issue of civil war. The Government will not assail *you*. You can have no conflict without being yourselves the aggressors. *You* have no oath registered in Heaven to destroy the government, while *I* shall have the most solemn one to 'preserve, protect, and defend' it."

The inauguration of Confederate President Jefferson Davis at Montgomery, Alabama. (Harper's Weekly, March 9, 1861)

Two views of the inauguration of Union President Abraham Lincoln at Washington, D.C. (Library of Congress)

Lincoln thereupon took that oath.

The next morning, Joseph Holt, who was remaining on as Secretary of War until Simon Cameron arrived in Washington to take over, handed Lincoln a letter from Major Anderson that had arrived on Inauguration Day. It stated that the Sumter garrison had only forty days' food left and that the Confederate batteries at Charleston were now so formidable that to reinforce and supply the fort would require "twenty thousand good and disciplined men" in order to succeed.

Lincoln was dismayed. His declared intention to "hold, occupy, and possess" the forts was threatened with becoming so many hollow words, at least as it applied to the most important fort of all. Anderson's communication also implied strongly that he believed that his garrison should be evacuated—that indeed there was no alternative.

Did Holt, asked Lincoln anxiously, have any reasons to suspect Anderson's loyalty? None, replied Holt. Had there been any previous indication from the major that he was in such a precarious plight? Again Holt said no—which was not quite accurate. During February Anderson had kept the War Department fully informed about the increasing power of the Confederate armaments at Charleston and the decreasing level of his food reserves. What he had not done was to state explicitly, in accordance with his January 19 instructions from Holt, that he *needed* supplies and reinforcements. He knew that to do so would result in another relief expedition which in turn would lead to war.

Faced with this unexpected crisis on his first day in office, Lincoln asked General Scott's advice. That night Scott gave it: "I see no alternative but a surrender, in some weeks." He also informed Lincoln of the Buchanan-Mallory "truce" with respect to Fort Pickens—another disturbing bit of news.

Though Scott's opinions on military matters carried great weight, Lincoln, the one-time militia captain, was unwilling to give up on Sumter without further consideration. Therefore he directed Scott to make a thorough study of the problem of relieving the fort.

On March 11 "Old Fuss and Feathers" reported: To "supply and re-enforce" Sumter would require such a large force of warships, transports, and troops that it would take six to eight months to assemble it. Thus, "As a practical military question the time for succoring Sumter . . . passed away nearly a month ago. Since then a surrender under assault or from starvation has been merely a question of time."

But even this did not convince Lincoln that Sumter was doomed. There *must* be some way of relieving it, or at least some alternative to meek surrender. In any case, there was one thing that could be done to

affirm his determination to retain possession of the surviving Federal outposts in the seceded states: Reinforce Fort Pickens. To be sure, there was the Buchanan-Mallory truce, but he did not consider himself bound by it, and obviously the Confederates were taking advantage of it to prepare an attack on the fort. So he instructed Scott to order the commander of the troops aboard the *Brooklyn*, Captain Israel Vogdes, to land them as soon as possible and hold Pickens at any cost. Scott sent the order to Vogdes the following day, March 12.

William Henry Seward was the new Secretary of State. He believed he should be President. As a senator from New York he had been playing a leading role in national affairs while Lincoln was just a country lawyer in Illinois. Only bad luck had prevented him from getting what he thought should have been his: the Republican nomination in 1860.

But if he could not be President in name he proposed to be so in fact. Twice before he had been the power behind the White House throne—first with William Henry Harrison, then with Zachary Taylor. There should be no difficulty in establishing the same sort of domination over Lincoln. Already the Illinoisan was revealing his inexperience and incompetence by his hesitation over what to do about Sumter.

Seward knew what to do: Evacuate the fort immediately. Indeed, do everything possible to avoid an armed showdown with the secessionists. For he was convinced—utterly convinced—that the majority of Southerners remained in their hearts loyal to the Union, and that sooner or later their latent patriotism would assert itself, thereby setting the stage for North-South reconciliation. On the other hand, for the Federal Government to employ force against the Confederates, or even threaten to do so, would only intensify and spread the secessionist distemper and result ultimately in civil war.

From the vantage point of historical hindsight it is easy to condemn Seward for underestimating Lincoln and overestimating Southern Unionism. But it should be remembered that few people sensed Lincoln's greatness in the spring of 1861, and that Seward himself was among the first to recognize it. Also it should be pointed out that some of the seven original Confederate states approved secession by very narrow margins, that the other slave states either rejected it or refused even to consider it prior to the actual outbreak of hostilities, and that many knowledgeable people in the South as well as the North shared Seward's belief that the secessionist fever would ultimately burn itself out. Indeed Lincoln himself hoped that the South's love of Union would prevail over its hatred of the North, and had sought to appeal to this in his inaugural address.

Nevertheless, the fact remains that Seward's unrealistic view of Lincoln's ability and of Southern attitudes caused him to pursue a course that was morally dubious and nearly disastrous for the Union cause.

First, via pro-Southern ex-Senator William Gwin of California, he assured Confederate commissioner Crawford, now in Washington, that Lincoln's announced intention to "hold, occupy, and possess" the forts actually meant only "so far as practicable." Next he implied to Crawford and another of the commissioners (again through Gwin) that the evacuation of Sumter was being delayed only by "the difficulties and confusion incident to a new administration." At the same time he told his good friend James Harvey, Washington correspondent of the New York *Tribune*, that the government had decided to withdraw Anderson. As he no doubt anticipated, Harvey, a native of South Carolina, telegraphed this intelligence to Charleston on March 11—the same day that Scott, who also had close personal ties with Seward, reported to Lincoln that it was impossible to relieve Sumter.

Seward said and did these things without Lincoln's knowledge, much less approval. But he believed that sooner or later the President would abandon Sumter. He would have no other choice.

But there was another choice, declared Postmaster General Montgomery Blair. When on March 11 Lincoln informed him and the other cabinet members that Scott had stated that Sumter could not be relieved and so must be evacuated, he telegraphed his brother-in-law Gustavus Vasa Fox in Massachusetts to come to Washington immediately.

Blair was more than just a Postmaster General—the lowest ranking cabinet post. His father, Frank, had been Andrew Jackson's right-hand man; his brother Frank, Jr. was a congressman from Missouri. Together the three Blairs constituted the most politically influential family in America.

Nor was Gustavus Fox an ordinary brother-in-law. Thirty-nine and an Annapolis graduate, he had served with distinction in the navy before entering the textile business. Back in February he had submitted to Scott a scheme for relieving Sumter. Now on the morning of March 13 he arrived at the White House, accompanied by Montgomery Blair, to present his plan to Lincoln.

Organize, he said, an expedition of two warships, a transport, and three tugboats. When it arrives outside Charleston Harbor, transfer troops and supplies from the transport to the tugs, then at night run the tugs in to Sumter. Darkness would protect them from

the Confederate shore batteries and the warships from naval attack. It all could be done within a few days and Fox would be proud to command the operation.

Here was an alternative to the impossibly large force of ships and soldiers deemed necessary by Anderson and Scott. But would it work? And would it not put the Federal Government in the role of the aggressor? As Lincoln had declared in his inaugural, if war came, it would have to be by an act of the South.

On March 14 Lincoln informed his cabinet of Fox's plan, then the following day asked each member to give a written answer to the question: "Assuming it to be possible to now provision Fort Sumter, under all the circumstances is it wise to attempt it?"

Later in the day Seward promised Supreme Court Justice John A. Campbell, a Virginian who had replaced Gwin as his go-between with the Confederate commissioners, that Sumter would be evacuated in three days. Exactly three days later the cabinet members submitted their replies to Lincoln's question. Five of them—Seward, Secretary of War Cameron, Secretary of the Navy Gideon Welles, Secretary of the Interior Caleb Smith, and Attorney General Edward Bates—advised withdrawing the garrison. Only Blair and Secretary of the Treasury Salmon P. Chase favored making an effort to maintain it—and the latter did so with many qualifications.

Obviously Seward had expected this outcome—hence his promise to Campbell. But to his dismay Lincoln still refused to order an evacuation. Instead he adopted a suggestion from Blair and sent Fox to Sumter for an on-the-spot investigation. He also had two of his Illinois friends, Stephen Hurlbut and Ward Hill Lamon, go to South Carolina to sound out Unionist sentiment.

General view of Charleston and its harbor. (The Soldier in Our Civil War)

While Lincoln's three agents were away, Davis' three commissioners repeatedly asked Seward (via Campbell) when the promised evacuation of Sumter would occur. Seward repeatedly assured them that it was just a matter of time. The commissioners hoped, but did not fully believe, that what he said would prove true. In any case, for the time being it did not make much difference. Davis had instructed them to "play with Seward"—that is, hint to him that the seceded states would voluntarily return to the Union if the Federal Government gave certain guarantees regarding slavery. That way additional time would be gained for the Confederacy to arm.

On March 25 Fox returned to Washington and reported to Lincoln. During a quick visit to Sumter Anderson had told him that relief from the sea was impossible. However, after studying the situation himself he was more confident than ever that his plan was feasible. Anderson had also stated that by putting his men on short rations he could hold out longer than previously estimated. Possibly because he distrusted the major's loyalty, he made no arrangements with Anderson for supplying or reinforcing the fort, nor did he reveal his plan for doing so.

Officers' quarters at Fort Sumter, while occupied by Robert Anderson and his men. (Harper's Weekly, February 23, 1861)

L-R: Postmaster General Montgomery Blair, Secretary of War Simon Cameron, Navy Secretary Gideon Welles (all Library of Congress), Attorney General Edward Bates. (Century Magazine)

Two days later Lamon and Hurlbut likewise came back from Charleston. The former had accomplished worse than nothing. Having been led by Seward to believe that Lincoln intended to evacuate Sumter, he had not only told Governor Pickens, but also Anderson. Hurlbut, on the other hand, brought valuable information. A native of South Carolina, he had talked with many intelligent and informed people there. All agreed that Unionism in the Lower South was as good as dead. Furthermore, even "moderates" in South Carolina would approve resisting any attempt to provision Sumter.

Throughout the night of March 28 Lincoln lay in bed sleepless, his mind churning. A decision on Sumter could not be postponed any longer—in two, at most three weeks, the garrison would be starving. But what should it be? An attempt to supply the fort would certainly result in war and probably the secession of most, perhaps all, of the slave states still in the Union. On the other hand, evacuation would discredit him, undermine the already sagging authority of the Federal Government, demoralize the North, and increase the prestige and strength of the Confederacy. Moreover, it would not settle anything. The crisis would merely be transferred to Fort Pickens or to some other issue.

When Lincoln got up in the morning he felt depressed—but he had made his decision. That afternoon he proposed it to his cabinet: a relief expedition to Sumter. Governor Pickens would be informed that it was on the way and that if it met no resistance, supplies only would be landed. Otherwise, troops as well as provisions would be sent into the fort under cover of cannon fire.

Every member of the cabinet approved except Seward. And even he based his opposition on the grounds that it would be better to have the war start at Pickens than Sumter. His stated reasons for so contending were deficient both in logic and sincerity.

Having made his decision, Lincoln proceeded to implement it. He ordered the Navy Department to assemble ships and the War Department 300 troops and supplies at New York, then sent Fox there to take charge.

Seward, however, was far from abandoning his effort to impose his leadership and policy on Lincoln. On the evening of March 29 he went to the White House, accompanied by Captain Montgomery C. Meigs of the Army Corps of Engineers, for the purpose of discussing the situation at Fort Pickens. Two days earlier Lincoln had learned from a newspaper report that the *Brooklyn*, which he had sent to reinforce Pickens early in March, had appeared at Key West (which the Union also retained) with troops still

aboard. Obviously, as Lincoln put it, the Pickens expedition had "fizzled out." Would Meigs, he asked, prepare a plan for relieving and holding the fort?

Meigs said he would and left to do so. Seward was pleased. He was hopeful now that Lincoln would call off the Sumter expedition in order to concentrate on holding Pickens. In addition, Seward had influenced certain New York businessmen to withhold the assistance needed by Fox to acquire ships and supplies.

On March 31 Meigs presented his Pickens plan to Lincoln, who approved it and instructed Scott that "he wished this thing done and not to let it fail." He adopted this peremptory tone toward the ancient general because several days before Scott had shocked him with a proposal to evacuate the Florida fort as well as Sumter.

On April 1 confirmation that the order to reinforce Pickens had not been executed reached Lincoln in a letter from Captain Vogdes, commander of the

Southern gentlemen sharpen their marksmanship at the Ordnance Bureau in Charleston. (The Soldier in Our Civil War)

troops on the *Brooklyn*. Vogdes neglected to explain this failure, but did speak of "uncertain" communications with Washington and warned that the Confederates might attack Pickens "without a moment's notice."

This alarming news hastened preparations for the Pickens expedition. All through the day Meigs and Navy Lieutenant David D. Porter sat in a White House office drawing up orders for Lincoln to sign. Seward, who in a sense was sponsoring the expedition, personally handed many of the orders to Lincoln. One of them was a telegram to the New York Naval Yard to "Fit out *Powhatan* to go to sea at the earliest possible moment." Meigs and Porter planned to use this warship to support the landing of men and stores at Pickens.

Pickens, however, was not the only thing on Seward's mind that day. There was still Sumter. On March 30 he had promised Justice Campbell that on April 1 he would give him definite word about the

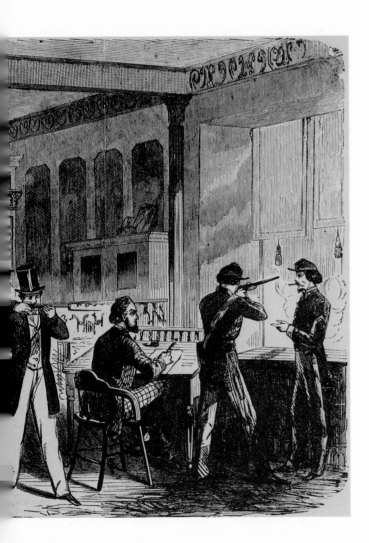

government's intentions concerning that fort to pass on to the Confederate commissioners. Now Campbell came to Seward for that word.

Seward excused himself, visited Lincoln, then returned and wrote a message to be delivered in Campbell's name to the commissioners: "I am satisfied the government will not undertake to supply Fort Sumter without giving notice to Governor Pickens."

Campbell protested that this was a betrayal of Seward's oft-repeated promises, which Campbell had personally guaranteed, that Sumter would be evacuated. Seward, however, somehow persuaded him that this was not so, with the incredible result that Campbell reported to the commissioners that Seward's promise still held good.

But the commissioners themselves were not so easily fooled. They telegraphed Robert Toombs, the Confederate Secretary of State, that Lincoln would not issue an order to evacuate Sumter because he feared the North's reaction. Instead, they reported, he intended to "shift responsibility upon Major Anderson by suffering him to be starved out."

Meanwhile, on this same eventful April Fool's Day, Seward, during one of his frequent calls at the White House, handed Lincoln the most remarkable memorandum ever submitted by a cabinet member to a President. Entitled "Some Thoughts for the President's Consideration," it stated that the government was "without a policy either domestic or foreign." Regarding the former, it proposed abandoning Sumter but defending Pickens. This, for reasons unexplained, would "change the question before the Public from one upon Slavery . . . for a question upon Union or Disunion." As for foreign policy, let the government initiate war with France (which was meddling in Mexican affairs), or with Spain (which had occupied Santo Domingo), or with both. Then, faced with a common alien foe, the people of North and South would forget their differences and the Union would be restored.

Seward concluded the memorandum by declaring that "whatever policy we adopt, there must be an energetic prosecution of it. . . . I neither seek to evade nor assume responsibility."

In brief, Seward offered to take command.

Lincoln would have been perfectly justified in demanding his resignation both for insubordination and incompetency. Instead, later in the day he sent a reply to Seward which calmly, tactfully, and firmly said: No.

Seward now realized that he could not dominate Lincoln. But he still hoped to influence him—and to head off the Sumter expedition.

The President, he knew, was especially anxious to

keep Virginia in the Union, for should she pull out, the rest of the Upper South soon would follow. Therefore on the morning of April 4 he brought to the White House John B. Baldwin, a leading Unionist member of the Virginia Convention, which had been called to consider secession. His object was to arrange a deal whereby Lincoln would agree to evacuate Sumter in exchange for the adjournment of the Virginia Convention.

Lincoln and Baldwin conversed long and earnestly—but to no avail. Baldwin somehow got the impression that Lincoln was simply asking for the disbandment of the convention. Lincoln, on the other hand, concluded that Baldwin had contemptuously rejected his offer to give up Sumter in return for the non-secession of Virginia. Following the interview he denounced Virginia Unionists as nothing but "white crows." Again Seward experienced frustration.

That afternoon Lincoln and Fox, who had returned to Washington, made final preparations for the Sumter expedition. Despite the Seward-inspired obstacles he had encountered in New York, Fox had obtained the passenger steamer *Baltic* and three tugboats. In addition he had authority to employ the warships *Pawnee* and *Pocahontas* and the revenue cutter *Harriet Lane*. Lincoln instructed him to rendezvous this flotilla outside Charleston Harbor, then to send an unarmed supply boat toward Sumter. If the Confederates opened fire, the boat was to turn back at once, and Fox would endeavor to land troops and provisions at Sumter by means of tugboats covered by the cannons of his warships and of the fort.

In order to make sure that *this time* the fort's cannons would fire, Lincoln also had Secretary of War Cameron send Anderson a letter (by regular mail) notifying him of the relief expedition and urging him to hold out, "if possible," until it arrived. However, should surrender become a necessity, he was "authorized to make it."

Before returning to New York, Fox asked Secretary of the Navy Gideon Welles for another and more powerful warship for use in repelling Confederate naval attack and transporting 300 sailors, with howitzers and landing boats. Welles, who had been kept totally in the dark about the Pickens expedition, promptly sent orders to Captain Samuel Mercer to take command of the *Powhatan* as part of the Sumter expedition.

The result was a farce. On April 5 Captain Meigs and Captain Mercer both showed up at the New York Naval Yard, where the *Powhatan* was berthed. Meigs insisted that his authority to assume control of the ship took precedence because it was signed by the President. No, maintained Mercer—his order from

Welles bore a later date. Finally Meigs telegraphed Seward asking him to settle the dispute.

Feeling rather embarrassed, Seward notified Welles of the mix-up. Welles, understandably enough, was angry over not being informed of the Pickens expedition. Together he and Seward hastened to the White House, arriving shortly before midnight.

Lincoln apologized to Welles, explaining that he had confused the *Powhatan* with the *Pocahontas!* Welles asked him to confirm his order assigning the *Powhatan* to Mercer. Seward, however, insisted that the ship go to Meigs—possibly he hoped even yet to thwart the Sumter expedition by denying it the means for success.

In any case, Lincoln supported Welles; Sumter was more urgent and important than Pickens. He instructed Seward to telegraph the New York Naval Yard to deliver the *Powhatan* to Mercer. Seward did so, but (perhaps deliberately) signed the message "Seward," not "Lincoln" as he should have.

As a consequence the officer in charge of the New York Naval Yard, Commander Andrew H. Foote (whose gunboat operations on the Tennessee and Cumberland rivers soon would make his a household name), decided to turn over the ship to Meigs's colleague Captain Porter (who also would become a Union naval hero). After all, the President's authority was supreme.

And so it was that on the afternoon of April 6 the *Powhatan*, unknown to Lincoln and against his desire, left New York as part of the Pickens' expedition. By the same token, two days later Fox, confident that the *Powhatan* soon would do the same, headed for Charleston aboard the *Baltic*, which carried 200 troops, sixteen launches, and supplies. The three tugboats were to follow him, and he expected to meet the *Pawnee*, *Pocahontas*, and *Harriet Lane* outside Charleston Harbor. Strangely, no one thought to inform him that the *Powhatan* had been turned over to Porter, nor did he bother to check on the ship despite the fact that she and her landing boats and sailors were now a key element in his plan to relieve Sumter.

As Fox steamed out of New York, Lincoln dispatched Robert Chew, a State Department clerk, to Charleston with the following unaddressed and unsigned message to Governor Pickens:

> I am directed by the President of the United States to notify you to expect an attempt will be made to supply Fort Sumter with provisions only, and that if such attempt be not resisted, no effort to throw in men, arms or ammunition, will be made, without further notice, or in case of an attack upon the Fort.

By thus giving advance notice of his intention to supply Sumter, Lincoln created a situation in which there was at least a chance that the Confederates would decide to withhold their fire. If they so decided, fine—Sumter would be relieved and United States sovereignty upheld. But if not, then they would have been maneuvered into firing the first shot.

Lincoln did not know it and many historians have failed to realize it, but Jefferson Davis already had decided to shoot first.

His reasons were a mirror image of Lincoln's motives for sending the relief expedition to Charleston. As long as the United States flag flew over Sumter and Pickens, the Confederacy's claim to independence was a self-evident fiction. Unless that flag came down the authority of the Confederate Government would melt away with the coming of the hot Southern summer. On the other hand, by forcing the Federal Government to relinquish the forts the Confederacy not only would establish itself but grow in power as the other slave states flocked to join it.

So the question was when and where to use force. By April "when" could be soon, for the preceding weeks had been put to good use in raising, organizing, equipping, and deploying troops. As for the "where," on April 3 Davis addressed an "unofficial" letter to General Bragg at Pensacola: Was he ready yet to take Fort Pickens? If so, he was to take it.

On April 8 Bragg's reply arrived. If ordered, he would attack Pickens. Unfortunately, however, he could not guarantee success—and casualties would be severe.

That same day another message reached Davis. It came from Governor Pickens. Chew had delivered Lincoln's message. A relief expedition was heading for Sumter.

Now Davis had an answer to "where." It would be at Charleston. Immediately he had his Secretary of War, Leroy P. Walker, telegraph Beauregard: "Under no circumstances are you to allow provisions to be sent to Fort Sumter."

The previous day, April 7, Davis' commissioners had demanded, through Campbell, that Seward make good on his assurances that Sumter would be evacuated. On April 8 Seward replied: "Faith as to Sumter fully kept; wait and see. . . ." Even now he was unwilling to admit that he had promised what was not his to promise. But later in the day he followed this message with an official memorandum, delivered to Campbell at the State Department, in which he flatly denied Confederate independence and refused to negotiate with the commissioners. The

Brigadier General Pierre G.T. Beauregard, commander of the Confederate forces in Charleston. (National Archives)

game he had been playing with them, and they with him, had ended.

The commissioners, who meanwhile had learned of Lincoln's note to Governor Pickens, were incensed by what they deemed to be Seward's duplicity. On April 9 they addressed to him a letter which asserted that Lincoln's announced intention of supplying Sumter "could only be received as a declaration of war." They also telegraphed Davis that the Federal Government "declines to recognize our official character or the power we represent."

Davis, on reading this message, perceived that there was no longer the slightest possibility of establishing Confederate independence by negotiation. It would have to be done by war. And so it was that late on the morning of April 10 Davis laid before his cabinet a proposal that Beauregard be instructed to demand the surrender of Fort Sumter and to attack it if the demand was rejected. Citing in support a telegram just received from Beauregard himself, Davis declared that Sumter had to be taken before the Federal relief expedition arrived, for once supplied and reinforced the fort would be practically impregnable.

All the cabinet concurred except Secretary of State Toombs: "The firing upon the fort will inaugurate a civil war greater than any the world has yet seen. . . ."

Davis realized that this probably would be the

46

consequence. Yet it would have to be risked. He saw no alternative if the Confederacy was to survive. Consequently he had Secretary of War Walker telegraph Beauregard to demand Sumter's evacuation, "and if this is refused proceed . . . to reduce it."

At 3:30 p.m. on the afternoon of April 11 a small boat flying a white flag tied up to the wharf of Fort Sumter. Three men climbed out—Captain Stephen D. Lee, Lieutenant Colonel A.R. Chisholm, and Colonel James Chesnut, an ex-U.S. Senator from South Carolina. All were members of Beauregard's staff.

They handed Anderson a letter from Beauregard demanding the surrender of the fort. In it Beauregard, who as a cadet had studied artillery tactics at West Point under Anderson, stated that means would be provided for the removal of the garrison, and that "The flag which you have upheld so long and with so much fortitude . . . may be saluted by you on taking it down."

Anderson had been awaiting—and dreading—such an ultimatum since April 7. On that date he had received Cameron's message that Fox's expedition was on the way and that he was to hold out as long as possible. Until then he had both expected and hoped for an order to evacuate: Expected it not only because of Lamon's assurance but also because he considered it impossible to relieve the fort; hoped for it because he believed it was the only way to avert the calamity of civil war, his prime objective from the start. Consequently, in the words of one of his officers, Cameron's letter "deeply affected" him.

However, in responding to it he wrote: "We shall strive to do our duty, though I frankly say that my heart is not in the war which I see is to be thus commenced." And in keeping with that statement he gave Beauregard's aides a reply that read:

> General: I have the honor to acknowledge the receipt of your communication demanding the evacuation of this fort, and to say, in reply thereto, that it is a demand with which I regret that my sense of honor, and of my obligations to my Government, prevent my compliance.

The aides, without a word, headed for the wharf. Anderson accompanied them. As he did so, he suddenly thought of something that might even yet stop civil war from beginning at Fort Sumter. For the past week the Confederates had not permitted the garrison to purchase fresh food in Charleston. The fort had only a few barrels of salt pork remaining.

"Will General Beauregard," he called to the aides, "open his batteries without further notice to me?"

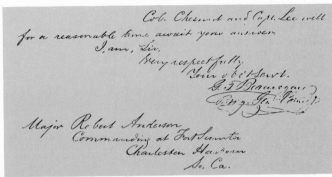

Part of Beauregard's letter to Anderson demanding the surrender of Fort Sumter. (Benson Lossing, Civil War in America)

"No, I can say to you that he will not," replied Chesnut after some hesitation.

"Gentlemen," said Anderson, "if you do not batter the fort to pieces about us, we shall be starved out in a few days."

Surprised by this important admission, Chesnut asked if he might repeat it to Beauregard. Anderson gave him permission to do so. In effect he was telling the Confederates: Wait a few days—if the relief expedition does not show up, Sumter will be yours without a shot.

Less than an hour later Beauregard sent a telegram to Montgomery in which he described Anderson's remark and asked for further instructions. Davis pondered, then had Walker telegraph Beauregard:

> Do not desire needlessly to bombard Fort Sumter. If Major Anderson will state the time at which, as indicated by him, he will evacuate, and agree that in the meantime he will not use his guns against us, unless ours should be employed against Fort Sumter, you are authorized thus to avoid the effusion of blood. If this, or its equivalent, be refused, reduce the fort as your judgment decides to be most practicable.

This meant that unless Anderson agreed to a prompt surrender he was to be attacked at once. Davis did not intend to risk the relief of Sumter. One way or another it must be occupied before Fox's expedition arrived. And above all, he was determined to assert the power and independence of the Confederacy.

Forty-five minutes past midnight, April 12, Chesnut, Chisholm, and Lee again docked at Fort Sumter. Remaining in their boat was Colonel Roger Pryor, an ex-congressman from Virginia and ardent secessionist, also a member of Beauregard's staff. Anderson read the message they brought from Beauregard: "If you will state the time at which you will evacuate Fort Sumter we will abstain from opening fire upon you."

While the three Confederates waited with growing impatience, Anderson conferred with his officers for over two hours. All of them rejected immediate surrender—even Lieutenant Meade of Virginia, who later joined the Confederate Army. However, in two more days, April 14, the garrison's food supply would be exhausted. Accordingly Anderson wrote a letter to Beauregard stating that he would "evacuate Fort Sumter by noon on the 15th instant . . . should I not receive prior to that time controlling instructions from my Government or additional supplies."

Beauregard's aides, who had been authorized by him to determine whether or not Anderson met the terms of his ultimatum, read the reply. Chesnut pronounced it "manifestly futile." Then, standing in a casemate, Captain Lee (who was 27 and destined to become the youngest lieutenant general in the Confederate Army) wrote the following, which both he and Chesnut signed before giving it to Anderson:

Fort Sumter, S. C., April 12, 1861, 3:20 A. M.—Sir: By authority of Brigadier-General Beauregard, commanding the Provisional Forces of the Confederate States, we have the honor to notify you that he will open the fire of his batteries on Fort Sumter in one hour from this time.

Anderson read these words, displaying great emotion as he did. Then he escorted the Confederates to the wharf where he shook hands with them and said, "If we never meet in this world again, God grant that we may meet in the next."

Instead of proceeding directly to Beauregard's headquarters in Charleston, Chesnut's party went to Fort Johnson. There, at 4 a.m., Chesnut ordered the fort's commander, Captain George S. James, to fire the gun that would signal the other batteries trained on Sumter to open up. Chesnut acted under authority previously given him by Beauregard and obviously felt no need to check with the general. The

Confederates mount cannon on Morris Island, preparatory to the attack on Fort Sumter, to the north, early on April 12, 1861. Wash drawing by William Waud. (Library of Congress)

Rabid secessionist Edmund Ruffin fired the first shot from the Iron Battery against Fort Sumter. (Library of Congress)

the first shot directed at the fort and struck it. Support for this contention comes from his own diary, in which he wrote:

> The night before, when expecting to engage, Capt. [George B.] Cuthbert had notified me that his company [the Palmetto Guard] requested of me to discharge the first cannon to be fired, which was their 64 lb. Columbiad, loaded with shell. By order of Gen. Beauregard, made known the afternoon of the 11th, the attack was to be commenced by the first shot at the fort being fired by the Palmetto Guard, & from the Iron Battery. In accepting & acting upon this highly appreciated compliment, that company had made me its instrument. . . . Of course I was highly gratified by the compliment, & delighted to perform the service—which I did. The shell struck the fort, at the north-east angle of the parapet.

However, it seems in fact that Ruffin merely fired the first shot from the Iron Battery on Cumming's Point, and that he did not do so until after other batteries had opened up. In his official report of April 17, 1861, Captain Cuthbert stated:

> The mortar battery at Cummings Point opened fire on Fort Sumter in its turn, after the signal shell from Fort Johnson, having been preceded by the mortar batteries on Sullivan's Island and the mortar battery of the Marion Artillery. . . . At the dawn of day the Iron battery commenced its work of demolition. The first shell from columbiad No. 1, fired by the venerable Edmund Ruffin, of Virginia, burst directly upon the parapet of the southwest angle of the fort [a more likely place for it to strike than the northeast angle referred to by Ruffin].

Other Confederate accounts, official and unofficial, confirm Cuthbert's statement.

If the signal shell from Fort Johnson be considered the opening shot of the Civil War, as it should, then Lieutenant Henry S. Farley fired it. He commanded the mortar that lobbed the shell over Sumter and according to his own testimony, which is supported by two eyewitnesses, he personally yanked the lanyard.

Beauregard's guns—thirty cannons and seventeen mortars—pounded the fort during the rest of the night and on into the dawn. Thousands of Charlestonians—men, women, and children, many in nightclothes—crowded the Battery, rooftops, and wharves to watch the pyrotechnics. In her excitement Mary Chesnut, wife of the colonel, sat down on a chimney atop the Mills House with the result that her dress caught fire! Friends beat out the flames before much more than her dignity was damaged.

Sumter's cannons remained silent. This disappointed the spectators and caused some of the Confederate soldiers to feel like bullies hitting a man who

prospect of civil war did not unduly disturb him. Back in November he had declared, "The man most averse to blood might safely drink every drop shed in establishing a Southern Confederacy."

Captain James offered Colonel Pryor, the Virginian, the "honor of firing the first gun of the war." But Pryor, who two days before had made a speech urging the Charlestonians to "strike a blow," declined. "I could not fire the first gun of the war," he said huskily.

Chesnut and his companions thereupon returned to their boat and continued across the bay toward Charleston. At 4:30 they heard James's cannon boom. They turned and saw a shell burst one hundred feet directly above the fort.

The Civil War had begun.

Soon nearly all of the Confederate batteries were blazing away. According to many historical accounts, the elderly Virginia secessionist Edmund Ruffin, now an honorary member of the Palmetto Guard, fired

Bursting of the signal shell from Fort Johnson over Fort Sumter. In the foreground: Confederates at the iron-clad battery at Cumming's Point. (Battles and Leaders of the Civil War)

will not fight back. Ruffin was "fearful that Major Anderson, relying on the security of his men in the covered casemates . . . did not intend to fire at all. It would have cheapened our conquest of the fort, if effected, if no hostile defence had been made—& still more increased the disgrace of failure."

Ruffin need not have worried. Anderson intended to fire back—but not until daylight. His guns lacked breech sights, and although Captain Doubleday and another officer had devised notched sticks as imperfect substitutes, they could not be aimed accurately in the dark. Moreover, he had a stockpile of only 700 powder bags (the cartridges used to discharge the cannons), which his men had made out of sheets and shirts. It would be foolish to squander them in nocturnal pot shots.

At 6 a.m., their regular time, the soldiers assembled in the bombproofs for reveille, ate a quick breakfast of pork and water, and then manned the guns on the lower tier. To the irritation of many of them, Anderson previously had decided not to operate the pieces on the more exposed upper tier (the parapet) because he feared excessive casualties to the small garrison, which would leave it with insufficient strength to repel a landing attempt (something, however, which the Confederates did not plan, as they considered it a hopeless enterprise). It is possible, too, that he wished to save these guns to cover Fox's relief expedition.

Anderson offered Doubleday, his second-in-command, the honor of firing (at least in the figurative sense) the first Union shot of the war. The New Yorker gladly accepted it. As far as he was concerned the war was "simply a contest, politically speaking, as whether virtue or vice should rule" in America.

Shortly before 7 a.m. Doubleday aimed a 32-pounder at the Iron Battery, then stepped back and shouted "Fire!" The gunner (apparently his name has

gone unrecorded) yanked the lanyard and the cannon belched forth an iron ball that whizzed across the bay and bounced off the slanting roof of the Iron Battery.

Following this shot the other gun crews went into action. At first they concentrated their fire on the Iron Battery and the Floating Battery, which had been anchored off the western tip of Sullivan's Island. The musicians and most of the workmen assisted by carrying ammunition to the casemates. Also some of the latter sewed up more powder bags, handicapped because only six needles were available! Owing to the lack of manpower and powder bags, the garrison after awhile employed but six cannons. On at least one occasion a group of workers took the place of the soldiers in serving a piece.

When it became apparent that no damage was being done to the Floating Battery, Anderson autho-

Captain Abner Doubleday, Anderson's second-in-command, prepares to fire the first gun in Fort Sumter. (CWTI Collection)

Bombardment of Fort Sumter, sketched from Morris Island. (The Soldier in Our Civil War)

rized a shift of fire to Fort Moultrie. However, most of the projectiles directed against it merely buried themselves harmlessly in piles of sandbags. Equally futile were the few shots aimed at the mortars on James Island. As for the Iron Battery, a Union cannonball put one of its guns out of action by jamming the steel shutter protecting its embrasure, but the Confederates soon repaired the shutter.

The Federals' fire would have been more effective, especially against Moultrie, had they been able to use shells. But they lacked the fuses necessary to explode the shells, and an attempt to improvise them failed. Likewise the 8-inch and 10-inch columbiads on the parapet almost certainly would have made things rougher on the Confederates. Not only did they shoot projectiles weighing 65 and 128 pounds, but their angle of fire was superior. Frustrated by the ineffectiveness of the 32-pounders that were being used, Private John Carmody ignored orders and went to the top parapet where he single-handedly fired a number of the big guns that already were loaded and trained on Moultrie. In addition, two sergeants managed to get off a couple of shots from a 10-inch columbiad aimed at the Iron Battery. No one, however, attempted to drop a cannonball on Charleston from one of the guns mounted as mortars in the parade ground.

Initially the Confederates tended to fire too high. But with daylight they soon got the range, with the result that numerous mortar shells exploded inside the fort and solid shot riddled the walls. On three different occasions the supposedly fireproof barracks began burning. The first two times parties of workmen headed by Peter Hart, an ex-sergeant serving as Anderson's personal aide, put out the flames. The third time, however, only the coming of an evening rainstorm completely doused the blaze.

Despite the hurricane of shot and shell, none of the garrison was seriously injured. The same held true of Sumter itself. Although the parapet and gorge wall were badly battered, its defensive capacity remained substantially unimpaired. On the other hand, the closest the Confederates came to suffering some casualties was when Doubleday put a couple of 42-pound balls through the roof of the Moultrie House, a resort hotel located near Fort Moultrie. These, a Charleston newspaper reported, caused the men inside to scatter "miscellaneously." Doubleday's excuse for firing on the hotel was that prior to the bombardment it flew a secessionist flag. As a joke, he told a Confederate officer that once he had received poor service there.

At nightfall Anderson ordered firing ceased in order to conserve the fast-dwindling supply of powder bags. The Confederates for their part slackened off to an occasional shot designed to prevent the garrison from resting. However, most of the weary Federals could have echoed Private Thompson, who wrote, "I for one slept all night as sound as ever I did in my life."

April 13 dawned bright and sunny, and some people in Charleston witnessed what they hailed as an omen of victory: A gamecock alighted on the tomb of Calhoun, flapped its wings, and crowed! Beauregard's batteries resumed a heavy barrage; the fort responded sporadically. At midmorning flames again engulfed the barracks. Desperate efforts to extinguish them proved futile. Moreover, they threatened to reach the powder magazine, which as a result of very bad planning was located on the ground floor of one of the buildings. Falling embers prevented the removal of more than a small portion of the powder.

By noon, wrote Doubleday later, "The roaring and crackling of the flames, the dense masses of whirling smoke, the bursting of the enemy's shells, and our own which were exploding in the burning rooms, the crashing of the shot, and the sound of masonry falling in every direction, made the fort a pandemonium." According to Private Thompson, the "only way to breathe was to lay flat on the ground and keep your face covered with a wet handkerchief." Yet Anderson's gunners still managed occasionally to fire a cannon as a token of continued resistance. Each time

A 10-inch columbiad, mounted as a mortar in Fort Sumter. Drawn by an officer of Major Anderson's command prior to the start of hostilities. (Harper's Weekly, February 16, 1861)

Scene on the floating battery in Charleston Harbor during the bombardment of Fort Sumter, prepared from a drawing by a Confederate officer. (The Soldier in Our Civil War)

they did so the Confederates gave forth with a cheer in admiration of the garrison's gallantry.

Since early afternoon on April 12 both the garrison and the Confederates had observed ships lying off the bar of the harbor. They were Fox's. At 3 a.m. on April 12 he had arrived in the *Baltic*, having been delayed by gales. He found the *Harriet Lane* waiting for him, and three hours later the *Pawnee* showed up. None of the three tugboats appeared. A storm had driven one into Wilmington, North Carolina, and chased another past Charleston to Savannah, and the owner of the third had refused to let it leave New York.

During the rest of the day Fox waited, then searched for the *Pocahontas* and the all-important *Powhatan*. Not until the morning of April 13 did he learn from the commander of the *Pawnee* that the *Powhatan* had been detached from the expedition. Without the tugs and without the *Powhatan's* supplies, launches, and 300 sailors, his whole plan for relieving Anderson fell through.

Frustrated but undaunted, Fox then considered trying to reach Sumter in longboats from the *Baltic*,

but the heavy sea forced him to reject this idea. Next he proposed to use a commandeered ice schooner to make a run for the fort at night, even though he realized that such a venture would be suicidal: "I should certainly have gone in, and as certainly been knocked to pieces," he subsequently reported. For-

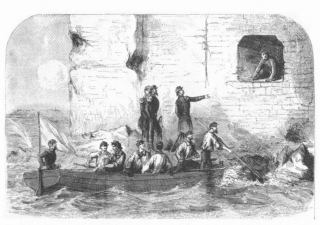

Anderson's interview with Colonel Louis Wigfall, through the porthole of Fort Sumter, during which Wigfall asked for Anderson's surrender. (Pictorial Battles of the Civil War)

tunately, however, he did not have an opportunity to make the attempt.

At 12:48 p.m. a shell cut Sumter's flagstaff. Peter Hart, assisted by several others, quickly replaced it and the banner it bore. But not long after he did so Louis Wigfall of Texas, now (like seemingly all Southern politicians) a colonel on Beauregard's staff, appeared outside one of the fort's embrasures waving a sword with a white handkerchief tied to its point. Having seen the flag go down, on his own initiative he had crossed the harbor to Sumter in a small boat to demand that Anderson surrender.

Anderson agreed to do so on the same terms Beauregard previously had offered. Flames were raging out of control through the fort. At any time the magazine might blow up. Nearly all the powder bags—including two dozen pairs of Anderson's socks—had been expended. The main gate had been blasted away and the fort lay open to a storming party. Above all it appeared obvious that no help could be expected from Fox. Hence there was no point in subjecting his hungry, exhausted, and half-suffocated men to further pounding. They had done their duty. So had he.

The flames in the fort burned down before blowing up the magazine. On the afternoon of April 14, a Sunday, the garrison marched out with drums playing "Yankee Doodle" and boarded a Confederate boat that transferred it on the following day to one of Fox's ships. That morning Anderson's soldiers, who had made additional powder bags out of scraps of blanket and even paper, had begun firing what he intended to be a hundred-gun salute to the flag before lowering it. However, midway in the ceremony a cartridge exploded prematurely. Five cannoneers were wounded, one mortally, and another killed outright. His name was Daniel Hough. He was the first soldier to die in the Civil War. Four years and some weeks and days later, over 600,000 others would be dead also.

On April 15 Lincoln issued a call for 75,000 volunteers to put down the Southern rebellion. Promptly Virginia, North Carolina, Tennessee, and Arkansas seceded, and Maryland, Kentucky, and Missouri threatened to do likewise. At the same time the vast majority of Southerners rallied enthusiastically behind the Confederacy, confident of victory and independence. Davis' decision to force a showdown at Sumter appeared justified by the outcome.

But the attack on the fort had outraged the North. There, too, men flocked to the colors and crowds cheered them as they marched off to do battle for the Union. On May 1, 1861, Lincoln was able to state quite accurately in a letter to Fox consoling him for

Following Andrerson's surrender on April 14, Confederates occupied Fort Sumter, cleaning up damage caused by the bombardment and posing for photographs. (National Archives)

The Confederate flag flies over Fort Sumter. Not until February 1865, when the Confederates were forced to leave Charleston, did the fort return to Union control. (National Archives)

Confederates inspect the 10-inch columbiad. Wade Hampton, whose father served under Thomas Sumter in the Revolutionary War, is top-hatted figure nearest gun. (National Archives)

the failure of his expedition: "You and I both anticipated that the cause of the country would be advanced by making the attempt to provision Fort Sumter, even if it should fail; and it is no small consolation now to feel that our anticipation is justified by the result."

In years to come historians would debate the question: Who caused the Civil War to begin at Fort Sumter—Lincoln or Davis?

The answer is simple: Both.

Lincoln as President of the United States had a duty to preserve a nation. Davis as President of the Confederacy had a mission to create one. Each decided to do what had to be done. The difference is that Lincoln's decision ultimately led to the success of his cause.

The firing on Fort Sumter decided that war would determine whether the North and South would be two or one. In the war itself the fort did not play a decisive part. Yet its role was prominent. To both Federals and Confederates it symbolized the Confederacy. Hence the former resolved to take it, the latter to keep it.

On April 7, 1863, nine Union ironclad ships tried to blast their way into Charleston Harbor. Sumter's cannons helped repulse them. In August 1863, the Federals opened on the fort with dozens of huge siege guns implanted on Morris Island. Their navy joined in. By September Sumter was a ruin, its cannons silenced. Yet when on the 9th 500 sailors and Marines tried to storm it, 320 Confederate defenders drove them back with heavy losses.

In December a second "Big Bombardment" took place. This, combined with an explosion in the powder magazine, reduced Sumter to a "volcanic pile." Nonetheless the gray garrison held on, crouch-

ing in bombproofs, its musicians defiantly playing "Dixie" whenever there was a lull in the shelling.

In July 1864, the Federals made a third and last attempt to pulverize Sumter into submission. It was no more successful than the first two. In fact, the fort emerged stronger than ever. As a later generation of American soldiers were to learn at Monte Cassino, rubble makes good defense.

Sumter did not fall into Northern hands until February 1865, when the approach of Sherman's army forced the Confederates to evacuate Charleston. By then the "Cradle of Secession" was a ruin, a "city of ashes." First there had been a devastating accidental fire in December 1861—the anniversary of secession. Then during 1863 and 1864 shellfire smashed and burned what was left. Even Calhoun's tomb was empty; the Charlestonians had reburied the coffin in an unmarked grave to prevent the Yankees from getting hold of it.

Shortly before noon, April 14, 1865, a Good Friday, Robert Anderson, now a general on the inactive list, returned to Fort Sumter. With him were his 6-year-old son and Peter Hart. The latter carried the same flag that had been hauled down there four bloody years before. A large crowd stood around a newly erected flagpole; many other people watched from boats in the harbor.

Hart attached the flag to the halyards of the pole; Anderson made a short speech, then seized the halyards and pulled the flag to the top of the pole. Sumter no longer was the symbol of the Confederacy. It now was the symbol of the victorious Union.

That night in Washington, D.C., the last important shot of the Civil War was fired. It came from a derringer aimed at the back of Abraham Lincoln's head.

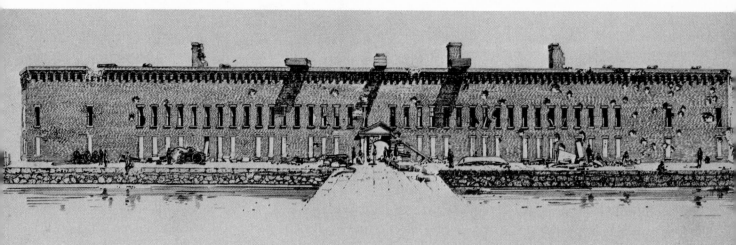

Drawing of Fort Sumter following bombardment by the Confederates. Pockmarks in the fort's wall made by shells are shown, as are the damaged chimneys. (Grey Castle Press)

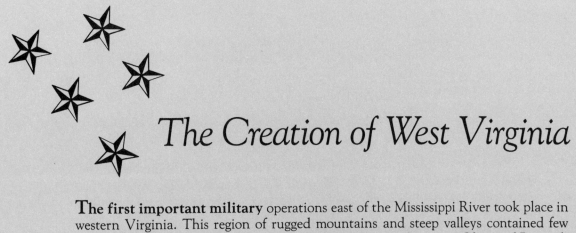

The Creation of West Virginia

The first important military operations east of the Mississippi River took place in western Virginia. This region of rugged mountains and steep valleys contained few slaves or plantations. Its small-farm economy was oriented more to Ohio and Pennsylvania than to the South. The largest city, Wheeling, was 330 miles from Richmond but only 60 miles from Pittsburgh. The people of Virginia west of the Shenandoah Valley were unionist in sympathy and their delegates to the Virginia convention had voted overwhelmingly against secession. They returned home from Richmond determined to detach western Virginia from the rest of the state and return it to the Union.

To do so they would need help from the Union army. By June 1861 help was on the way. Ten thousand soldiers from Ohio and Indiana joined two thousand West Virginians and moved against a small Confederate force of five thousand defending

West Virginia flag borne by the 13th Infantry. West Virginia managed to secede from the Confederacy and rejoin the Union, but its early history was hardly peaceful. (CWTI Collection)

two mountain passes through which ran the principal roads between eastern Virginia and the Ohio River. The Union troops were organized and commanded by George B. McClellan, with William S. Rosecrans second in command. Their achievements in western Virginia would launch meteoric Civil War careers of early prominence and ultimate failure for both men.

On July 11 Rosecrans led a flank attack against Confederate troops at Rich Mountain that routed the rebels in confusion. Commanding the main Union force, McClellan demonstrated the caution and hesitancy that became his trademark. His failure to throw in his men at the crucial moment allowed most of the Confederate defenders to escape. Nevertheless, by July 13 Yankee forces had captured 1,000 enemy troops and driven the rest out of western Virginia. The Confederate commander, Robert Garnett, was killed in the fighting, becoming the first of seventy-seven southern generals killed in action during the war.

This Union success had two important consequences. First, McClellan took credit for the victories and was hailed in the northern press as a "young Napoleon" who could lead the North to victory. After the Union defeat at Bull Run in eastern Virginia on July 21, Lincoln called McClellan to Washington to take command of the Army of the Potomac. Second, behind the shield of northern military occupation the unionists of western Virginia proceeded to organize the new state of West Virginia. A complicated series of political and legal maneuvers by conventions in Wheeling and by Congress in Washington led to formal creation of the new state in 1862 and its admission to the Union in 1863.

The early history of West Virginia was scarcely peaceful, however. The Confederates made a determined effort to regain control of the region in the fall of 1861. Jefferson Davis sent his military adviser, Robert E. Lee, out to the mountains in August to take overall command of some 20,000 Confederate troops and drive the Yankees out. One of the most promising officers in the pre-war army, Lee had opposed secession. When Virginia left the Union he faced an agonizing choice. Should he remain loyal to the country he had served for thirty-five years? "I must side either with or against my section," he told a northern friend. But he did not hesitate. "I cannot raise my hand against my birthplace, my home, my children." Lee resigned from the U.S. army and joined the Confederacy, where his initial duty was to organize Virginia's troops. His assignment to western Virginia was his first field command. It almost ruined his reputation.

Lee's efforts to regain western Virginia were frustrated by bad weather; by sickness and inexperience among his unseasoned troops; by feuding between his subordinate commanders John Floyd and Henry A. Wise, both of them former governors of Virginia who thirsted for military glory but possessed little military ability; and by the skillful opposition of Union military commanders William Rosecrans and Jacob Cox. Continual rains bogged Lee's army down in the mud while measles and dysentery put more than one-third of his men on the sick list, forcing him to call off an attack on the Cheat Mountain pass in mid-September. Subsequent efforts to dislodge Rosecrans from the Kanawha Valley also failed. Confederate forces gave up the offensive in October 1861 amid loud criticism from Virginia newspapers, which derided their commander as "Evacuating Lee" and "Granny Lee." Guerrilla warfare would plague West Virginia for the next three years, but Union military control remained firm enough to enable political creation of the new state to go forward.

To most contemporaries in both North and South these operations in the Virginia mountains were a sideshow. The main action occurred in the lowland corridor between Washington and Richmond, where the first major battle of the war took place near the sluggish stream of Bull Run twenty-five miles from Washington.

—*James M. McPherson*

FIRST MANASSAS

by V. C. Jones

Capitol at Washington. Lincoln's inauguration, March 4, 1861. Note unfinished dome on which work was continued during the war.

When a hot, relentless sun rose on Sunday, July 21, 1861, Bull Run and Manassas were names that meant virtually nothing throughout the world. By nightfall they were on their way to immortality.

That morning, the casual observer casting his eyes over the sweep from Centreville Ridge on the east to the hazy-blue Bull Run Mountains ten miles to the west would see nothing to indicate that over a part of that area within the next few hours would be fought one of the great battles of modern history and the first major conflict of the Civil War, America's internecine struggle between the North and South.

Here lay deceiving country. Pastoral in appearance, with rolling, gentle hills a mile or so apart, it was wooded mostly, but here and there occasional cleared acreage marked moderately prosperous farms. Scattered about, too, were houses of varying proportions and construction, some far apart, some close, but none closer than the pair separated by only a few hundred yards on the brow of Henry Hill, where the crux of the battle would occur. This hill, six miles from the little railroad junction of Manassas, meeting point of the Orange & Alexandria and Manassas Gap lines, overlooked Bull Run, a meandering stream. With Cub

Run and Rocky Run to the east, it was the largest of the three, all parallel. The first two would play proportionately important roles in the forthcoming conflict, one of the bloodiest of all time.

Other factors would come into play. On a thirty-odd-foot tower near Manassas a signal officer would stand with binoculars, meticulously scanning the countryside and bringing to warfare a new mode of communication. He would wigwag Boy Scout fashion an important message. And miles to the west, onto the dirty, smoke-blackened cars of the little Manassas Gap Railroad running from Manassas to Strasburg over in the Shenandoah Valley, soldiers under Joseph E. Johnston would clamber by the thousands, en route to a union of forces that would turn out to be one of the major coups of the day.

The man on the tower, Captain E. P. Alexander, later a prominent Confederate general, and many others like him, of little fame at the time, would rise into prominence like shooting stars. By the close of day, records and actions would be shaping up names for the history books—Beauregard, Burnside, Jubal Early, Ewell, Hampton, A. P. Hill, Jackson, Longstreet, Sherman, Stuart, and many more—a bevy of "greats" whose names would ring on the tongues of succeeding generations without respect to the side on which they fought. But at least two of those who participated—George A. Custer and John S. Mosby—would have to wait until a later day for the chroniclers to find them.

On the Northern front there was a frantic impatience for troops to march upon the Confederate Capital. "On to Richmond!" was the cry. The United States Congress had gone into extraordinary session on July 4 in Washington, D. C., the Federal Capital. Early on the agenda was a message from President Abraham

Confederate Capitol at Richmond, from photograph taken in April 1865 after evacuation. Observe the broken windows.

Lincoln reviewing hostilities that had gone on in the seceded states since the preceding fall and urging steps to save the Union.

On Tuesday, July 16, troops started marching out of Washington. They were clad in a heterogeneous mixture of uniforms, few of which gave definite indication of the allegiance of the men who wore them. Their leader was a physically powerful man named Irvin McDowell, 43, only two months a brigadier general. He had been educated in France and at the United States Military Academy, and had distinguished himself in the Mexican War. He was looked upon as an officer well informed outside and inside of his profession. Though inexperienced as a leader and no military genius, he knew the 30,000 troops under his command were mostly untrained and ill-equipped for the assignment ahead of them. But the word was "Go!"

Behind, he was leaving Winfield Scott, General in Chief, on whose staff he had served. Scott, actually a year older than the Federal Constitution and a hero of the War of 1812 and the Mexican War, was too decrepit to take the field. From his desk near the White House, however, he would play a part in the unfolding drama.

Not all the urgency for battle action rested with the North. The Southerners had their notion about when fighting should begin, too.

At Richmond, an officer who would take his place with Alexander the Great and Napoleon as one of the military leaders of all time surveyed the terrain in the vicinity of Washington. He was Robert E. Lee, newly resigned from the United States Army to defend his native state of Virginia and serving at the moment as adviser to the Confederacy's President, Jefferson Davis.

Lee's eyes focused on Bull Run, flowing southeast from the Bull Run Mountains and only thirty miles from the Union Capital. This narrow, crooked stream, with alternately precipitous and marshy banks, seemed to him to be a good base line for the protection of the railroads at Manassas and possibly for offensive operations against the enemy.

On May 8, Brigadier General Philip St. George Cocke, West Point graduate and well-to-do Virginia and Mississippi plantation owner, was stationed at the junction with four companies of infantry and cavalry. This force was soon increased to a dozen companies, and camps of instruction sprang up. Before the month was out, Brigadier General M. L. Bonham, Indian fighter, Mexican War veteran, and ex-United States Congressman, arrived with a brigade, and on June 1 Brigadier General Pierre Gustave Toutant Beauregard took over as commander of all the Confederate forces in northeastern Virginia, bundled together as the Army of the Potomac. This last officer, a West Point-trained, Mexican War veteran who had served on General Scott's staff, had more recently been superintendent of the Military Academy and still more recently toasted as the hero of Fort Sumter, where he was in command of the Confederate attack. He was a military engineer, more curbed by personality than lack of ability.

General Pierre Gustave Toutant Beauregard. Portrait by B. F. Reinhardt, painted December 19, 1861.

General Joseph Eggleston Johnston, whose reinforcements to Beauregard turned the tide of battle.

Beauregard began early to think of offensive action, but it was July 14 before he was well enough along with his plans to express them to others. They revolved around General Johnston and his army of 12,000 men facing an army of 18,000 under Brevet Brigadier General Robert Patterson over in the Shenandoah Valley. Here was a veteran of the regular service confronting a leader who had received his training through the Pennsylvania militia. Johnston was a West Pointer, Indian fighter, and Mexican War veteran who had personally led the storming column at Chapultepec. He had been wounded numerous times. While Patterson had served with the militia in the War of 1812 and also the Mexican War, he had no such extensive battle experience as Johnston.

On July 14, Beauregard sent his plan to Richmond via Colonel James Chesnut, a South Carolina lawyer who had served in the United States Senate with Jefferson Davis. It was briefly this:

General Johnston should leave from 3,000 to 5,000 men in the passes of the Blue Ridge Mountains to hold Patterson in check, while with the bulk of his army he should move by the Manassas Gap Railroad to join forces with Beauregard. The two of them would advance rapidly on Fairfax Court House, establishing themselves between the lines of Union troops around Falls Church and Alexandria and attacking them separately with large forces, exterminating them or driving them into the Potomac River. Johnston would then, with a part of Beauregard's troops and those left in the passes, attack and destroy Patterson at Winchester or wherever he might be. The attack would next be on Washington, Johnston moving from the Maryland side and Beauregard from Virginia. There must be no delay.

At least one part of this plan had been under consideration since the Confederates first started fortifying at Manassas. As early as May 15, General Cocke, in a dispatch to Lee, had pointed out the importance of the Manassas Gap line, which would enable troops to be moved from the Valley to Manassas, or vice versa.

But Beauregard's grandiose plan to take the offensive never materialized, for at 3 o'clock on the afternoon of July 16 the vanguard of the Federal army started from Washington. Experienced officers and men of distinction were at the head of the units involved, as follows:

1st Division—Commanded by Brigadier General Daniel Tyler, West Pointer and authority on artillery maneuvers. The division consisted of the 1st Brigade, under Colonel Erasmus D. Keyes, West Point graduate and instructor, Indian fighter, and specialist in coastal defense; 2d Brigade, Brigadier General Robert C. Schenck, former U.S. Congressman and minister to

Brazil; 3d Brigade, Colonel William T. Sherman, West Pointer and Mexican War veteran; and 4th Brigade, Colonel Isaac B. Richardson, West Pointer and Indian fighter, known as "Fighting Dick" because of his record in the Mexican War.

2d Division—Under Colonel David Hunter, West Pointer and Mexican War veteran. His command included: 1st Brigade, Colonel David Porter, West Pointer and Mexican War veteran; and 2d Brigade, Colonel Ambrose E. Burnside, West Pointer, Mexican War veteran, and firearms manufacturer, distinguished also by his unusual growth of side whiskers.

3d Division — Led by Colonel Samuel P. Heintzelman, West Pointer, Indian fighter, and Mexican War veteran. His brigades were: 1st Brigade, Colonel William B. Franklin, West Point graduate and instructor and Mexican War veteran; 2d Brigade, Colonel Orlando Bolivar Willcox, West Pointer, Indian fighter, and Mexican War veteran; and 3d Brigade, Colonel Oliver O. Howard, West Point graduate and instructor and Indian fighter.

4th Division—Under militia Brigadier General Theodore Runyon, left seven miles from the battle area to guard communications.

5th Division — Commanded by Colonel Dixon S. Miles, West Pointer whose first assignment had been at Fort Leavenworth, Kansas. His division: 1st Brigade, Colonel Lewis Blenker, German officer who had served with the Bavarian Legion; and 2d Brigade, Colonel Thomas A. Davies, West Pointer and Indian fighter.

Later Major General Irvin McDowell, unfortunate Union commander at Bull Run.

National Archives

That night, most of the men reached Annandale, about ten miles to the west, and went into camp. Their movement was not unknown to General Beauregard. He had employed espionage to learn what the Federals were doing. A former clerk in one of the government departments in Washington volunteered to go into the city and bring back the latest information on the happenings there. Below Alexandria, just across the Potomac from the Capital, this man crossed by boat, carrying a small scrap of paper bearing the

words "Trust bearer." In the early morning he handed this to Rose O'Neal Greenhow, Southern sympathizer and a society leader who was able to move about with ease in political circles. She reacted promptly, and the agent was soon on his way back to Beauregard with this message: "Order issued to McDowell to march upon Manassas tonight."

Other things were happening on this important July 16. Over in the Shenandoah Valley, Colonel J. E. B. Stuart, another West Pointer and Indian fighter, commanding a regiment of Confederate cavalry, reported that General Patterson had moved from Martinsburg and halted at Bunker Hill, nine miles from Winchester, where the Confederates lay. This gave Johnston the impression that the Union leader was creating a diversion to keep him occupied while Beauregard was being attacked at Manassas.

On July 17, the Federal troops pushed on to Fairfax Court House, another ten miles from Washington. There they began to encounter the Confederates, who departed hastily leaving behind camp equipage and forage. The Northerners paraded through town four abreast, with bands playing and flags waving.

That day Colonel Chesnut returned from Richmond. He had found Davis sick in bed, but the President received him "with great kindness and cordiality." Later the emissary unfolded Beauregard's plan of action at the Spotswood Hotel in a meeting with Davis, Lee, Inspector General Samuel Coper and Colonel John S. Preston, successful planter and brother-in-law of Wade Hampton. The scheme was considered "brillant and comprehensive," yet Davis and Lee found two faults with it: 1) Johnston's army was not strong enough to allow the withdrawal of enough troops to effect the object and keep Patterson from coming down on Beauregard's left; and (2) —this mainly—the Federals were still so close to cover that they could fall back upon their intrenchments or be reinforced by their reserves. Later, when the lines were longer, the plan could work, they advised, but not now.

Failure of the plan to get approval from Richmond actually made little difference. Already the Federals were clogging the roads west out of Washington, and by the 18th they were gathering along the heights of Centreville. Beauregard, in the meantime, completed the withdrawal of his troops behind Bull Run, General Bonham's 1st Brigade barely getting across unscathed after midnight. If unable to get reinforcements from the Valley, Beauregard still had hopes of support from the Aquia District of the Department of Northern Virginia below Fredericksburg. It was commanded by Brigadier General Theophilus H. Holmes, veteran of the Seminole and Mexican Wars and a West Point classmate of Jefferson Davis.

The Confederate forces lay along an eight-mile stretch of Bull Run, concentrating at or near seven crossing points—six fords and a bridge—with reserve units in supporting distance. In the array, as in the case of the North's high command, were fighting strength and talent. The defense stations from east to west were:

Union Mills Ford, near the railroad—three regiments of infantry, four 12-pounder howitzers, and three companies of cavalry, under Colonel Richard S. Ewell, Mexican War veteran and Indian fighter.

McLean's Ford—three regiments, two brass 6-

Post-war photograph of signal tower similar to the one used by the Confederates in detecting McDowell's flank march against the Confederate left.

pounders, and one company of cavalry, under Brigadier General D. R. Jones, West Pointer, Indian fighter, Mexican War veteran, and chief of staff during the bombardment of Fort Sumter.

Blackburn's Ford—three regiments and two 6-pounder guns, under Brigadier General James Longstreet, West Pointer, Indian fighter, and Mexican War veteran.

Mitchell's Ford, in the center—four regiments, two batteries of artillery, and six companies of cavalry, under General Bonham, closing out his second month of service at Manassas.

Ball's and Lewis' Fords, three miles farther west and near Stone Bridge—three regiments, one battery, and one company of cavalry, under General Cocke, first commander on duty in the area.

Stone Bridge—one regiment and a battalion of infantry, four 6-pounder guns, and two companies of cavalry, under Colonel Nathan G. "Shanks" Evans, West Pointer and Indian fighter.

During the 17th, Beauregard sent a message to Richmond by telegraph, a system of communication then in use for only seventeen years. This would be its first use in a war. The message read:

"The enemy has assaulted my outposts in heavy force. I have fallen back on the Bull Run, and will make a stand at Mitchell's Ford. If his force is overwhelming I shall retire to the Rappahannock Rail-

Above: Scene at Manassas Junction, Union-held in 1864. Box cars are considerably smaller than those now in use. Below: Post-war photograph of the famous Stone Bridge over Bull Run.

road Bridge, saving my command for defense there and future operations. Please inform Johnston of this, via Staunton, and also Holmes. Send forward any reinforcements at the earliest possible instant and to every possible means."

At 1 o'clock on the morning of July 18, General Johnston received a telegram from Inspector General Cooper at Richmond that indicated Beauregard's plan of action had not been ignored altogether. It stated: "General Beauregard is attacked. To strike the enemy a decisive blow a junction of all your effective force will be needed. If practicable, make the movement, sending your sick and baggage to Culpeper Court House either by railroad or by Warrenton. In all the arrangements exercise your discretion."

Johnston was a man of action, and the telegram from Richmond got immediate attention. "The best service which the Army of the Shenandoah could render was to prevent the defeat of that of the Potomac," he later wrote. His decision was to elude Patterson, a speedier course than trying to defeat him. Quickly he made dispositions of the advance guard to bring about the evasion, provided for his sick at Winchester, and started moving his army through Ashby's Gap to Piedmont, a station on the Manassas Gap line. What he was doing would bring Patterson's dismissal from the Federal Army in a matter of days.

Meanwhile, pursuing his advance, McDowell moved with confidence. He had been assured by Scott that

64

Patterson would prevent Johnston from reinforcing Beauregard. At 8:15 a.m. July 18, he sent a message ahead to General Tyler, commanding the 1st Division and in the advance:

"I have information which leads me to believe you will find no force at Centreville, and will meet with no resistance in getting there. Observe the roads to Bull Run and Warrenton. Do not bring on an engagement, but keep up the impression that we are moving on Manassas."

At 9 a.m., the 4th Brigade of Tyler's division, under "Fighting Dick" Richardson, moved into Centreville. It found the enemy had indeed gone, so it turned along the road to Manassas and halted to obtain water. Tyler came up and, despite his instructions not to bring on an engagement, took a squadron of cavalry and two light companies from the brigade and, with Richardson, went to make a reconnaissance.

"We soon found ourselves overlooking the strong position of the enemy situated at Blackburn's Ford, on Bull Run," he reported. "A moment's observation discovered a battery on the opposite bank, but no great body of troops, although the usual pickets and small detachments showed themselves on the left of the position.

"Suspecting from the natural strength which I saw the position to possess that the enemy must be in force, and desiring to ascertain the extent of that force and the position of his batteries, I ordered up the two rifled guns, Ayres' battery, and Richardson's entire brigade, and subsequently Sherman's brigade in reserve, to be ready for any contingency. As soon as the

Scouting party from 1st Ohio Infantry near Fairfax Court House, June 1861. Wash drawing by A. R. Waud. Four of the men are wearing the later discarded havelocks.

rifled guns came up I ordered them into battery on the crest of the hill, nearly a mile from a single battery which we could see placed on the opposite side of the run. Ten or a dozen shots were fired, one of them seeming to take effect on a large body of cavalry who evidently thought themselves out of range."

But the Confederates refused to satisfy Tyler's curiosity. They threw a few shells and sent out a few skirmishers, after which they remained in the woods. Tyler made more advances and sent out a section of a battery supported by a squadron of cavalry. Suddenly the Southerners came alive "with volleys which showed that the whole bottom was filled with troops."

Two Federal officers watching the action from a hill in the rear became alarmed at this new turn of affairs. They were Major J. G. Barnard of the U. S. Corps of Engineers, a Mexican War veteran who had served as superintendent of the Military Academy and more recently as Chief Engineer of Washington, D. C., and Captain J. B. Fry, Assistant Adjutant General, West Point graduate and artillery teacher, and Mexican War veteran. They sent a messenger to remind Tyler that McDowell had advised against bringing on an engagement. This seemed to have its effect. Anyway, Tyler had learned all he wanted to know: "This attack . . . showed that the enemy was in force and disclosed the position of his batteries."

It was Tyler's intention to withdraw in orderly fashion, but something went wrong. Some of the men left the scene in confusion, especially a regiment of New Yorkers, who panicked and ran a mile and a half before they could be rallied.

Above: Union soldiers pose exuberantly on the roof of Fairfax Court House. Below: Centreville was the jump-off point and later the Union rallying point in the First Bull Run Campaign.

Harper's Weekly, Aug. 3, 1861

"Fall's Church, Virginia, the advanced post of our army on the Potomac."

"The fire which the regiment encountered was severe, but no excuse for the disorganization it produced," Tyler reported. Longstreet, commanding the Confederates on the other side of the stream, dismissed the incident with the observation that the presence of his regiments "probaby intimidated the enemy as much as the fire of the troops that met him."

The action had begun about noon and continued with an exchange of gunfire until 4 o'clock in the afternoon. The Confederates answered the Federals gun for gun, but discontinued the moment Tyler ordered a halt. There were casualties on both sides.

That night McDowell called a council of some of his officers to discuss plans. He had made some reconnaissance during the day and had reached a definite decision. Originally it was planned to make a sweep to the left of Manassas, from Fairfax Court House and Centreville to Fairfax Station and on to Wolf Run Shoals, but he had had a look and so had some of his Engineers, and they had determined that the country in that direction was unfit for the operations of a large army. Therefore the movement must be by the right, turning the enemy's left. This would mean that their advance would be along the Warrenton turnpike out of Centreville, instead of along the road toward Blackburn's Ford, where Tyler's men had been repulsed.

But there would be time to see, he advised. The provision trains were just beginning to come in, and the troops would require at least another day to cook their provisions for the continued march, which would afford opportunity to examine the country more carefully. Major Barnard, who was present, promised to

have a look the next day and try to bring in more information.

The 19th was spent in contemplating the best way to get around the Confederate left. McDowell's engineers had information that there was a ford about three miles above Stone Bridge at a place listed on the maps as "Sudley Springs." They were reliably informed—some of the details came from Mathias C. Mitchell, a local resident who represented himself as a Union man and was secured as a guide—that Bull Run was passable at this point even for wheeled vehicles. Moreover, maps indicated a farm ford between Sudley and Stone Bridge that was also said to be good, though little used. They were further advised that a road branched off in the direction of Sudley a short distance after passing over Cub Run, which was spanned by a suspension bridge.

As promised, Major Barnard went out on reconnaissance. With him rode Captain Daniel Phineas Woodbury, of the engineers, who had had experience in constructing roads on the east coast and even on the frontier, and Governor William Sprague of Rhode Island, commanding a regiment of militia and a battery of light horse artillery from his state. A company of cavalry escorted them. They passed over Cub Run and, truly enough, found a road that seemed to lead to Sudley. It was a tortuous, narrow trace of a rarely used byway, much of its course lying through a dense

Continued on page 70

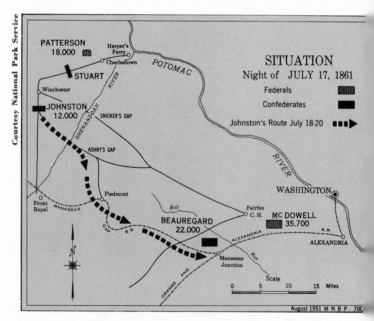

On July 17, with McDowell's army of more than 35,000 men advancing from Washington, Confederate forces were divided between Winchester and Manassas. By means of the Manassas Gap Railroad, Johnston's force was transferred to Manassas in time to reinforce Beauregard.

PRINCIPAL FEDERAL OFFICERS AT FIRST BULL RUN

Captain James B. Ricketts, afterward a major general.

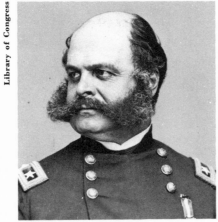

Colonel (later Major General) Ambrose E. Burnside.

Colonel (subsequently Brigadier General) Louis Blenker.

Captain Charles Griffin, later a major general.

Colonel (later Lieutenant General) William T. Sherman.

Brigadier (later Major) General Robert C. Schenck.

Brigadier General Daniel Tyler.

Colonel (later Major General) Samuel P. Heintzelman.

Colonel (subsequently Major General) David Hunter.

PRINCIPAL CONFEDERATE OFFICERS AT FIRST BULL RUN

Captain Edward P. Alexander, later a brigadier.

Colonel (later Lieutenant General) Thomas J. Jackson.

Colonel James E. B. Stuart, who rose to major general.

Colonel Wade Hampton, afterward a lieutenant general.

Brigadier General Barnard E. Bee.

Kean Archives

Brigadier (later Lieutenant) General James Longstreet.

Battles and Leaders of the Civil War

Colonel F. S. Bartow.

Library of Congress

Colonel (later lieutenant general) Jubal A. Early.

Library of Congress

Brigadier (later Lieutenant) General Richard S. Ewell.

Library of Congress

Colonel Arnold Elzey (Jones) later became a major general.

Library of Congress

Captain John D. Imboden, became a brigadier.

Cook Collection, Valentine Museum

Brigadier General Philip St. George Cocke.

Kean Archives

Colonel (later lieutenant general) Ambrose P. Hill.

Uniforms of Federal units which fought at Bull Run. Left to right: 2d Ohio, Blenker's 8th New York, 1st Massachusetts.

Continued from page 66

woods. For some distance they followed it, opening gates and passing through private grounds, but stopped when they encountered enemy patrols. To go farther would be dangerous, not so much for fear of their personal safety, but because they did not wish to attract attention to their designs in this quarter.

Captain Woodbury suggested that he make a reconnaissance at night with a few Michigan woodsmen, but this later turned out to be a failure. There were too many Confederates wandering around through the woods.

While the Federals were having their troubles on the 19th in deciding what to do, so was Beauregard at Manassas. During the day this telegram came in from Inspector General Cooper:

"We have no intelligence from General Johnston. If the enemy in front of you has abandoned an immediate attack, and General Johnston has not moved, you had better withdraw your call upon him, so that he may be left to his full direction. All the troops arriving at Lynchburg are ordered to join you. From

this place we will send as fast as transportation permits. The enemy is advised at Washington of the projected movement of Generals Johnston and Holmes, and may vary his plans in conformity thereto."

Beauregard did not consider the telegram an order in terms, but rather an "urgency" from Richmond that left him technically free to decide his further course. He determined to make every effort to bring about the prompt arrival of the Shenandoah forces and, should they come before McDowell attacked, to take the offensive himself. Fortunately for him, the Union commander was delaying, partly because of lack of rations and partly due to the need for more information.

Centreville is an old village; in the early days it was a stage stop on the route from Washington to Winchester and a busy crossroads with an inn known far and wide as Newgate Tavern. The village had been incorporated in 1798, lots and streets laid off, and plans made for a considerable community. To some of the Union soldiers who halted there on the march to Bull Run it did indeed seem a thriving community,

Left to right: Garibaldi Guards, 14th New York, 11th New York (Fire Zouaves).

although they noticed only a few houses, and most of these on the west side of the ridge running north and south.

July 20 of 1861 also found it busy. Troops seemed everywhere, although most of them were quartered along the eastern slope of the ridge, the road to Blackburn's Ford, and Braddock Road, coming into the village from the southeast. This latter route was an old one from Williamsburg built by Braddock's army during its advance on Fort Duquesne in 1755.

Even though almost within cannon range of the Confederates, the bivouacs of the Union soldiers swarmed with visitors during both the 19th and 20th. Some were official and some unofficial, but they all moved about without military restraint, passing to and fro among the troops as they pleased. Many of them had come out from Washington in carriages and had brought their own supplies. Some of the women had even packed along their best finery, for it was common knowledge that there would be dancing at Fairfax Court House after the Northerners had driven the Southerners back to Richmond. Surveying the scene,

Fry was impressed that it had the "appearance of a monster military picnic." Two factors detracted from the jolly atmosphere: the heat and the dust. Clouds of the latter were stirred from the clayey soil by even the slightest movement.

Throughout the 20th campfires burned everywhere. Soldiers were cooking the rations sent out by wagon train from Washington. They had received orders that they must have at least two or three days' supply in their haversacks when the march was resumed. The daily ration consisted of a pound of hardtack, three quarters of a pound of pork or bacon or a pound and a quarter of fresh or salt beef, an ounce and a half of coffee, twenty-four ounces of sugar, and a small quantity of salt.

McDowell had definitely made up his mind that the swing must be to the right along the Warrenton turnpike. The affair at Blackburn's Ford had convinced him that the enemy position was too strong at that point for passage to be forced without great loss. As for the movement to the right, Stone Bridge was the problem. He had information that it was

Confederate troops en route to Manassas. Allen C. Redwood sketch.

mined, defended by a battery in position, and further fortified by heavy abatis. But this point could be avoided by making only a feint there and swinging the bulk of his troops across Bull Run at Sudley Springs. Then they would go on to break the Manassas Gap line and prevent Johnston from joining Beauregard.

It was his intention to move the several columns out on the road a few miles on the evening of the 20th, so they would have a shorter march in the morning and thus be fresher for whatever fighting might be in store. But his officers gave him some bad advice. They urged starting in the early dawn and making only one move. McDowell consented, thus giving the Southerners more time in which to bring up reinforcements.

McDowell summoned his brigade commanders to headquarters for a final meeting as night closed in. Each was told what he was to do. Most of the troops would move off at 2:30 a.m. and head down the Warrenton turnpike, but the 5th Division under Colonel Miles, along with the 4th Brigade, 1st Division, commanded by Colonel Richardson, would remain behind and guard Blackburn's Ford to make sure the Confederates did not execute a turning movement from that direction while the Union thrust was being made to the right. As soon as cannon fire was heard from upstream around Stone Bridge, Richardson, nearest to the ford, was to open with his guns for the purpose of making a diversion.

A few other matters were on McDowell's mind. He was anxious over the inability of his troops to make their rations last as long as they should, and he was especially bothered by the fact that the term of service of some of them was expiring. This had been one of the reasons for the impatience in the North. The men had signed up for three months, and the three-month period was drawing to a close for some of them. Even that day it had ended for the 4th Pennsylvania and the 8th New York Militia, and these regiments turned a deaf ear to pleas that they remain a few days longer. On the morrow they would move to the rear "to the sound of the enemy's cannon." The Union commander, expecting within the next few days to lose thousands of the best troops in the army for this reason, ironically noted that every day made the enemy's force stronger and his weaker. He believed that the repulse at Blackburn's Ford on the 18th was largely to blame for the attitude of the retiring units.

Battles and Leaders of the Civil War

Still other things were bothering him. He had word from a man who said he had just come from the Valley that Patterson was falling back. And there were rumors that Johnston had actually joined Beauregard.

At Manassas during the 20th, the biggest development was the arrival of the vanguard of troops from the Shenandoah Valley, confirming the rumor at Centreville. In came the 7th and 8th Georgia regiments, and then the 1st Brigade under Brigadier General Thomas J. Jackson, consisting of the 2d, 4th, 5th, 27th, and 33d Virginia regiments. About noon, in chugged a train bringing General Johnston and, with him, Brigadier General Barnard E. Bee, with Alabama and Mississippi troops. For the first time in history, steam-propelled locomotives had been used for the rapid movement of troops.

The Manassas Gap line was young and poorly equipped, with little rolling stock of its own. Some of the engines in use had been run out of Alexandria before that city was occupied by the Federals. Many of the cars were captured in May when the Confederacy took over more than 100 miles of the Baltimore & Ohio's main line and transported them, as well as locomotives, over the turnpikes by animal power to railroads farther south.

"Listening for the first gun at Manassas." A. C. Redwood sketch.

Johnston was in an optimistic mood when he stepped off the train at Manassas. The president of the railroad had assured him that the remainder of his troops should arrive during the day. His cavalry and artillery were coming by turnpike, and he knew they were well on their way. Moreover, he had eluded Patterson without trouble, although he suspected the Union commander would follow as soon as he learned the size of the force confronting him. This might be as early as the 22d.

Sherman's battery of light artillery, engaged at First Bull Run.

Harper's Weekly, June 8, 1861

Without delay, Johnston rode to look over the field and found Beauregard's position so extensive and the ground so densely wooded that he knew it would be virtually impossible for him to gain knowledge of it and the enemy's position in the brief time at his disposal, so he informed Beauregard that he would rely upon his judgment, having full confidence in it.

Beauregard also was feeling good about developments. Johnston was bringing 8,340 men and twenty guns from the Valley, and General Holmes already had arrived with 1,265 rank and file, with six pieces of artillery, from Aquia. The latter force, with the 6th Brigade of the Army of the Potomac under Colonel Jubal A. Early, at forty-five a profane, tobacco-chewing Indian fighter, Mexican War veteran, and lawyer, would be placed back of the fords on the right as a reserve. The others would be stationed so as to strengthen the left center and left, the latter being particularly weak owing to lack of available troops.

Little sleeping went on in the Federal camp at Centreville the night of the 20th. The men had their canteens filled and their haversacks packed. But many of them, untrained and unaccustomed to the physical effort that had been involved in the march from Washington, were already fatigued almost to the point of exhaustion, not to mention the trouble they were having with sore feet and the suffering from the heat. Much of the latter was due to the heavy uniforms they were wearing, certainly not the light material necessary for mid-July weather in Virginia.

From the start there was delay as the troops were aroused from their billets before the hour set by McDowell for the start of the march. The artillery was ready on schedule, but the infantry was not, and there was nearly an hour of waiting before Tyler's division took to the road. Three of his brigades were to go straight down the turnpike to Stone Bridge and had to clear the turnoff point beyond Cub Run so that Hunter's and Heintzelman's divisions could turn to the right and cross Sudley Ford at least by 7 a.m. The movement had been scheduled so as to avoid the burning heat that would come as the day advanced.

It was about two miles to the turnoff, but it took hours to cover that distance. March was route step and, despite their aches and pains, the soldiers were in a light mood. Most of them knew nothing about the horrors of war. They sang and they joked in the dark, knowing that the eyes of the North were upon them. The vocal press and the even more highly vocal element exempt from military service had assured them that it should be no problem to drive the Confederates toward whom they were marching back to the rebellious homes whence they had come.

Federal army advancing at the start of the Battle of Bull Run. Note civilian (lower right) "consulting" with officer.

The road from Centreville was not winding. It was downhill half a mile or so, then it curved slightly to the left and climbed gently uphill, the last rise before the descent to the suspension bridge over Cub Run. But it was dusty, and this slowed the marchers as they choked and fell out of line to catch their breath. Then, as the dawn began to break, they made out blackberry bushes in the fields on each side, and this was an irresistible lure. They fell out, picked handfuls of the ripened berries, and then sauntered back to their lines.

Another delaying factor was a 30-pounder Parrott gun attached to Tyler's division. It was to open the

The Soldier in Our Civil War

firing at Stone Bridge and might even turn out to be the deciding factor, for it was looked upon as a mighty weapon. Thus it had the green flag for the advance, but its nineteen-horse team found difficulty in moving it along the narrow and sometimes rough road. A cloud of dust hovered over it whenever it was moved. And when it arrived at Cub Run there was considerable delay, while the men in charge made up their minds to gamble that the suspension bridge would not collapse under the gun's considerable weight. As it turned out, the span was equal to the test, and the Parrott rolled on toward Stone Bridge.

The progress of Tyler's division was so slow that Hunter's and Heintzelman's columns found it took them two to three hours to cover the distance from Centreville, something a fast-walking man could do in half an hour easily. It was far past the scheduled time before they were able to turn off on the road toward Sudley—this had been set for early daylight or about 4 a.m.—and then they gradually realized something they had not expected. The route was much longer than information gathered by the Engineers had indicated. Fry put it at twelve miles instead of six; both figures were exaggerations, but toiling over a little-

Harper's Weekly, Aug 3, 1861

The 30-pounder Parrott of Carlisle's battery fires the first shot at Bull Run.

used trail in dust and oppressive heat distorted the best of estimates.

Some time after daylight the first shot was fired from the 30-pounder Parrott. The exact time of this action and the exact person who pulled the lanyard have been lost to history. The gun was attached to the battery of Captain J. Howard Carlisle, commanding Company E of the 2d Artillery, and was under the direction of Lieutenant Peter C. Hains of the U.S. Artillery Corps.

McDowell recorded: "General Tyler commenced with his artillery at 6:30 a.m." From Tyler came this report: "After examining the position and posting Sherman's and Schenck's brigades and the artillery, I fired the first gun at 6:30 a.m., as agreed upon, to show that we were in position." Lieutenant John M. Wilson of the 2d Artillery stated: "At 5 a.m. exactly the first gun was fired by Captain Carlisle. . . ." Lieutenant Stephen C. Lyford, 1st U.S. Dragoons, attached to Schenck's brigade, wrote: "We arrived in view of the enemy's position about 5 a.m., and immediately opened fire with the 30-pounder rifled gun attached to our battery. . . ."

The Confederates also gave their version as to the actual time. Colonel Evans, at whose forces the gun was aimed, recorded: "The enemy made his appearance in line of battle on the east side of the bridge . . . and opened fire with rifled cannon at 5:15 a.m." Beauregard differed with him, reporting: "About half-past 5 o'clock, the peal of a heavy rifled gun was heard in front of the Stone Bridge."

Lieutenant Hains, who, in view of his assigned responsibility for the gun, would seem to have been the individual who fired the first shot of the first major engagement of the war, apparently left no record.

Regardless of when the shot was fired and who fired it, two others followed in quickly succession. One of these went through the tent of Signal Officer Alexander, but it did not harm him, for he was off on the tower at Manassas scanning the countryside. The Confederate artillery made no reply.

Almost immediately after the three shots were heard, Richardson's guns opened at Blackburn's Ford. Confederates watching from across Bull Run at that point saw Federals moving about in force, maneuvering as though they were about to launch a major attack.

At 6:30 a.m. Beauregard, directing action with Johnston's approval, received a message from Evans. It announced that some 1,200 men were deployed in his front.

This news brought about an immediate change of plans at Confederate headquarters. Only two hours earlier Johnston had given his approval in writing to an offensive plan of action prepared by Beauregard. Now both leaders knew that the Union had taken the initiative away from them. The Federal movement from Centreville definitely put them on the defensive. Beauregard ordered Evans and also Cocke (the latter commanding at adjacent Ball's and Lewis' Fords) if attacked, to maintain their positions to the last extremity.

"In my opinion," wrote Beauregard later, "the most effective method of relieving that flank [his weak left] was by a rapid, determined attack with my right wing and center on the enemy's flank and rear at Centreville, with due precautions against the advance of his reserve from the direction of Washington. By such a movement I confidently expected to achieve a complete victory for my country by 12 m."

After sending off the message to Evans, Beauregard ordered Jackson's brigade to take up such position along Bull Run that, in case of need, he could sup-

port Bonham on his right, at Mitchell's Ford, or Cocke on his left. With him were to move the battery of Captain John D. Imboden, Virginia lawyer turned soldier, and five pieces of the battery of Major J. B. Walton of the Washington Artillery, crack outfit with thirteen guns. The parts of Bee's and Georgia Colonel F. S. Bartow's brigades that had arrived from the Valley—about 2,800 men—were sent forward to the support of Evans at Stone Bridge.

Tyler had deployed his troops on each side of the road leading to the bridge, Schenck's brigade below and Keyes's and Sherman's brigades above it. The demonstration they made was not vigorous, for the main drive was to come farther upstream at Sudley. A moderate fire from a battery of rifled pieces was maintained. It was directed for a while against the bridge and then was turned farther downstream toward Cocke's position. Skirmishers moved forward from both sides and kept up a brisk fire for about an hour.

Confederates could be seen in groups beyond the bridge, some out of range in the edge of the woods,

Harper's Weekly, Aug 3, 1861

"Colonel Hunter's attack at the Battle of Bull's Run."

Photograph of the Stone House, at the junction of the Sudley-Manassas road and the Warrenton turnpike taken long after the war. Utility poles and outbuildings have since been removed.

but maintaining their silence. The silence bothered McDowell, now making his way with Hunter's and Heintzelman's columns toward Sudley. Did it mean the Confederates were not in any force in his front? Did they intend themselves to make an attack—and at Blackburn's Ford? As time passed, this seemed to the Union commander to be more and more a possibility. He gave orders for one of Heintzelman's brigades to be held in reserve, in case it should be necessary to send troops back to reinforce Miles. His anxiety would have been relieved had he known that the Southerners were silent because their guns were smoothbores, too short-ranged to shell the Federal line effectively.

Around 8:30 a.m., Evans began to wonder. The Federal attack did not increase in boldness and vigor. He could see dust clouds in the distance toward Centreville, indicating that troops were on the move, and wisps seemed to be rising in places off to the left.

They were vapory at first, and then increased in density as marching feet ground the dry earth into powder.

Suddenly a signal officer—one of the occupants of that tent through which Tyler's shell from the Parrott had passed—uttered an exclamation and focused his binoculars anew. From the tower on Signal Hill beyond Manassas Alexander was signalling, for he had seen the sun glittering on bayonets and brass cannon up toward Sudley Ford. The officer repeated the message as it was wigwagged to him:

"Look out for your left! You are turned!"

Evans stared with increased interest at the dust clouds gathering off to his left. Forces definitely were moving toward Sudley Ford, a passage he did not have enough troops to guard.

He sent Cocke word of the enemy's movement and of his own plans to meet it. Leaving four companies under cover at Stone Bridge, he hurriedly marched upstream three quarters of a mile with the remainder of his force, about 1,100 men—six companies of the

Liberia house, General Beauregard's headquarters.

4th South Carolina and five companies of Louisiana Zouaves under the colorful Major Chatham Roberdeau Wheat, prominent criminal lawyer and preacher's son, an adventurous man who had fought in the Mexican War, in Latin America, and with Garibaldi in Italy.

They moved across the valley of Young's Branch, Bull Run tributary coursing from the west, and went toward Sudley, taking along two 6-pounder howitzers. Most of the concentration of troops in the beginning had centered around the point at which the road from Sudley to Manassas crossed the road from Centreville to Warrenton. Near this crossroad, in the northeastern angle, sat a stone farmhouse already in use as a hospital. After this day, history would call it the Stone House; shells would damage but not destroy it.

From the other side of Bull Run, the Parrott gun occasionally sent off a shot to let the Confederates know the Federals meant business. A high tree had been found that could be used as an observatory for

Tyler's forces, and a lookout was maintained from its topmost branches.

Reaching high ground on a shoulder of Matthews' Hill above the Stone House and about 400 yards in rear of "Pittsylvania," the home of the Carter family, Evans formed a battle line at right angles to his former position. His left rested on the road running past the Carter mansion, with troops distributed on each side of a small copse where they could take advantage of such cover as the ground afforded. They lay facing open fields, with woods beyond, along which the Federals must advance. A howitzer was placed at each end of the line. Later, discovering that the road along which they waited was a branch of the main highway from Sudley, he swung his force farther to the left onto Matthews' Hill and stationed some of his men in a shallow ravine. Union officer Fry later wrote in admiration: "Evans' action was probably one of the best pieces of soldiership on either side during the campaign."

Evans had not long to wait. The march of Hunter's and Heintzelman's columns had been anything but a success from the standpoint of timing. It was not 7 a.m. but at least two hours later before the leading brigade, Burnside's, reached Sudley. Some of the delay had been caused by Tyler's slow advance during the dark hours of morning, but most of it was due to the circuitous route the engineers serving as guides had followed in an effort to conceal their movement from the enemy.

When McDowell reached Sudley Ford, he found that a part of Burnside's brigade had crossed, but the men following were slow in getting over. The scene about them was not altogether one of war. Picnickers in groups had accompanied the column and engaged the soldiers in conversation. Across the way stood the Sudley Church, later to be used as a hospital, and about its lawn stood a crowd of worshippers, waiting for the Sunday sermon that would not be preached.

Burnside's men were hot, sweaty, dusty, and thirsty, and they stopped to drink and fill their canteens. The water they gulped was mostly from Bull Run, but some managed to take advantage of the cooling flow from Sudley Springs, the center of a swarming, shouting horde of desperately dry men. The Union commander urged them to hurry. He could see clouds of dust rising from the direction of Manassas and feared that the Confederates might come down on the head of his column and scatter it before it could be reinforced.

Orders were hurried back to urge the commanders of regiments in the rear to break from the column and come forward separately as fast as possible. McDowell also sent word to the reserve brigade of Heintzelman's division to come by a nearer road across the field, and sent an aide-de-camp to tell Tyler to press forward his attack, as large bodies of the enemy were passing in his front to head off the force at Sudley. This was a sharp change of plans. It had been hoped the defenses of Stone Bridge could be taken in rear and that it could be passed without force.

When they finally broke away from the refreshing coolness at Sudley Ford, Burnside's men moved southward along the road toward Matthews' Hill. Evans' troops had orders to open fire as soon as the enemy approached. This they did at 9:15 a.m., causing the first of the Federals who came in sight to halt in confusion and then fall back. A vigorous burst of fire from the Southerners followed, and Wheat charged with his battalion, later falling severely wounded in both lungs.

Colonel Burnside's Rhode Island brigade and the 71st New York open the flank attack at Bull Run. Pencil and wash drawing by A. R. Waud.

Hunter came up. Major Barnard of the Engineers was with him and suggested confining operations to the left flank, so as to drive the Southerners from the immediate vicinity of Bull Run and form a junction with Tyler at Stone Bridge. Hunter moved forward to judge better how to direct the attack. As he advanced, a fragment of shell struck him and took him out of action.

Shortly thereafter, as he left the field, Hunter met Burnside and asked him to take charge. It was 9:45 a.m.

Burnside immediately began debouching troops from the woods into the open fields. He threw forward skirmishers, and they became engaged with Wheat's command. Up came the 2d Rhode Island, with its vaunted battery of six 13-pounder rifled guns. More Union troops were crossing at Sudley and on the way.

For about an hour Evans maintained his position on Matthews' Hill, but at the end of that period he began to waver, for the Federals were coming up rapidly. Acting on McDowell's order to press his attack, Tyler directed Sherman's and Keyes's brigades to cross Bull Run at the farm ford shown by the maps about 800 yards above Stone Bridge and go to the aid of Hunter's column. Before Keyes's troops could get fully under way, an enemy battery on the other side of the stream threw twenty-five or thirty rounds of shot and shell upon the 1st and 2d Regiments of Connecticut Volunteers, causing temporary confusion and wounding several men.

More Union artillery was crossing at Sudley and

pushing on toward the battle action. Soon there would be five batteries—Griffin's, Ricketts', Arnold's, the Rhode Island, and the 71st regiment—twenty-four pieces. Their shells would add further to the pressure now building up, especially on the Confederate right toward which Barnard had suggested the attack be aimed.

Shortly after McDowell arrived at the front, Burnside rode up to him and said his brigade had borne the brunt of the battle and was out of ammunition; he asked permission to withdraw and refit. In the excitement of the moment, the commander gave consent. The brigade marched to the rear, stacked arms, and took no further part in the fight.

Long believed a photo of Confederate dead on Matthews Hill, this was a shot posed by Federals.

As directed earlier in the morning, General Bee, the South Carolinian, moved his column nearer Stone Bridge and brought it to a halt on Henry Hill overlooking Young's Branch, some distance to the rear of where Evans' troops were fighting. From there, Imboden's batteries were able to drop shells with telling effect upon the oncoming Federals. It was Bee's hope to get Evans to fall back to this hill, a superior position, he felt, but Evans insisted on continuing the battle near the Matthews house and urged the other officer to join him. Finally Bee gave in and moved forward, taking with him the 7th and 8th Georgia, 4th Alabama, 2d Mississippi, two companies of the 11th Mississippi, and Imboden's battery.

The morning advanced. Meanwhile, the sound of firing convinced General Johnston, waiting with Beauregard near Mitchell's Ford, that a major battle was under way and that the enemy's great effort was to

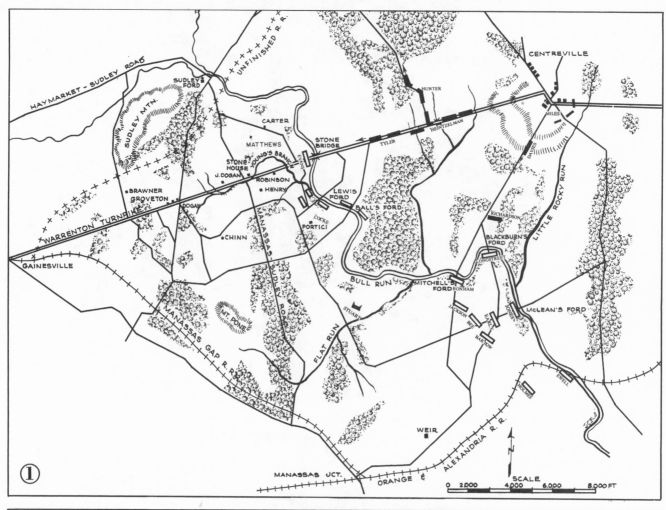

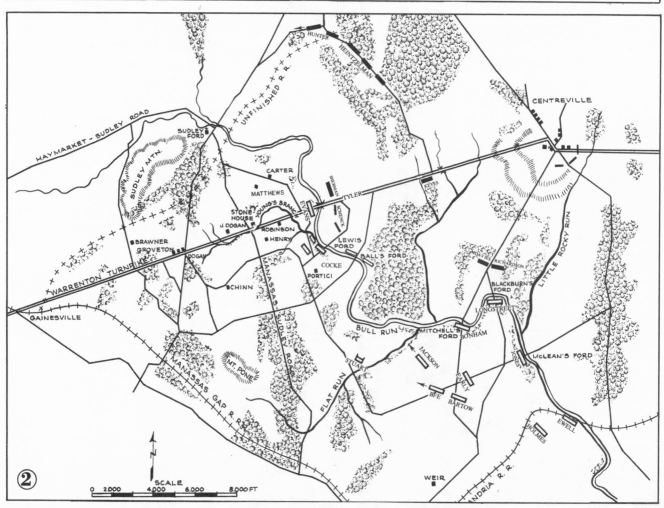

Maps and Text by Col. W. S. Nye

Map 1. Situation at Sunrise, July 21, 1861.

TYLER, commanding the holding or secondary attack, was supposed to clear Centreville at 2:30 a.m. But he was two hours late, thus delaying the march of the other brigades. The main attack force, the divisions of Hunter and Heintzelman, is just leaving the turnpike to start the movement to envelop the Confederates from the north. One of Tyler's brigades, that of Keyes, was halted where shown, as a reserve. Miles has one brigade in and around Centreville as a reserve; Richardson's brigade of Tyler's division, is still opposite Blackburn's Ford, where it has been since the 18th; the other of Miles' brigades, Davies', is moving to reinforce Richardson.

The Confederates are disposed to cover the fords, with Holmes, Early, Jackson, Bee, and Bartow in reserve.

Map 2. Actions Between 5:30 a.m. and 7:30 a.m.

TYLER has started his demonstration at the Stone Bridge over Bull Run. Beauregard, about 7 a.m., ordered Jackson to a position between Bonham and Cocke, and Bee and Bartow to move to support the troops guarding Stone Bridge. Ewell was ordered to join Longstreet and Jones in an advance on Centreville, but he did not receive the orders, and this movement did not get under way.

Map 3. Situation at About 8:45 a.m.

HUNTER and Heintzelman are approaching Sudley Ford. Evans, who has detected the flanking movement and has correctly diagnosed Tyler's effort as being a demonstration or feint, is sending part of his brigade north to occupy the high ground above the turnpike as a defense against the force coming down on the Conferedate left flank. Bee and Bartow are moving to reinforce Evans. Jackson, first ordered to support Bonham, afterwards Cocke, has moved forward so as to be able to reinforce the defense of Stone Bridge.

Map 4. Actions From About 9:45 a.m. to About 10:45 a.m.

BURNSIDE'S brigade of Hunter's division arrived at Sudley Ford at 9:30 a.m. and after resting for a half hour moved south, debouched from the woods and advanced against Evans, who had taken a position on the high ground north of Stone House. Bee and Bartow had arrived on the Henry House plateau, which Bee thought was the best position for defense. At Evans' request, however, he is moving his brigade and that of Bartow up to assist Evans.

Burnside attacked about 10:30, and was reinforced soon by Sykes' battalion of Regulars. Porter's brigade is still at Sudley Ford at 10:45, but soon thereafter moved south to join in the battle. Heintzelman had not yet reached the ford.

Sherman's and Keyes' brigades of Tyler's division are moving to cross at a ford north of Stone Bridge.

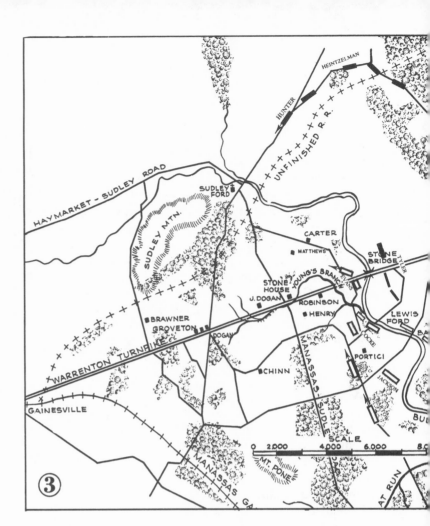

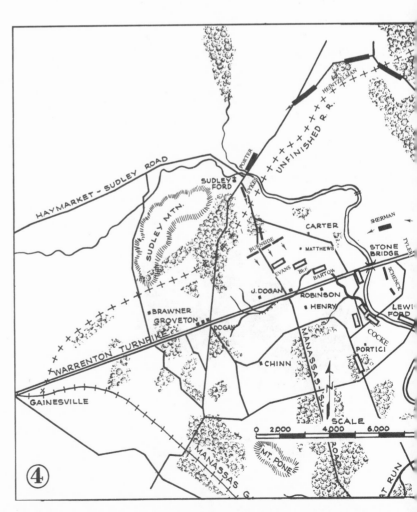

be made with his right. They had been expecting for some time to hear action that would indicate the turning movement against the Union left was taking place. This did not come, for orders had failed to reach some of the officers involved. So the plan was abandoned, and dispositions were made to meet the enemy's drive instead of giving him some of his own medicine.

Accordingly, orders were sent to General Holmes and Colonel Early, waiting in reserve back of the fords to the east, to move with all speed to the scene of action. Generals Ewell, Jones, Longstreet, and Bonham were instructed to make demonstrations on their respective fronts. The two commanding officers then left headquarters and galloped off toward Stone Bridge, having four or five miles to cover.

When Heintzelman reached Sudley Ford after 11 a.m., one brigade of Hunter's division was still on the eastern side of the run. Smoke was rising from two points on the left, indicating the battle front. McDowell had already gone forward, and soon he sent word for two regiments to be hurried forward. Heintzelman accompanied one of them, leaving orders for the remainder of his division to follow.

As noon approached, the Confederates, with Bee in over-all command, fell back. The pressure upon them was too great. Porter's Union column, and then the brigades of Franklin and Willcox, arrived to extend the Union right across the fields to the Warrenton turnpike west of the stone house at the crossroads. Threatened with disaster, and despite the efforts of Bee and Bartow and Evans to rally them, the demoralized Southerners retreated across Young's Branch and back toward Henry Hill where Jackson waited with his brigade, as stolid and calm as the nickname he was about to receive.

Battles and Leaders of the Civil War

The rebuilt Henry house, showing the Union monument of the first battle. From an 1884 photograph.

The open, level top of this hill is more than 200 yards across. On the western brow sat the home of the bedridden widow, Judith Carter Henry, born in 1777 at "Pittsylvania," near where the fighting had raged. She was a direct descendant of Colonel Robert "King" Carter, a man greatly responsible for the settlement of this portion of Virginia. Her two semi-invalid sons had managed to get her out of the house on a mattress and had started toward a neighbor's. But as the fighting in the distance grew hotter, she insisted on being returned to what she considered the safety of her bedroom, where she now lay cared for by a young Negro woman named Rosa Stokes. Only a few hundred yards away at the northeastern end of the plateau stood the modest home of James Robinson, a free Negro.

Carried back with the tide of his retreating regiments, Bee reached the brow of the hill and spied Jackson, standing with his men in line of battle in the edge of a pine thicket from which their fire could sweep the plateau. Whether in praise or derogation—there are two schools of thought—he shouted to the panicky men around him:

"Look! There stands Jackson like a stone wall! Rally behind the Virginians!"

It was that sudden. A nickname that would live forever—"Stonewall"—had been given a man who would prove during the next two years that he deserved it.

Above: Troops of Bee, Bartow, and Evans rally behind the Robinson house. From painting by Thure de Thulstrup. Below: J. E. Taylor painting of Jackson at Bull Run. But unlike this painting, Jackson was dressed in his old Mexican War uniform.

Even in the beginning, it inspired soldiers who heard it. They steadied and began to form a solid line, while off to the right around the Robinson house the Hampton Legion, 600 strong and just arrived after twenty hours on the train from Richmond, carried on some desperate, confused fighting to check the Union pursuit. This gallant outfit had been organized by the wealthy and aristocratic South Carolina planter, Colonel Wade Hampton, a man renowned for his intellect and physical strength.

Some time after noon, Johnston and Beauregard reached Henry Hill. The fighting was still in progress, though not at its previous rapid pace. Finding that most of the field officers of the 4th Alabama had been disabled, Johnston led it forward, the regimental flag at his side. The sight among them of this veteran who had been wounded so many times in previous wars brought new spirit to the Confederates on the field, and they cheered as loudly as their dusty and parched throats would allow.

For some unexplained reason, a lull settled over the battle area between 1 and 2 o'clock. It was like a lunch break for the heat-exhausted men on both sides. Firing almost completely died out, and the only real activity for a time was in the background of each line, where more troops were coming up. Among those on the Federal side was Willcox' brigade, consisting of the 1st Michigan, 11th New York (Fire Zouaves), 38th New York, and Arnold's battery. And for the Confederates, just off the train at Manassas were 1,700 infantrymen

Battles and Leaders of the Civil War

Federal attack up the slope
of Henry Hill to recapture
the guns of Griffin's battery.
Drawing by Walton Taber.

from the Shenandoah Valley led by Brigadier General Kirby Smith, Indian fighter, Mexican War veteran, and ex-mathematics professor at West Point. Their arrival was a triumphant accomplishment for the Manassas Gap line. It had been having troubles—confusion in shunting trains back and forth on a single track, one collision, and overworked crews.

latest arrivals among the Federals were taking position. As soon as this was completed, Beauregard urged Johnston to leave the conduct of the field to him and to retire to "Portici," the nearby home of the Francis W. Lewis family at the rear, from which he could direct reinforcements to the front and have a better look at the entire Confederate line. Johnston reluctantly agreed.

This break in the fighting was a welcome development for soldiers on each side. Some of them had been awake since before 2 a.m. and fighting since shortly after 9 a.m. Their uniforms were wringing wet with sweat, their bodies and their clothes coated with dust. Water was an urgent necessity, especially at this season of the year; food was scarcely considered in the excitement.

With the two Southern commanders on the field, the line of battle was rearranged slightly and some troops were moved to strengthen it on the left, toward the Sudley road and toward the west where the

Battles and Leaders of the Civil War

The Henry house from Jackson's position.

Wartime photograph of the Matthews house.

McDowell had at hand the brigades of Franklin, Willcox, Sherman, and Porter, as well as a battalion of Regular cavalry. Howard's brigade was in reserve. Keyes's brigade, accompanied by Tyler, had become separated from Sherman and opened a gap in the line by marching down Young's Branch below Stone Bridge, entirely out of the battle. Close to the front were the crack batteries of Captain Charles Griffin, experienced soldier, Indian fighter, Mexican War veteran, and instructor in artillery at West Point—and Captain James B. Ricketts, veteran of the Mexican and Seminole Wars. But the Union commander had no equivalent officer like Johnston to look over the field from the rear and to forward reinforcements.

When McDowell's line again advanced, Sherman was on the left, Porter and Franklin in the center, and Willcox on the right.

Willcox' brigade had reached the front near the intersection of the Warrenton and Sudley roads. Troops on their left, in the vicinity of the Robinson house, the commanding officer noticed, were engaged in desultory firing. He posted the 38th New York in line and was moving up the Zouaves when he re-

The Robinson house from Jackson's position.

Slaughter and rout of Ricketts' battery by the 33d Virginia. Painting by Sydney King, after drawing by A. R. Waud.

ceived an order to detach a regiment for the support of Rickett's battery on a hill a quarter of a mile or more to the right. The Zouaves were turned in that direction.

It was now 2 p.m., and the fighting was picking up in force all along the front. Whereas the Southerners had been retreating before 1 o'clock, they now stood fast—Bee's, Bartow's, and Evans' commands merged with Jackson's brigade of fresh troops, 6,500 men, with thirteen pieces of artillery and Stuart's cavalry.

Some time early in the renewed fighting, Imboden, who had been going from battery to battery on Jack-

son's orders to see that the guns were properly aimed, came up to ask permission to return to his own command. As "Stonewall" gave permission, his eyes shining, he characteristically extended the open palm of his left hand toward the artillery officer. Suddenly he jerked it down. Blood was streaming from it. "General, you are wounded!" exclaimed Imboden. Jackson drew a handkerchief from his breast pocket. "Only a

scratch—a mere scratch," he said, galloping off.

Griffin's and Ricketts' batteries were soon ordered to cross the Sudley road and to move up Henry Hill, to within 330 yards of the opposing guns, a move that some military students have insisted was McDowell's blunder of the day. It is their contention that more would have been gained by sending one battery forward and leaving the other where it could enfilade

Stuart's 1st Virginia Cavalry charge and rout the New York Fire Zouaves supporting Ricketts' and Griffin's batteries on Henry Hill.

the hilltop. At any rate, the guns soon became engaged in a hot duel with Imboden's and other Confederate batteries.

As the tempo of the battle increased, the action became dramatic—and tragic. The infantry moved back and forth, first one side and then the other occupying the plateau. Suddenly Confederate snipers began firing at Ricketts' and Griffin's batteries from the Henry house, or from the cover of it. At last, in desperation, some of the Union guns were turned upon the building. Several shots passed through it, scattering shingles and boards and splinters over a wide area. Inside, the aged widow was struck by five fragments; she died before sundown. Her maid, Rosa Stokes, was wounded in the heel, an injury that would lame her for life.

The Confederate fire concentrated upon the two batteries. Stuart's 1st Virginia Cavalry, guarding Jackson's left, charged down upon the protecting Zouaves and routed them. Then Jackson's 33d Virginia came over a rise on Griffin's right. As the Parrott rifles prepared to open upon it with canister, Major William F. Barry, Chief of Artillery, assured Griffin it was a regiment that had been sent to their support by

Heintzelman. Uniforms worn by the advancing regiment gave no clue, and a fatal mistake was made. The Southerners came to within sixty or seventy yards and delivered a deadly volley, killing and wounding fifty-four officers and men and 104 horses. Griffin was among the wounded.

Another wounded was Adelbert Ames of East Thomaston, Maine, commanding a section of Griffin's battery. He refused to leave the field until he was so weak he was unable to sit on the caisson on which he had been placed by his men. Thirty-three years later, on June 22, 1894, he would be presented the Congressional Medal of Honor, an award originated during the Civil War. Ames established a record as the first to earn the honor, though he was not the first to receive it. In 1933, he would die as the oldest living graduate of the U.S. Military Academy.

The eleven guns in Griffin's and Ricketts' batteries were put out of action and temporarily lost. Soon there was a countercharge and they were regained, but remained unmanned and silent on the field. This was repeated two or three times as contending infantry surged around the stilled pieces, sitting amid the heaps of dead men and horses.

The over-all battle was just as changeable. Five assaults were made by the Federals, driving the Confederates from the plateau. Each time the Southerners would rally and drive the Northern troops back.

Beauregard, leading some of the charges in person, was constantly moving about, trying to "infuse into the hearts of my officers and men the confidence and determined spirit of resistance to this wicked invasion of the homes of a free people which I felt." He reminded them that they were fighting for their homes, their firesides, and the independence of their country. And he promised them reinforcements.

It was while watching for this new support that he noticed something wrong about the flag they were carrying. In the brightness of the hot July sun, it could scarcely be distinguished from that of the enemy. Later he would report this, and design a new banner to take the place of the Stars and Bars.

The promised reinforcements arrived at 3 p.m. in the form of Kirby Smith and the last units from the Valley. But soon Smith was severely wounded by a ball in the left breast, and the command devolved upon Colonel Arnold Elzey, another Indian fighter and Mexican War veteran, who at West Point had dropped his last name, Jones.

Now the time was 3:30, and the heat on the bare, sun-baked hilltop was intolerable. The Federals formed a crescent-shaped line covering three sides of the plateau, on and behind which waited the Southerners. The last Union brigade, Howard's, took position in two lines of battle on the extreme right.

"It was a truly magnificent, though redoubtable, spectacle as they threw forward in fine style on the broad, general slopes of the ridge occupied by their main line a cloud of skirmishers, preparatory for another attack," remembered Beauregard.

The Confederates braced. Up came more reinforcements, these some that should have been there sooner. An order sent Colonel Early at noon had failed to reach him in his reserve position back of the fords at the far end of the line until 2 p.m. He brought his brigade hurriedly to the front, arriving just in time. Passing through the woods behind Elzey, he spread his men on the Confederate left, facing Howard.

The final assault came after 4 o'clock. Beauregard sensed that the Confederates had the advantage and did his utmost to whip them into a frenzy of resistance. Jackson advised his men that the situation called for use of the bayonet. All along the line the Rebel Yell rang out for the first time in battle.

The two armies surged forward. But, almost as suddenly as the first gun had blasted forth in the early dawn, men from Alabama and Georgia, North Carolina and Virginia, and seven other seceded states swept onward. The balance of power had shifted to the side of the Southerners. An accumulation of delays—that permitted by McDowell on the 20th, the

A Louisiana Zouave drummer boy.

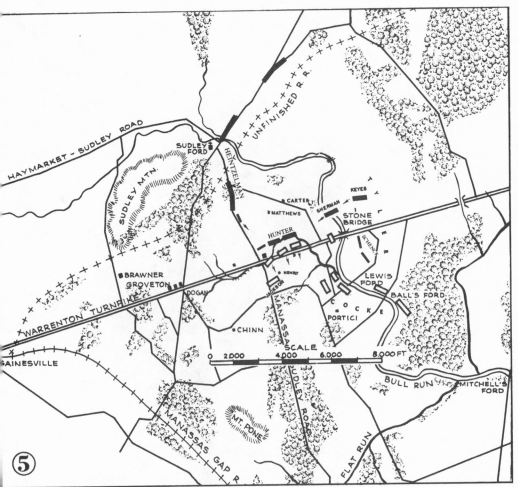

Map 5. Situation At About 11:30 a.m.

HUNTER has been wounded, but McDowell has arrived and assumed personal direction of the attack. Heintzelman's leading brigade (Franklin's) is coming on the field, but his next brigade (Willcox's) is still at Sudley Ford and will not march south for another half hour or more. The Confederates are being pushed back slowly toward the high ground south of the turnpike, where on the left Jackson has established a line. Two of Tyler's brigades (Sherman and Keyes) are fording Bull Run north of the Stone Bridge and heading for the field of action.

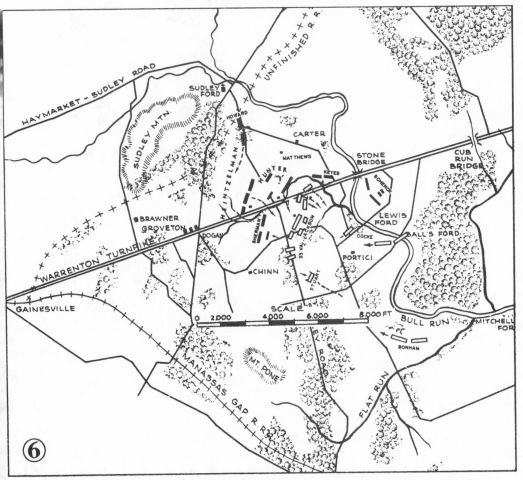

Map 6. Actions From 1 to 2 p.m.

McDOWELL'S main effort is developing, but is not being pushed as a coordinated effort. Some regiments are not attacking, others are being thrown in piecemeal. Howard's regiments, constituting Heintzelman's Third Brigade, are just coming on the field. Burnside has withdrawn from the line and stacked arms, for the alleged purpose of "issuing ammunition," a process that could have been completed in 30 minutes but was still in progress at the end of the battle. The Federals, nearly all raw militia, are showing courage but their musketry is faulty, the firing being ragged and highly inaccurate. Their powerful artillery, skilfully handled, is, however, forcing the Confederates back.

Jackson's brigade stands firm, and forms a line on which the Confederates form a new position as reinforcements are hurried up. Hampton's Legion (not shown) is thrown in on the right of Jackson to fill the gap caused by the withdrawal of the broken brigades of Evans, Bee, and Bartow, which up to now have withstood the Federal assault practically unaided. At this moment a Federal victory seems to be in the making.

Map 7. Actions Between 2 p.m. and 4 p.m.

McDOWELL'S troops drove the Confederates back on both flanks, taking the Robinson house and Henry house positions and threatening to turn both flanks. Confederate reinforcements were brought up, as shown, and the broken units of Evans, Bee, and Bartow were rallied. The battle swayed back and forth until about 4 p.m., when the whole Confederate line advanced. Gradually, and without orders, Federal regiments began to withdraw.

Many of the units shown hereon did not actually get into the fight.

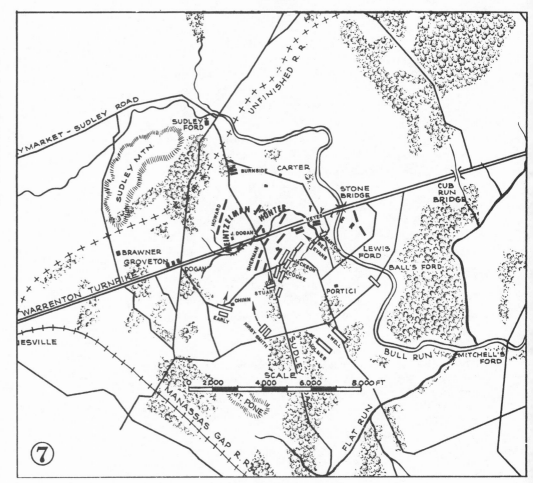

Map 8. The Federal Retreat

UNEXPECTEDLY, about 4:30 p.m., the Federal troops stopped fighting, broke ranks, and commenced to leave the field. At first the men were simply walking back quietly, though without orders. Individually and in little groups they made their way east along the turnpike, across the fields to other fords, and north along the road by which they had reached the battlefield. Sykes' Regulars and Sherman's brigade covered the withdrawal from a position near Stone Bridge. Later a Confederate shell smashed a wagon on Cub Run bridge, blocking this main route of withdrawal, and the retreat degenerated into a panic.

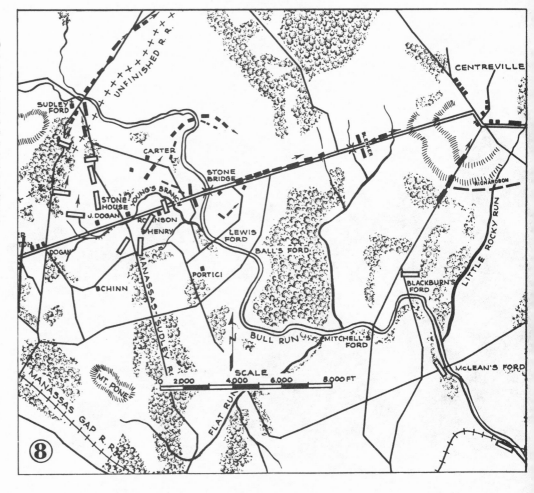

slow march from Centreville, and the respite after Evans' troops had been driven back from Matthews' Hill—made it possible for the South to bring together enough reinforcements to bring victory to their banners. Brigades all along the crest of Henry Hill drove against the Northerners, down the slope of the plateau, across the valley of Young's Branch, northward and eastward, in a fan-shaped phalanx of yelling, screaming, maddened warriors who realized that they had at last gained what they had hoped for.

"Under this combined attack," wrote Beauregard, "the enemy soon was forced first over the narrow plateau in the southern angle made by the two roads so often mentioned into a patch of woods on its western slope, then back over Young's Branch . . . and rearward, in extreme disorder in all available directions towards Bull Run. The rout had become general and complete."

The Sudley Springs road, looking north from the slope of Henry Hill. The Stone House on the Warrenton turnpike appears in the middle distance right. Matthews' Hill lies beyond the Stone House.

The Northerners ran over one another in a frantic effort to get away from the charging hordes coming down from the crest of Henry Hill, pushing in on Howard's brigade from the west, driving toward Stone Bridge. Some of the Union commands held temporarily and withdrew in order, but the vast majority ran away in a continuous trail of dust, most of them going back by Sudley Ford, the way they had come, instead of straight down the turnpike.

"The retreat soon became a rout, and this soon degenerated still further into a panic," wrote McDowell.

"Such a rout I never witnessed before," agreed Heintzelman. "No efforts could induce a single regiment to form after the retreat was commenced."

Heintzelman was particularly critical of troops from Minnesota, Michigan, and New York: "The want of discipline in these regiments was so great that most of the men would run from 50 to several hundred yards to the rear and continue the fire—fortunately for the braver ones, very high in the air—compelling those in front to retreat."

Union troops retreat in panic from the battlefield. Painting by Walter Russell.

But he manifested some sympathy: "Much excuse can be made for those who fled, as few of the enemy could at any time be seen. Raw troops cannot be expected to stand long against an unseen enemy."

After the rout got under way, many of the Confederates dropped to the ground, utterly exhausted. But some of them managed to administer a final sting to the fleeing Federals.

A battery under the command of Captain Delaware Kemper, Mexican War veteran, lawyer, and one day to be Virginia's governor, made its way across Bull Run near Stone Bridge and, on the opposite side, joined up with infantry and cavalry to hurry eastward along the turnpike. On topping the rise overlooking Cub Run, the Confederates looked down upon a fine target. Cannon, caissons, ambulances, wagons, and other vehicles, most of them abandoned by their drivers, were congregated in a confused mass around the turnoff to Sudley Ford. Civilians—men and women, including members of Congress—mingled with the mob.

Kemper unlimbered two guns. He signalled to a white-haired, 67-year-old, ardent secessionist who had ridden down from Stone Bridge astride the barrel of one of the weapons, a man who in 1865 would shoot himself to death rather than live under the U.S. Government. This volunteer was Edmund Ruffin, prominent agriculturist and writer, who had fired one of the first cannon aimed at Fort Sumter. Since morning he had been fighting. And now he pulled a lanyard that sent a shot into the center of the suspension bridge, overturning a wagon and completely blocking the span.

The confusion became greater than ever. Soldiers and teamsters fled. Some of them cut the horses from their traces, jumped upon their bare backs, and rode away, leaving behind fourteen artillery pieces, ammunition, forges, thirty wagons, and forty or fifty horses—and assorted Congressmen. Several persons were killed.

McDowell left the battlefield convinced that "could we have fought a day—yes, a few hours—sooner," the North would have won. He must have been among the first of the fleeing Federals to reach Centreville. At 5:45 p.m. he telegraphed Washington:

"We passed Bull Run. Engaged the enemy, who, it seems, had just been reinforced by General Johnston. We drove them for several miles, and finally routed them.

"They rallied and repulsed us, but only to give us

again the victory, which seemed complete. But our men, exhausted with fatigue and thirst and confused by firing into each other, were attacked by the enemy's reserves, and driven from the position we had gained, overlooking Manassas. After this the men could not be rallied, but slowly left the field. In the meantime the enemy outflanked Richardson at Blackburn's Ford, and we have now to hold Centreville till our men can get behind it. Miles's division is holding the town. It is reported Colonel Cameron is killed, Hunter and Heintzelman wounded, neither dangerously."

Cameron, brother of Secretary of War Simon Cameron, was dead, shot down while leading his men. So were Bee and Bartow and 844 others, Federal and Confederate. The wounded totaled 2,706—all shot in a matter of seven hours. This total of 3,553 killed and wounded would be compared nearly a century later with the casualties of later wars—3,178 at Tarawa in 4 days, 20,326 at Iwo Jima in 36 days.

The fleeing Federals hurried on past Centreville and through the night toward Washington, leaving the road behind them littered with guns, haversacks, blankets, canteens, camp equipage, clothing, and other property. They would arrive next morning in a pelting rain.

Back on the battlefield, Johnston and Beauregard made their separate ways toward their headquarters at Manassas. Awaiting them was Jefferson Davis. He had come by train during the afternoon and ridden hurriedly toward the sound of firing, arriving too late to witness the fighting.

Days would pass before the two Confederate leaders issued a congratulatory proclamation to their soldiers. It began with these two paragraphs:

"One week ago a countless host of men, organized into an army, with all the appointments which modern art and practical skill could devise, invaded the soil of Virginia. Their people sounded their approach with triumphant displays of anticipated victory. Their generals came in almost royal state; their great ministers, senators, and women came to witness the immolation of our army and the subjugation of our

Edmund Ruffin fired the last shot of the battle.

Ruins of the Stone Bridge in 1862 looking along the Warrenton turnpike toward the battlefield.

people, and to celebrate the result with wild revelry.

"It is with the profoundest emotions of gratitude to an overruling God, whose hand is manifest in protecting our homes and our liberties, that we, your generals commanding, are enabled, in the name of our whole country, to thank you for that patriotic courage, that heroic gallantry, that devoted daring, exhibited by you in the actions of the 18th and 21st, by which the hosts of the enemy were scattered and a signal and glorious victory obtained."

The battle had been fought mainly by Johnston's troops. His men and officers made up two thirds of the killed and wounded.

No effort was made on the part of the Southerners to pursue the Federals into Washington. There were many reasons, chief of which was that the soldiers after their hard day of fighting, were exhausted. Furthermore, they had neither equipment nor supplies for such a pursuit.

The first battle of Bull Run ended with Edmund Ruffin's shot at the suspension bridge over Cub Run. Quite evenly matched in numbers were the two armies —30,000 Federals and 32,000 Confederates—but only about 18,000 on each side saw action.

Although a victory for the South, this battle would turn out to be a poor bargain. The North profited by its repulse, licked its wounds, and prepared for a long, relentless, and bloody war. The Southerners on the other hand were lulled into underestimating the fighting capacity of the forces they still had to defeat. Many who fought that day went home feeling the war was over and the South had won. They would not so readily take up arms again.

Comparative quiet settled down over the Manassas battlefield after July 21. But matters were not to remain that way. Little more than a year later, Stonewall Jackson would slip through Thoroughfare Gap in the Bull Run Mountains with his "foot cavalry" and drop down behind a railroad bed that had never had rails on it, an unfinished line that lay slightly to the west of where McDowell's men had marched from Sudley Ford. There he would wait to pounce upon the army of Union General John Pope, steadily marching eastward on the Warrenton turnpike and unaware that the Confederates were in force anywhere in their vicinity. For four days, August 29-September 1, 1862, there would be bloody fighting, with 19,514 killed and wounded.

But the Second Battle of Bull Run was the continuation of a war and not the beginning. It had not the "firsts" of the First Battle, and its centennial, unlike that of July 21, 1961, would pass almost unnoticed.

The Long Bridge, Washington. Retreating Union troops passed into the Capital over this bridge.

Battles and Leaders of the Civil War

Above: Union soldiers among Confederate fortifications at Centreville in March 1862. Below: Dedication of First Bull Run monument, June 10, 1865 in yard of Henry house.

Speaker Judge Olin stands with cane behind boy in white shirt. To his left are Generals Thomas, Willcox, Heintzelman, and Dyer. The monument still stands.

Goodbye to the Three-Months' War

The debacle at Manassas put an end to northern notions of suppressing the rebellion in a few months. Some former optimists now wondered if it could be suppressed at all. "On every brow sits sullen, scorching, black despair," wrote the mercurial but influential editor Horace Greeley, whose *New York Tribune* editorials "Forward to Richmond!" had done much to harry Union leaders into premature action. "If it is best for the country and for mankind," Greeley wrote Lincoln, "that we should make peace with the rebels, and on their own terms, do not shrink even from that."

But Lincoln had no intention of giving up. "The fat is in the fire now," wrote his private secretary John Hay, "and we shall have to crow small until we can retrieve the disgrace somehow. The preparations for the war will be continued with increased vigor by the Government." The day after Manassas, Lincoln signed a bill authorizing the enlistment of 500,000 three-year volunteers in the Union army. Three days later he signed a bill for another 500,000. Galvanized by the crisis, volunteers flocked to recruiting offices. By early 1862 the North had 600,000 men under arms (compared with 325,000 in the South). Lincoln called George B. McClellan to Washington to reorganize the most important Union field army and whip it into shape for a new offensive.

McClellan proved to be superb at this task. He created the Army of the Potomac and drilled it into a large, well-oiled machine during the next six months. But as a military commander McClellan had a fatal flaw. He was reluctant to damage this machine by committing it to combat. He sought and found excuses for postponing the expected offensive through the rest of 1861 and several months into 1862. His men were not yet ready, he said; the enemy outnumbered him (McClellan consistently overestimated by a factor of two the number of Confederate troops facing him); he was short of arms, equipment, supplies. Lincoln's confidence in McClellan gradually eroded as time passed and the excuses for inaction mounted. But the officers and men in the army loved their commander, and Lincoln had to defer to McClellan's judgment about the best time and place for an offensive in Virginia. The time would not come until the spring of 1862.

Meanwhile the Union navy took up the slack and won some much-needed victories to bolster northern morale. The navy's main task was the blockade of southern ports that Lincoln had ordered on April 19. Possessing too few ships at first to make the blockade effective, the navy gradually built up its strength by purchase and construction. By 1862 the blockade was beginning to strangle the export of cotton and import of military goods essential to the Confederacy's war economy.

One of the navy's most serious problems in 1861 was a lack of sufficient bases for the blockade fleet. Union forces had retained control of Hampton Roads at the mouth of the James River in Virginia, and built it into the main naval base for the South Atlantic. But the length of time required to come and go for supplies and repairs from this base to the principal Confederate ports of Charleston, Savannah, and Wilmington severely restricted the navy's blockade efficiency. So a naval strategy board planned to seize additional bases along the South Atlantic coast.

Union troops land at Hatteras in August 1861. Panic reigned along the tidewater as North Carolinians feared that hordes of Yankees would soon follow. (Franklin D. Roosevelt Library)

The first task force for this mission rendezvoused off Cape Hatteras in late August 1861. Seven warships carrying 141 guns battered the two Confederate forts guarding Hatteras Inlet, the entry to Albemarle and Pamlico sounds behind the North Carolina barrier islands. Union army troops took control of the forts after they had surrendered to the navy. This victory paved the way for a much larger army-navy expeditionary force commanded by General Ambrose Burnside of Rhode Island, which gained control of the North Carolina sounds and several coastal cities with a series of victories in February and March 1862.

The principal Union naval achievement in 1861 occurred at Port Royal, South Carolina, halfway between Charleston and Savannah. Seventeen warships mounting 157 guns accompanied by twenty-five colliers and thirty-three transports carrying 12,000 infantry and 600 marines had headed southward from northern ports under sealed orders in late October. A gale off Cape Hatteras scattered and almost wrecked the fleet, but most of the ships made it through and assembled outside Port Royal Sound, one of the finest natural harbors in the South. Steaming in an oval pattern, Union warships bombarded the two Confederate forts with tons of shells, forcing them to surrender on November 7. The troops poured ashore and occupied the rich cotton-growing sea islands along the South Carolina and Georgia coasts. This region became a mecca for slaves escaping from the interior and a starting point for further Union assaults along the coast, as well as a base for the blockade fleet. This Union victory, the most important of 1861, did much to offset the defeat at Manassas.

During these same months of 1861 and early 1862, fighting in Missouri, Arkansas, and faraway New Mexico had also, on balance, resulted in significant Union gains.

—James M. McPherson

THE CIVIL WAR WEST OF THE MISSISSIPPI

The Contest for Missouri

by James M. McPherson

The origins of the Civil War lay in the conflict over expansion of slavery into new territories west of Texas and Missouri. Secession had been narrowly averted by the Compromise of 1850 which, among other provisions, allowed slavery to go into New Mexico if the settlers there wanted it. In 1854 Congress opened a new sore by passing the Kansas-Nebraska Act, which repealed earlier legislation barring slavery from the new territories of Kansas and Nebraska. Proslavery and antislavery settlers poured into Kansas, where they began to fight each other in small-scale guerrilla warfare that flared up and died back for a half-dozen years until it helped kindle the big war of 1861. The chief actors in this violent drama

along the Missouri-Kansas border were proslavery "border ruffians" from Missouri, who repeatedly rode into Kansas to stuff ballot boxes and to clash with the free-soil Kansas "Jayhawkers." The free soilers ultimately won this battle, bringing Kansas into the Union as a free state on the eve of the Civil War in 1861.

The contest then shifted to Missouri itself. As a border state, Missouri was torn between North and South. Only 10 percent of its people were slaves and only 11 percent of its white population belonged to slave-holding families (compared with 40 percent and 32 percent, respectively, in the eleven Confederate states). But most Missourians were descended from

Missourians read a Mayor's Proclamation at St. Louis, Missouri. The struggle for Missouri was marked by much violence and terrorism. (Harper's Weekly, June 1, 1861)

Events in St. Louis caused many conditional unionists to join the ranks of secessionists. Above: a mob attacks U.S. volunteers at the corner of Fifth and Walnut Streets in St. Louis. Sketched by M. Hastings. (Harper's Weekly, *June 1, 1861*)

southern settlers. A significant exception was the large German-American population in St. Louis, which formed the core of unionist sentiment in the state. As other southern states were seceding in 1861, Missouri voters elected a majority of unionists to a convention which voted down a resolution of secession in March. But when Lincoln called on all loyal states for troops to help suppress insurrection after the fall of Fort Sumter, Missouri's governor defied the president and declared his allegiance to the Confederacy. A majority of the Missouri legislature held similar sentiments. The governor began organizing pro-Confederate militia regiments and plotting to seize the U.S. arsenal in St. Louis, with 60,000 muskets and other arms in storage. To counter these plans, U.S. army Captain Nathaniel Lyon organized unionist regiments in St. Louis.

These actions set the stage for an armed showdown in May 1861, which launched four years of bloody war within Missouri that echoed the larger Civil War on the national stage. Unionists retained precarious control of the state, while pro-Confederate elements formed a government-in-exile whose representatives were admitted to the Confederate Congress. Missouri became the twelfth star in the Confederate flag (Kentucky, likewise divided between North and South, became the thirteenth).

The bitter, vicious warfare between the two sides in Missouri spilled over into neighboring Arkansas and Kansas. The fighting in Missouri led to the second major battle of the Civil War, at Wilson's Creek on August 10, 1861, and to subsequent military operations that helped determine the fate of the vast region west of the Mississippi.

Wilson's Creek
by Dee Brown

"The Charge of the First Iowa Regiment," at Wilson's Creek, General Lyon in the lead.

On February 6, 1861, a short, spare, red-bearded captain of infantry reported for duty with an under-strength company of troops at the St. Louis, Missouri, arsenal. He was 42-year-old Nathaniel Lyon, one of the few confirmed abolitionists in the United States Army. Not long after his arrival in St. Louis, Lyon set forces in motion which made inevitable the second great battle of the Civil War. This battle followed Bull Run by less than three weeks and was much the same kind of amateur action—confused, blundering, indecisive, and very bloody. The Confederates named it Oak Hills. For the Union soldiers it was the Battle of Wilson's Creek, and it is now best known by that name.

Nathaniel Lyon was a West Point professional who had served with distinction in the Mexican War. Prior to his transfer to St. Louis, he spent six years at posts in Kansas where he developed an intense dislike for the pro-slavery element. To Lyon's dismay he found St. Louis and much of Missouri, including its governor, leaning toward the South. When the war began his ire was aroused by an encampment of pro-Confederate state militia just outside the city. Suspecting that the militia planned to capture the vital arsenal, Lyon surrounded the camp with a force of Regular troops and pro-Union volunteers and informed the militiamen that they were prisoners. As the captives were being taken back to the city, a riot broke out in the streets and Lyon's men fired into a mob of civilians, killing twenty-eight of them. The incident immediately widened the breach between pro-Union and pro-Confederate Missourians. Men such as former Governor Sterling Price, who had opposed the state's secession, now became fully committed to the Southern cause. Price soon took command of the Confederate state troops, and Lyon, who was promoted from captain to brigadier general on May 31, began moving up the Missouri River in pursuit of Price. After winning easy victories at Jefferson City and Boonville, Lyon established a base at Springfield from which he hoped to drive Price's Confederates completely out of Missouri.

By the end of July 1861, however, Lyon was in a precarious position. Terms of service of his three-months

Brigadier General Nathaniel Lyon, Union firebrand who led his army to Wilson's Creek, and his own death.

volunteers were nearing expiration, and his commander, General John Frémont, seemed unwilling to send reinforcements or supplies. "God damn General Frémont," Lyon shouted in exasperation after receiving a final curt refusal of aid from St. Louis. "He is a worse enemy to me and the Union cause than Price and the whole damned tribe of Rebels!"

Early in August, after an indecisive fight at Dug Springs, Lyon fell back on Springfield, fully aware that he must either withdraw from southwestern Missouri or defeat Price in a quick victory before too many reinforcements reached him from Arkansas. From scouts and spies, Lyon learned that Confederate troops under Generals Ben McCulloch and N. Bart Pearce had already joined Price's Missourians, forming an army of more than ten thousand men, and they were now camped ten miles southwest of Springfield. Lyon had only about five thousand ready for battle, but on August 9 he informed his officers that he intended to attack the Confederates before they attacked him.

During the council of war, Colonel Franz Sigel proposed that the Union force be divided; he would take his regiment of St. Louis Germans, a few Regular cavalrymen, and six pieces of artillery by side roads and attack the Confederates from the rear while Lyon attacked simultaneously from the front. All officers present were opposed to dividing five thousand men to attack a superior force of ten thousand, but for some reason Lyon accepted Sigel's plan.

Perhaps Lyon had fallen under the spell of the Sigel myth—the German's haughty manner, his thick-accented allusions to intricate military tactics, and boasts of his superior European military training and experience. Sigel had been a mathematics teacher in St. Louis, but somehow in his uniform he looked more like an officer than anybody else. (During the next three years, Franz Sigel would humbug far more experienced men than Lyon and not until 1864 would the Sigel myth explode in a final bloody fiasco in the Shenandoah Valley.)

Late in the evening of August 9, the two columns moved out of Springfield by separate roads. Rain began drizzling on Lyon's regiment about midnight, and not long afterward advance scouts sighted the campfires of the Confederates. Lyon ordered a halt until first daylight, and then after borrowing a rubber coat from his adjutant, Major John M. Schofield, he stretched out between two corn rows and went to sleep.

At 4:15 a.m. Lyon's column was moving again in gray light under broken clouds with the 1st Missouri Volunteers in advance, Company H deployed forward as skirmishers. The grass was wet from the night drizzle, and as they began marching up a slope their formations were broken by stunted oaks and underbrush. From the summit, the men in the first ranks could see the Confederate camps, smoke hanging over them, in the half-mile-wide valley of Wilson's Creek, "a thousand tents, stretching off into the distance, and partially screened from view by a hill jutting into an angle of the creek." The hill would later be called Bloody Hill, and Lyon made it his immediate objective.

At 5:10 the forward skirmishers of the 1st Missouri opened fire on Confederate pickets, and Lyon began deploying his troops for battle. Off to the left and across the creek into a cornfield went Captain Joseph Plummer with his 1st U. S. Infantry, supported from the hill slope by Lieutenant John Du Bois' four pieces of light artillery. To the right went Major Peter Osterhaus and a battalion of the 2d Missouri. Charging up through the blackjacks of Bloody Hill, the 1st Kansas at left and the 1st Missouri at right center quickly took the high ground, but they were separated by sixty yards of broken ravine. Behind them bounced the six light guns of Captain James Totten's battery of 2d U.S. Artillery.

A cloud was passing over the rising sun when Totten's gunners fired their first shot. It was a signal to Sigel, who was supposed to be at the other end of the valley, and artillery somewhere off to the southwest replied immediately. In the creek bottom below, Confederates from the nearest camp (Brigadier General James S. Rains' 2d Division, Missouri State Guard) were scattering southward on foot and on horseback. A St. Louis newspaper reporter, who had just reached the crest of Bloody Hill, observed the flight and said: "We have completely surprised them."

"General Lyon attacked us before breakfast," Lieutenant W. P. Barlow, one of the Missouri Confederates later reported. "We were surprised completely." The main reason for this apparent carelessness on the part of the Confederates was the loose chain of command which existed in their hastily combined army. On July 28 at Cassville, Missouri, General Price had joined his forces with those of Generals McCulloch and Pearce. McCulloch, a former Texas Ranger, had been commissioned a brigadier by President Jefferson Davis, and his C.S.A. command consisted of well-trained soldiers from Texas, Louisiana, and Arkansas. Pearce's troops were Arkansas Volunteers who were "cooperating" with McCulloch.

During the week between July 28 and August 4, McCulloch let Price know that he was planning to take his troops back into Arkansas in order to be closer to his supply base. Price was so dismayed that he offered to put himself and all his forces under McCulloch's command, provided the latter would help him defeat Lyon. "If you refuse to accept this offer," Price said, "I will move with the Missourians alone, against Lyon." At first McCulloch declined Price's offer, but on August 4 he changed his mind and agreed "to take the command and march upon the enemy." On the 6th, this loosely organized army reached Wilson's Creek. For three days the Confederates camped there while McCulloch waited for his scouts to bring him reliable information on the

Franz Sigel, as a brigadier, played an undistinguished part in the Federal defeat at Wilson's Creek.

strength and exact location of Lyon's army. Finally, on the morning of the 9th, General Price confronted McCulloch. "Are you going to attack Lyon or not?" he demanded. When McCulloch refused to commit himself, Price bluntly asked for the Missouri troops to be returned to his command so that he could lead them into battle. Knowing that Price meant what he said, McCulloch issued an order for the army to move out for Springfield at 9 p.m.

Just before time for the march to begin, a summer storm threatened. Horses were already saddled and pickets had been called in, but when a light rain began falling, McCulloch conferred with Price. Fewer than a fourth of the soldiers had ammunition boxes, and if the 20 to 25 rounds which they carried in their cotton sacks became wet, they would have no ammunition to fire. McCulloch sent orders to all troop commanders to see that their men took special care to keep their ammunition dry and be prepared to move at a moment's notice when the rain ceased. It continued falling until 11 o'clock, slacked to a drizzle, and then stopped about midnight, but McCulloch issued no order to march. A few commanders sent pickets back out to their camp perimeters; most did not. For this reason, Lyon was able to secure his position on Bloody Hill before the Confederates knew he had even left Springfield.

McCulloch, Price, and Colonel James McIntosh were breakfasting in Price's tent on roasted green corn when a horseman galloped in from General Rains's camp to warn that Lyon's army was approaching. McCulloch

The Wilson's Creek battlefield as viewed from Pearce's camp east of the stream.

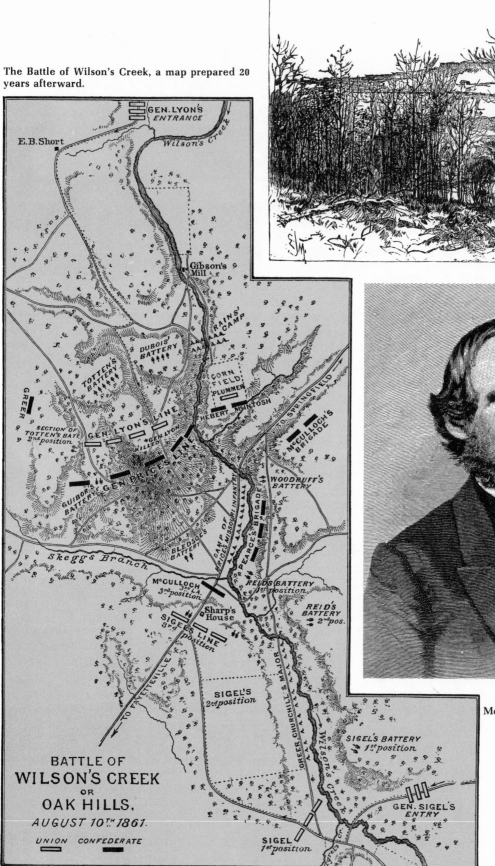

SHARP'S HOUSE (SIGEL'S POSITION).

The Battle of Wilson's Creek, a map prepared 20 years afterward.

GEN. LYON'S ENTRANCE

E.B.Short

Wilson's Creek

Gibson's Mill

DUBOIS' BATTERY

RAINS' CAMP

TOTTEN'S BATTERY

CORN FIELD

PLUMMER

GREER

HEBERT McINTOSH

GEN. LYON'S LINE

SPRINGFIELD

McCULLOCH'S BRIGADE

SECTION OF TOTTEN'S BATT. 2nd position

GEN. LYON KILLED

WOODRUFF'S BATTERY

GUIBOR'S BATTERY GEN. PEARCE'S LINE

CAMP OF PRICE'S MISSOURI INFANTRY

PEARCE'S BRIGADE

BLEDSOE'S BATTERY

Skeggs Branch

REID'S BATTERY 1st position

McCULLOCH 3rd La. 3rd position

Sharp's House

REID'S BATTERY 2nd pos.

SIGEL'S LINE 3rd position

TO FAYETTEVILLE

SIGEL'S 2nd position

GREER, CHURCHILL & MAJOR

Wilson's Creek

SIGEL'S BATTERY 1st position

BATTLE OF
WILSON'S CREEK
OR
OAK HILLS.
AUGUST 10TH 1861.

GEN. SIGEL'S ENTRY

UNION   CONFEDERATE

Tyrel's Cr.

SIGEL 1st position

Brigadier General Ben McCulloch led the Confederates at Wilson's Creek.

BLOODY HILL, IN THE DISTANCE.

BATTLES AND LEADERS OF THE CIVIL WAR

and McIntosh were skeptical. Neither man had much respect for the Missouri Volunteers, especially Rains's division which had over a thousand mounted men unarmed or poorly armed and with little military training. McIntosh referred to them as "Price's stupid fools," and McCulloch despaired of their discipline and complained that "instead of being a help, they are continually in the way." Not long after the messenger arrived, however, the distant rattle of rifle fire was unmistakable, and to the northwest a confused mass of retreating horsemen and wagons was plainly visible. McCulloch quickly devised a counter attack: Colonel McIntosh would lead the trained Louisiana and Arkansas troops to the right along the creek and strike for Lyon's flank while Price and his Missourians would drive to the left, straight up through the underbrush on Bloody Hill.

McCulloch and McIntosh, who were in uniform, mounted to ride back to their troops. Price, in a suit of rough linen, was buttoning his suspenders as he ran for his horse. "A stout farmer-looking old gentleman," one of the soldiers there described him. In his haste, Price forgot his hat, but later in the morning, some one gave him a black plug hat to shield his head from the August sun. An Arkansas artilleryman said that throughout the battle that tall black headpiece "ranged over the field like an orriflamme to the Missourians."

Meanwhile the first troops ordered into battle were tying pieces of white cloth around their left arms to distinguish them from the enemy. (Lack of distinguishable uniforms caused more confusion at Wilson's Creek than in any other Civil War battle. Many men on both sides had no uniforms; others wore state militia uniforms of varying colors, including blues and grays on both sides. Most of the 3d Louisiana companies wore new bluish-

gray uniforms, while the 1st Iowa Volunteers on the Union side wore uniforms of a similar shade of gray.)

When General McCulloch came galloping along the slope where Colonel Louis Hébert's 3d Louisiana was camped he found the men scurrying about in search of their uniform coats. McCulloch reined his horse and stood in his stirrups; he was a wiry man of about 50 with piercing blue eyes. "Colonel Hébert," he shouted, "why in hell don't you lead your men out!" Hébert immediately started his columns, and many of the infantrymen marched off without their coats, tying strips of white canvas over their shirtsleeves.

To the left across the creek, Price was positioning four small "divisions" (about 2,000 men altogether) under Brigadier Generals William Slack, J. H. McBride, John B. Clark, and Mosby M. Parsons. With Captain Henry Guibor's battery in support, the infantrymen rushed up through the hazel and blackjack of Bloody Hill. Because of the full-leafed cover their old short-range rifles and shotguns were as effective as the longer-ranged rifles of their Union opponents. On the left of the crescent-shaped line of battle it was Missourian against Missourian as McBride's Ozarkers stopped Lyon's 1st Missouri Volunteers; on their right Slack's division tangled with the 1st Kansas.

On the opposite side of the creek Colonel McIntosh was forming a battle line with his 2d Arkansas Mounted Rifles, Lieutenant Colonel Dandridge McRae's Arkansas infantry battalion, and Hébert's 3d Louisiana. The cornfield into which Captain Plummer's U.S. Regulars were advancing was McIntosh's objective. As the Louisianans moved off the open slope where they had been camped, Major Totten's Union artillerymen saluted them with a blast of shot. By this time Captain William Woodruff's Arkansas battery was ready to reply, and the

The Battle of Wilson's Creek, as painted by N. C. Wyeth for a mural in the Missouri State Capitol, Jefferson City.

Arkansans' cannon fire helped check the advance of Lyon's forces on Bloody Hill. Ironically, young Woodruff had been drilled and instructed by none other than the man with whom he was dueling. Major Totten as commander of the Little Rock arsenal had trained the local militia, but when Arkansas seceded he had been forced to surrender the arsenal and the very guns that Woodruff was now firing upon him.

McIntosh's infantrymen pushed on through shoulder-high bottomland brush toward the cornfield fence. Most of the grain had already been harvested and the stalks were trampled down. "We could see the enemy's line advancing in beautiful order," said Sergeant William Watson of the 3d Louisiana, "with skirmishers in front."

Along one section of the fence, the opponents came together before a shot was exchanged. Two U.S. Regulars climbed upon the rails to confront the raised rifle of a Confederate who was wearing a blue uniform. "Don't shoot!" cried one of the Union infantrymen, "We are friends." To his surprise he learned a moment later that he and his comrade were prisoners of the Confederates. When firing began, the lines were so close together that officers on either side could hear the others' commands. By coincidence the opposing leaders, McIntosh and Plummer, had been classmates at West Point. Also Major Samuel Sturgis, who was in the field as Lyon's second-in-command, had been McIntosh's commander only a few months earlier.

At first the old-style phalanx formation of the U.S. Regulars made them easy targets for the Confederates

kneeling in the brush, but in a short time powder smoke became so thick in the humid air that the Confederates could see no targets until the advancing ranks were almost upon them. Fearing that Plummer's Regulars would overrun his troops, McIntosh ordered a bayonet charge. Superior numbers forced the Regulars back across the field, but as soon as the Confederates were in the open, Lieutenant Du Bois' flanking artillery checked them. "The ground was black with their dead," Du Bois later reported, but he should have added that many of the casualties were Union soldiers. His artillery bombardment split McIntosh's troops apart, half of them taking cover in woods to the right of the creek, the others crossing the stream into a brushy hollow. As soon as Captain Plummer withdrew his Regulars up Bloody Hill, a company of determined Louisianans made a quick thrust at Du Bois' battery. When Du Bois saw their bluish-gray uniforms through the thick underbrush he thought they might be Union soldiers from one of Sigel's regiments trying to break through the Confederate lines. At twenty yards, however, they opened fire on the artillerymen with rifles and pistols. "They nearly carried my guns," Du Bois said. "This only lasted ten minutes, but it was very bloody."

To Du Bois' right along the crest of Bloody Hill, heavy fighting was now in progress, the lines moving back and forth in the blackjack woods. Sometimes the contending Missourians came so close together they recognized the faces of former friends and acquaintances, and Price and Lyon could hear each other's commands. After almost two hours of hard fighting, the lines drew apart like two winded, blooded, but undefeated animals. "The most remarkable of the battle's characteristics," said one of the participants, "was the deep silence which now and then fell upon the smoking field—while the two armies, unseen to each other, lay but a few yards apart, gathering strength to grapple again in the death struggle for Missouri."

During the first long pause in the fighting, Lyon brought up the gray-uniformed 1st Iowa to relieve the 1st Kansas, and the 2d Kansas to relieve the battered 1st Missouri. On the Confederate side, McCulloch ordered Pearce's Arkansas Volunteers and some of McIntosh's troops into Price's front ranks on Bloody Hill. Forming into three ranks, the Confederates began moving upward through the bullet-shattered blackjack. "On they came in overwhelming numbers," said the New York *Herald* correspondent. "Not a breath was heard among the Iowans till their enemies came within thirty-five or forty feet." Then there was the sharp click of a thousand rifles and the battle was resumed. The time was now between 9 and 10 o'clock in the morning.

From his Confederate battery across the creek, Captain Woodruff noted the gray-clad Iowans moving into a position which gave him an excellent opportunity to enfilade the regiment. "We opened on it with the effect of breaking its beautiful line and scattering it its full length." At the same time, Major Totten sent a section of Union artillery forward to open at close range upon the Confederate infantry. A Confederate officer afterward described this action as "the most terrific storm of grape and musketry ever poured out upon the ranks of any American troops."

General Lyon on horseback was dashing recklessly about, trying to rally his outnumbered troops. He kept asking: "Where is Sigel? What has happened to Sigel?" Blood flowed from surface wounds in his head and leg. When he galloped to the rear to give an order to Totten, the major offered him some brandy, but he declined. As he turned toward the front again, his horse was shot and fell dead. While his adjutant, Major Schofield, was obtaining another mount for him, Lyon wiped blood from his face and remarked despondently: "Major, I fear the day is lost." Schofield tried to reassure him, but it was evident that the Iowa and Kansas regiments were beginning to break apart. Without Sigel's troops, they could not long contain the mass of attacking Confederates. "Everything," Lieutenant Du Bois noted tersely, "was covered with blood." The 1st Iowa had lost thirteen of its twenty-seven officers, and its entire color guard was cut down. As companies fell back to re-form ranks, they became mixed with retreating companies of the 2d Kansas.

In a desperate move to save the day, Lyon hurried to the front. "Swinging his hat in the air," Major Schofield reported, "he led forward the troops, who promptly

rallied around him." A few seconds later a bullet tore into Lyon's chest and killed him. Some accounts of his death say that he dismounted and then fell into the arms of his orderly. Others say that his horse was felled first and that he was standing upon the animal's prostrate body, waving his sword and cheering his men on when he was shot. Most pictorial representations of the event show him dying in the saddle. Major Schofield was convinced that Lyon, despairing of victory without Sigel's missing troops, threw away his life in desperation. Moments after Lyon died, Schofield was at his side; the major had to catch a loose "secesh" horse to ride to Major Sturgis and inform him that he was now in command.

What *had* happened to Colonel Franz Sigel? Exactly as the haughty German had planned, he arrived at the southwest end of the Confederate camps just as dawn was breaking. His forward cavalry units cut off forty Confederate soldiers who were getting water from Wilson's Creek. After passing the prisoners to the rear, Sigel placed his battery of six guns on a hill and sent his infantry across the creek. At 5:30, upon hearing the rattle of Lyon's first rifle attack, he ordered his battery to begin firing into the tented camps of Colonel Thomas J. Churchill's 1st Arkansas Mounted Rifles and Colonel Elkanah Greer's Texas Rangers. While the Confederates were taking cover in the woods to the north, Sigel sent his infantry in pursuit of them—but only as far as the Springfield-Fayetteville road. As soon as he heard Major Totten's opening artillery signal, he brought his own battery across the creek and placed it on low bluffs overlooking Skeggs Branch.

With his troops and guns astraddle the Fayetteville road, Sigel was now in perfect position to strike the Confederates from the rear while Lyon was attacking in front. Instead of pushing forward, however, Sigel formed a line and waited for Lyon to drive the Confederates to him. While he waited, his idle troops wandered through the abandoned Confederate tents along the creek collecting souvenirs. Sigel himself obtained a Texas Ranger's hat. All that he had accomplished thus far was to drive several hundred Arkansas and Texas troops to the base of Bloody Hill where McCulloch promptly added them to the force that was cutting Lyon's regiments to pieces.

During the 9 o'clock lull in the fighting on Bloody Hill, Sigel's men sighted a column of troops approaching along the Fayetteville road. Through the dust and smoke their uniforms appeared to be a shade of gray. Because of the silence which had fallen over the battlefield Sigel assumed that the Confederates had fled the fighting in disorder and that these oncoming troops must be the Iowa regiment in their militia gray. Sigel ordered his men to hold their fire and wave their flags so that the Iowans would not fire upon them.

The approaching soldiers were not Union, however. They were led by General McCulloch, who had observed Sigel's threatening presence in his rear, and had hastily collected some scattered units of cavalry and three companies of infantry from the 3d Louisiana to launch an attack. Because he met with no challenging fire all the way to the base of the low bluff where Sigel's battery was placed, McCulloch began to wonder if the guns and men above him were Union. He knew that two light Confederate batteries were supposed to be somewhere in the area.

"Whose forces are those?" he demanded of a soldier posted beside a huge oak.

"Sigel's," the soldier replied in a German accent.

McCulloch's shaggy eyebrows lowered in a questioning frown. "Whose did you say?" he shouted.

"Union. Sigel," the man replied and raised his rifle.

The death of Lyon.

Before the soldier could fire, Corporal Henry Gentles of the Pelican Rifles dropped him with a quick shot. McCulloch turned and glanced at Gentles. "That was a good shot," he said, and then quickly shouted an order to Captain John Vigilini: "Take your company up, captain, and give them hell!" Even as the Louisianans swarmed over Sigel's batteries, the Union artillerymen were still shouting: "Don't shoot! We're friends!" But a few minutes later, Sigel's entire command was shaken by the realization that a Confederate force had penetrated their lines and captured the artillery.

At the sight of Confederate bayonets, most of Sigel's artillerymen abandoned their guns and fled with their caissons, lashing the horses down the road away from the battlefield. Panic quickly spread through the infantry and they also took flight, leaving only two small units of Regular cavalry on the flanks. Many of the fleeing men circled around to the rear of Lyon's line of battle, where they were badly needed, but there was no one to stop them. As they fled toward Springfield, they left small arms, blankets, coats, and knapsacks strewn along the road. Colonel Sigel himself took flight, donning the yellow slouch hat taken from the abandoned Confederate camp and throwing a blanket over his uniform so he would not be recognized as an enemy by pursuing Confederates. He was completely out of the fight by 10 o'clock, and reached Springfield before the main battle was ended. The Confederates had captured five of his six guns, a regimental standard, and more than 200 prisoners.

On Bloody Hill meanwhile, McCulloch had unloosed a cavalry thrust at his enemy's right flank. Assembling in woods cover on the west side of the hill, the horsemen startled Union rear support units with their sudden appearance. "The enemy tried to overwhelm us," Major Totten reported, "by an attack of some 800 cavalry, which unobserved, had formed below the crests of the hills to our right and rear." Totten wheeled a section of artillery upon them and Major Osterhaus' Missouri Union infantry soon checked the cavalry charge. In his official report, Totten was most uncomplimentary toward the Confederate cavalry: "It was so effete and ineffectual in its force and character as to deserve only the appellation of child's play. Their cavalry is utterly worthless on the battlefield." He made no allowance for the terrain, the dense brush and trees which made it impossible for horsemen to ride through in formation. Some of these Texas and Arkansas cavalrymen would later serve with Forrest and Morgan to disprove Major Totten's estimate of their prowess.

Between 10:30 and 11:00 a.m., the battlefield once again lay silent. "An almost total silence," Major Schofield described it. "As soon as the enemy began to give way and it became apparent that the field was at least for the present ours, the principal officers of the command were informed of General Lyon's death, and Major Sturgis assumed command. He at once called together the chief officers in his vicinity and consulted with them as to the course that should be pursued."

While the Union officers were discussing whether or not they should push forward and resume the battle, the Confederates settled the question for them by launching their third massive attack of the day. It proved to be the fiercest of the entire battle, and it began with a wild Rebel yell. In the forefront of the Confederate line was Colonel John Gratiot's 3d Arkansas Infantry, which had been supporting Woodruff's battery most of the morning. Upon receiving orders to enter the battle, the Arkansans marched up Bloody Hill in column of fours. "I advanced them until we came near the enemy," Gratiot reported. "We then faced toward them, and marched in line of battle about fifty paces, when we were attacked by a large force of the enemy in front and on the left flank."

During the next few minutes Gratiot's men were in the vortex of the final struggle for Bloody Hill. While they were fighting almost muzzle to muzzle with Kansas infantrymen, they were caught in enfilading fire from Lieutenant Du Bois' artillery. At the same time the 5th Arkansas coming up through thick powder smoke fired into them from the rear. In the very few minutes they were in action, the men of the 3d suffered 109 casualties. "It was," said one of the participants, "a mighty mean-fowt fight."

At one time, attacking Confederates almost overran Totten's battery. To prevent disaster, Captain Gordon Granger of the Regulars rallied scattered units of Kansans, Iowans, and Missourians and led them against the Confederate right flank. This surprise attack blunted the Confederates' forward motion, and Granger had pushed their right ranks half way down Bloody Hill when Sturgis called him back. "Most of our men had fired away all their ammunition," Sturgis explained in his report. "Nothing, therefore, was left to do but to return to Springfield."

The Confederates also had expended most of their ammunition, and they were as blooded and weary of the fighting as their opponents. "We watched the retreating enemy through our field-glasses," said General Bart Pearce of the Army of Arkansas, *"and were glad to see him go."*

After the Union forces withdrew toward Springfield with their wounded, the Confederates took over the contested ground of Bloody Hill. Among the many dead who lay there, they found the body of General Lyon. At the last moment, hospital orderlies evidently had removed Lyon's dead body from an army wagon and replaced it with a wounded man. Under a flag of truce, Confederate officers took the dead commander's body into Springfield and were received in a friendly manner by Union officers. "We gave the Confederates a good dinner and some whiskey," Lieutenant Du Bois recorded, "and when we sat on the ground afterwards, chatting gaily over our segars, one would not have supposed that we had been trying to take each others' lives only a few hours ago."

Like Bull Run in the East, Wilson's Creek in the West was acclaimed as a victory by Confederates because they

One of Frank Leslie's best artists, Henry Lovie, drew this on-the-spot sketch
depicting the Confederate cavalry charge against the 2d Kansas.

had forced Union soldiers to leave the field. Neither battle was decisive, of course, and many of Lyon's junior officers always looked upon Wilson's Creek as a standoff. Some believed that they would have been victorious had the men with Sigel been on Bloody Hill. Nine officers were so disgusted with Sigel's lack of leadership and his flight into Springfield that they signed a statement addressed to General H. W. Halleck requesting that he be removed from command. The statement was ignored, however, and General Frémont cited Sigel "for gallant and meritorious conduct in the command of his brigade."

Casualties at Wilson's Creek for the Union were 223 killed, 721 wounded, 291 missing, for a total of 1,235; for the Confederates 257 killed, 900 wounded, 27 missing for a total of 1,184. Considering the lesser number of men engaged, Wilson's Creek was a far bloodier battle than Bull Run. One-fourth of the Federal soldiers were killed, wounded, or missing. The 1st Missouri Union Infantry marched on the field with 720 men and left it with but 420; the 1st Kansas lost 300 of 800. More than half of the Confederate casualties were from Price's Missouri regiments, but the 3d Louisiana and two Arkansas regiments also took heavy losses.

So far as the war in the West was concerned, Wilson's Creek changed almost nothing. In or out of the Union, Missouri was doomed by geography to suffer four years of guerrilla fighting. Many of those who would be involved in that border terror—men such as William Quantrill, Frank James, Cole Younger, Wild Bill Hickok—were there at Wilson's Creek.

"Adanger Bissence"

(Richmond, Va.)

September 11, 1864 . . . . . . Dare Brother iwante you to Bee shore and tende to . . . Beney ande keepe hime outo this ware ite is note avary bade mater to git in this ware Bute ite is amiti harde mater to gite oute of ite . . . . and again . . . . Bute Dear Brother ican tel you that chargene yankes rite off thare Breste works is note the thinges that it is CraCked upe to Bee fore ite is adanger Bissence [a dangerous business] . . . . Beryamin Brame-Cate (?)

From the collection of Dr. Harold E. Simon, Birming-ham, Alabama, and furnished through his courtesy.

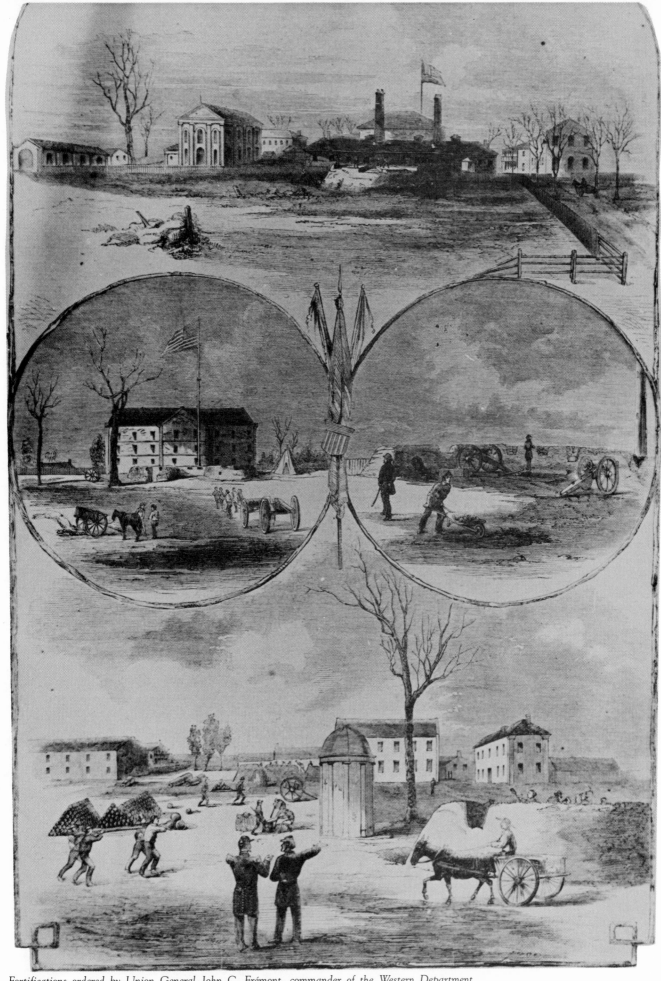

Fortifications ordered by Union General John C. Frémont, commander of the Western Department (mainly Missouri), to protect the U.S. arsenal at St. Louis. (Harper's Weekly)

The Siege of Lexington

by Albert Castel

THE Union defeat at Wilson's Creek opened the way for the Confederate take-over of Missouri. Or at least so thought Major General Sterling Price, whose pro-Southern Missouri State Guard had combined with Confederate forces under Brigadier General Ben McCulloch to win this battle, fought August 10, 1861 near Springfield, Missouri. Price, a former governor of Missouri, believed that the majority of Missourians sympathized with the South and were only awaiting an opportunity to stage a mass uprising against Northern domination. Consequently he proposed to follow up the Wilson's Creek victory by an advance through western Missouri, now devoid of Union defenders, to the Missouri River. Tens of thousands of volunteers, he was confident, would flock to his banner, and thus enable him to drive the Federal occupation army out of the state. And once the Confederacy was in control of Missouri its strategic position would be so impregnable as to leave the North little choice except to acknowledge the independence of the Southern states. In short, the war itself would be won by a quick, bold thrust into the heartland of Missouri.

But when Price asked McCulloch to join him in a march to the Missouri River, McCulloch (who disliked Price and despised the poorly disciplined Missouri State Guard) flatly refused. His army, he declared, lacked ammunition, it was needed to protect Arkansas and the Indian Territory, and several of his regiments were about to return home, leaving him with only 2,500 men. In addition he argued that a movement to the Missouri could not succeed without the support of the Confederate forces in the eastern part of the state—and they, he had just learned, had retreated to the Arkansas line.

McCulloch's negative response angered the disappointed Price, but it did not deter him. He was convinced that Missouri's hour of deliverance was at hand and that not to take action now would give the Federals a chance to recover from their defeat at Wilson's Creek and more time in which to consolidate their hold on the state. Hence, on August 25 he set out from Springfield with an army of about 7,000 men, a large portion of whom were mounted, and sixteen field pieces. He planned first to "clear out" some Kansas jayhawkers (as Union irregulars from that state were called) who were making "marauding and murdering" raids out of Fort Scott into Missouri, then swing north into the slaveholding counties south of the Missouri River. Here he would be in an area where pro-Southern sentiment was strong, and where he would be able to gather recruits from the upper half of the state.

ON THE evening of September 2 Price's advance guard encountered about 500 jayhawkers at Drywood Creek along the Kansas-Missouri border. The opposing

Battle of Lexington, seen from within the Federal works. (HW)

Major General Sterling Price. Engraved from photograph. (B&L)

Brig. General Ben McCulloch refused aid to General Price.

sides skirmished for about two hours, then the badly out-numbered Kansans fled. Content with thus "chastising" the jayhawkers, Price turned northward, passing through Osceola and Warrensburg. He met no significant resistance anywhere, and most encouraging of all, hundreds of eager volunteers joined his army.

On the morning of September 13 Price, at the head of his cavalry, approached the southern outskirts of Lexington, a tidy little town of about 1,000 population perched on a bluff overlooking the Missouri River. Union pickets opened fire and Price ordered his men to fall back while he brought up the main force and artillery. That afternoon he advanced again and after a brief action the Federal garrison retreated to its fortifications. These consisted of a rampart of sod and earth twelve feet high and twelve feet thick located on the north side of Lexington and surrounding the white-pillared, three-storied, brick building of the Masonic College. Beyond this bastion was an irregular line of earthworks and rifle pits, protected by traverses, ditches, sharpened stakes, and trip-wires. The garrison was composed of the "Irish Brigade" of Chicago (most of whose men, however, were not Irish), a regiment of Illinois cavalry, portions of two Missouri Federal regiments, and a battalion of Unionist home guards—in all about 3,500 troops. Mounted behind embrasures in the rampart were seven cannon.

The commander of the garrison was Colonel James A. Mulligan of the Irish Brigade, a thirty-one-year-old Chicago politician turned soldier. Although he had known for several days that Price was approaching and so could have easily escaped on the two steamboats he had available, he had decided to make a stand. His orders from his immediate superior were to hold Lexington "at all hazards," and in addition he wanted to protect the large quantities of confiscated Rebel property which he had buried in the basement of the college—property that included the Great Seal of the State of Missouri and nearly one million dollars taken from the Lexington bank. Besides, he was confident that Major General John C. Frémont, the top Union commander in Missouri, would waste no time in sending a relief column to his rescue. Frémont at this time was at St. Louis organizing a large army with which he proposed to sweep all Southern forces out of the state, then drive down the Mississippi to New Orleans.

PRICE had to wait for his ammunition wagons to come up from the south over muddy, rain-soaked roads before attacking the fort. Meanwhile his army continued to swell in numbers as each day more volunteers arrived. Among the reinforcements were nearly 2,000 troops from northeast Missouri under Brigadier General Thomas A. Harris, a division which earlier had included in its ranks a Mississippi River pilot named Sam Clemens. Although the future Mark Twain never fought under Price, another young man also soon to be famous (but in a totally different fashion) did serve with Price throughout the siege.

Arkansas troops, sketched in Beauregard's army in Virginia. (HW)

He was a native of Ohio and former Kansas resident named William Clarke Quantrill.

On September 18, the ammunition train having arrived, Price invested the Union fort. Mulligan himself later described the Confederate advance: "They came as one dark moving mass, their guns beaming in the sun, their banners waving, and drums beating—everywhere, as far as we could see, were men, men, men, approaching grandly."

The garrison poured a heavy artillery fire on the Missourians, causing most of their officers to dismount. But Price, a tall, portly man, galloped to the front, the plaid hunting shirt he wore during battle covered with dust, his face glowing with excitement. "Perfectly self-possessed," later wrote one of his men in admiration,

he seemed not to heed the storm of grape and canister, and taking position in the rear of Parsons' battery directed the handling of the guns. Many officers urged him to retire or dismount, but he refused. A grapeshot struck his field glass, breaking it in pieces, but without the slightest apparent emotion, he continued giving his orders. After twenty minutes he retired, leaving a lasting impression upon his men, who have ever loved him as their chief, and admired him as their "beau ideal" of honor and chivalry.

WITHIN a few hours Price's divisions, as the main units of the State Guard were rather inaccurately called, completely encircled the fort: Brigadier General William Y. Slack's on the west, Brigadier General Mosby M. Parsons' on the south, Brigadier General James S. Rains' on the east, and Brigadier Generals J. H. McBride's and Harris' on the river side. They then launched a general assault, moving forward in long, straggling lines, the men taking advantage of the cover provided by numerous trees, bushes, and ravines, and firing incessantly as they moved forward. Under the pressure of this heavy attack, the garrison quickly pulled back to the inner works, abandoning as it did so the outpost protecting the fort's water supply, a spring located in a ravine just north of the outer line of fortifications. In anticipation of this development, the Federals had filled cisterns inside the college with water, but much of this had already been consumed by wagon team and cavalry horses. Consequently at the very outset of the siege Mulligan's men began to suffer from thirst.

As the Missourians attempted to follow up their initial success, fierce fighting took place around the Anderson House, a large brick structure which stood (and still stands) on a hill only 125 yards from the Union ramparts on the west. The Federals were using it as a hospital, and when Price's men captured it they found a doctor, a priest,

and a number of wounded present. Incensed by what he considered to be a barbaric violation of the laws of warfare, Mulligan ordered first one, then another of his units to retake the house, but both refused to budge. Finally one of his Irish companies sallied forth and stormed the building, after which they murdered three Rebel prisoners in retaliation. But the Missourians soon drove the Irish out, then held on during the rest of the siege. Because of its location the Anderson House had great military value, and so should never have been used as a hospital.

DARKNESS ended the first day's fighting. On the second day of the siege (September 19) Price's troops kept up a steady musket and artillery fire on the fort. From behind their rampart the Federals returned the fire, or else sought desperately to obtain drinking water by wringing out their rainsoaked blankets into canteens. As they bit open their cartridges their dry lips cracked, sending blood streaming in tiny rivulets down their chins and into their whiskers. Several Rebel hot shot ripped through the walls of the college, but Mulligan's men used shovels to toss them out before a fire could start. In turn stray projectiles from the fort smashed into buildings in Lexington, including one that buried itself in a corner of the courthouse, where its mark can be seen to this day. But since Price had ordered the town evacuated, there were no civilian casualties. Some of the local inhabitants joined in the fighting, among them a 60-year-old farmer

who appeared every morning the siege lasted with a basket of food in one hand and an old flintlock in the other. Taking position behind a large tree, he banged away at the Yankees all day, then at dusk returned home.

The young and impetuous officers of Price's staff urged him to order a mass frontal assault on the Masonic College, arguing that unless the garrison was captured soon a Federal relief column would rescue it. But Price refused to follow this advice. "It is unnecessary to kill off the boys here," he said. "Patience will give us what we want."

Mulligan and his men were sustained by the hope of a relief column, which they expected to arrive that very day. And, in fact, such a column under Brigadier General Samuel D. Sturgis had set out from Mexico, Missouri and by September 19 was only fifteen miles from Lexington. But Price learned of its approach and sent 3,000 men under Parsons across the river to intercept it. A Negro warned Sturgis of Parsons' movement and caused him to turn off in the direction of Kansas City. Other Federal forces in the vicinity, ignorant of the situation at Lexington, dared not intervene. Thus the garrison was left to its fate.

ON THE evening of the 19th some of the Missouri soldiers, apparently on their own initiative, began using hemp bales, which they found in a warehouse on the riverfront, as mobile breastworks. Others followed their example, and General Harris requested additional bales

Colonel James A. Mulligan, Union defender at Lexington. (HW)

OVERLEAF: *Battle of Lexington, as pictured in "Frank Leslie's Illustrated Newspaper" Oct. 12, 1861. This woodcut bears the credit line: "From a sketch by F. B. Wilkie, a prisoner in the Rebel camp during the fight." The principal landmarks are clearly shown. L. to R.: Col. Anderson's house, boarding house, and Masonic College. The college was the final Union stronghold.*

from Price. He promptly obtained 132 of them, for several days previously Captain Thomas Hinkle of the State Guard and a resident of the Lexington area had suggested this use of the bales to a couple of Price's staff officers,

who in turn told Price. Liking the idea—after all, Andrew Jackson purportedly had constructed his defenses at New Orleans out of cotton bales—Price had Hinkle collect several wagon loads of bales from the countryside and then deposit them near his headquarters on the riverbank. This, at least, seems the most likely explanation of how the famous hemp bale stratagem came into being, for there is much conflicting testimony on the matter, with Price, Harris, and others claiming sole credit. Only four years previously Sepoy mutineers had employed mobile cotton-bale barricades in attacking the British at Cawnpore in India.

At first Harris had the bales soaked in the river (another device which Hinkle had suggested) so as to prevent them from catching fire when hit by bullets and hot shot. However this so increased their weight, which was tremendous in any case, that the tired and hungry Missourians were unable to haul them up to the top of the bluff. Harris thereupon instructed his men to wet the bales after putting them in position. By morning a long, snake-like line of bales faced the fort on the north and west, generally 400 yards distant, but in places as close as 100 yards.

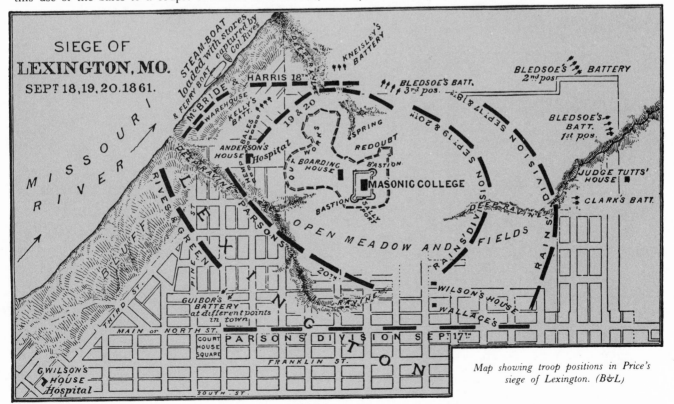

Map showing troop positions in Price's siege of Lexington. (B&L)

SHORTLY after 8 a.m. Price's soldiers began rolling the bales forward. In some cases they propelled them by poles or dragged them by ropes, but usually three men, unarmed, pushed them along by crawling on their knees and butting them with their heads. Behind the bales, firing as they came, advanced Harris', McBride's, and portions of other divisions. The Union troops opened a heavy fire in a frantic attempt to keep the hemp coil from closing, but to no avail. Bullets merely buried themselves harmlessly in the bales, and cannon balls caused them only to "rock a little and then settle back." Hot shot also failed, and fortunately for the success of the stratagem the Federals lacked shells. After several hours the Missourians were nearly close enough to the fort to take it in one quick rush.

By then the garrison's ammunition was almost exhausted, it was without food or water, and morale and discipline were beginning to crumble. One of Mulligan's officers, acting without orders, hoisted a white flag and the Union troops stopped firing. Price ordered his men to do likewise, then sent a note to Mulligan asking, "Why has the firing ceased?" The Irish colonel, unaware of his subordinate's action, returned the note with the gallant but rather absurd reply written on the back, "General, I hardly know, unless you have surrendered." A few minutes later Price's soldiers resumed firing—and pushing their hemp bales.

Mulligan knew that he was merely postponing the inevitable, that barring the sudden appearance of a strong relief column the only choice was surrender or massacre. He put the question to his senior officers, and by a large majority they voted in favor of the former. Immediately he sent out a flag of truce, at the same time asking for terms. Colonel Thomas L. Snead, Price's chief of staff, demanded unconditional surrender to be made within ten minutes, for he suspected that Mulligan might be trying to gain time in hopes of help arriving. Mulligan could only comply. A little after 2 p.m. the garrison marched out and laid down its arms—not, however, without much grumbling from the still defiant Irishmen. Mulligan and his officers came before Price and offered their swords. But Price, in a characteristic action, declined them: "You gentlemen have fought so bravely that it would be wrong to deprive you of your swords. Keep them. Orders to parole you and your men will be issued, Colonel Mulligan, without unnecessary delay."

Price was not simply being gallant. Lacking proper facilities and with even his own men on slim rations, he could not have kept such a large body of enemy troops prisoner in any case. After being lined up and forced to listen to a speech by the secessionist governor of Missouri, Claiborne Jackson, all the Federals were released except Mulligan. He refused a parole and remained with Price as a privileged captive, being joined by his pretty 19-year-old bride who had stayed near Lexington during the siege. The couple rode in Price's carriage and slept in a tent pitched next to his. On October 30 Price exchanged the Irish colonel for a Confederate prisoner of equal rank. After being hailed as a hero in the North, Mulligan served in Virginia, where on July 24, 1864 he was mortally wounded at the Battle of Winchester.

LEXINGTON was the most complete and spectacular victory achieved by Southern arms in the war up to that time. Besides nearly 3,500 Union troops, Price's army captured seven cannon, over 3,000 rifles, 750 horses, and a large quantity of other items, including sabers, saddles, and commissary stores. In so doing it inflicted 159 casualties and suffered fewer than 100. Coming on the heels of Wilson's Creek and dramatically enhanced by the ingenious use of the hemp bales, the siege of Lexington made Price a popular hero throughout the South, where some

Confederates fighting behind hemp bales at Lexington. (B&L)

Ex-Governor Claiborne Jackson of Missouri addressing Colonel Mulligan's troops after their surrender at Lexington. (HW)

politicians began talking about electing him the next President of the Confederacy.

Price remained at Lexington for over a week following Mulligan's surrender. During that period he distributed the captured equipment among his troops, received large numbers of recruits, and, in an action that was almost quixotic in view of his army's slender financial resources, restored all but $37,000 of the money taken by the Federals from the Lexington bank. He also called on McCulloch to send reinforcements or at least some percussion caps, but that general, who had withdrawn into Arkansas, declared that he could spare neither.

Meanwhile Frémont finally completed organizing his army, 38,000 strong, and on September 26 he took the field against Price. A day or two later Price learned that a Federal detachment had reached Sedalia, less than fifty miles southeast of Lexington. At once he began preparations for a retreat, for he now was in danger of being cut off. As McCulloch had anticipated, he could not maintain himself on the Missouri without the active support of Confederate forces in the eastern part of the state, and this was not forthcoming. Nor had there been a mass uprising against Union control which Price had counted on to compensate for the absence of such support. As one of his officers commented bitterly, "the sentiment on Missouri was not in harmony with the secession movement," and even those Missourians who did sympathize with the Confederate cause "were more interested in the conservation of their property and scalps than in abstract principle." One-third of Mulligan's garrison consisted of Unionist Missourians, and throughout the war Missouri was largely defended against the Confederates by its own militia, voluntarily enlisted.

TO BE SURE, thousands of volunteers joined Price during the Lexington campaign. But he lacked the arms and equipment to supply more than a fraction of them. Consequently he had to advise many to return home and wait for a more favorable opportunity to take the field. Hundreds of others simply began leaving on their own once the siege ended, declaring as they did so that they had to "arrange their business affairs, and set their houses in order." These latter were men who had joined in a holiday mood and had enjoyed themselves hugely in the balmy September weather peppering the Masonic College with bullets and buckshot. But the prospect of retreat, cold weather, long marches, and short rations was less appealing. And that was all Price could offer them.

On September 29 the State Guard marched southward out of Lexington. By the time it reached the Osage River nine days later it had dwindled from desertions to only 7,000, which was exactly its number when it left Springfield over a month before, and about 13,000 less than its peak strength immediately after Mulligan's surrender. Instead of a great campaign of liberation Price's march to the Missouri had merely been a raid, and the triumph at Lexington, however dramatic, had proved strategically barren. Federal control over most of Missouri remained firm, and early in 1862 a Union army would first drive Price out of the state, then defeat him and McCulloch at the Battle of Pea Ridge in Arkansas. Not until the autumn of 1864 would Price again invade Missouri, and then only to be routed at the battles of Westport and Mine Creek.

Pea Ridge
by D. Alexander Brown

WHEN THE Butterfield Company opened a stagecoach line between St. Louis and San Francisco in 1858, a shrewd Arkansas farmer who lived on the route converted his home into a tavern. His name was Jesse Cox, and his large two-story frame house stood just below the Missouri border at the east end of a swell of ground called Pea Ridge. To make certain that travelers would recognize and remember his tavern, Cox mounted the horns and skull of a huge elk at the center of the ridgepole. Elkhorn Tavern with its overhanging roof, wide porches, and big fireplaces soon became known as a place where "good cheer was most ample."

Three years later, war was raging northward in Missouri, and the transcontinental coaches were no longer running on that route. During 1861 the Confederates won some victories in Missouri, but after Brigadier General Samuel R. Curtis took command of Union forces on Christmas Day, the tide began to turn. Jesse Cox watched anxiously as Confederate Brigadier General Ben McCulloch slowly withdrew from Missouri with his Texas, Louisiana, and Arkansas troops. In February 1862, Brigadier General Sterling Price's Missouri Confederates also began retreating into the Boston Mountains of Arkansas, with Curtis' pursuing Federals not far behind.

Cox sympathized with the South, but he was also

The Battle of Pea Ridge. Engraved after a sketch by an officer in Brig. Gen. Franz Sigel's division. (HW)

Brig. Gen. Samuel R. Curtis.

concerned over the safety of his fine cattle herd. Thousands of soldiers foraging through the countryside could soon make short work of livestock without payment to the owner. Leaving his tavern in the care of his wife Polly and his young son Joseph, Cox set out for Kansas with the cattle herd. Before he returned, Elkhorn Tavern would become the vortex of one of the bloodiest battles fought west of the Mississippi River.

ON MARCH 3, Major General Earl Van Dorn, a handsome and flamboyant veteran of the Mexican War, arrived in the Boston Mountains to take command of the combined Confederate forces of Price and McCulloch. Responding to a forty-gun salute, Van Dorn promised his troops a victory after which they would sweep across Missouri to St. Louis. They numbered 16,000 men, including a thousand Cherokees fresh from Indian Territory under command of Brigadier General Albert Pike.

Van Dorn immediately set this army in motion northward, confident that he could smash the 10,500 Federals strung out across seventy miles of northwest Arkansas. He overlooked the fact that thousands of his men were without battle experience. Many were recent Arkansas volunteers, incensed by the invasion of their state. "Very few of the officers," General Price's adjutant noted, "had any knowledge whatever

of military principles or practices." As for the Cherokees, they knew nothing of discipline or firing by command.

For three days the Confederates marched through rain and melting snow, subsisting on scanty rations. On March 6, near Bentonville, Van Dorn's cavalry struck hard at one end of the Federals' extended line. General Curtis, however, had been alerted by his scouts, and had already begun concentrating his forces along Little Sugar Creek, two miles below Elkhorn Tavern. When the Confederates attacked at Bentonville, Brigadier General Franz Sigel's two divisions under Peter Osterhaus and Alexander Asboth were moving into their new positions. Sigel himself directed the rear guard withdrawal until nightfall of the 6th, fighting off slashing attacks from Joseph Shelby's Missouri cavalrymen, giving Osterhaus and Asboth time to prepare defenses.

In the extreme rear of Curtis' main line of defense was Elkhorn Tavern, still occupied by Polly Cox, her son Joseph, and his teenage wife, Lucinda. They were somewhat crowded by the addition of the Union army's provost marshal and his staff; the adjacent storehouses and barn were filled with army rations, and all about the grounds were wagons and tents containing ordnance and other supplies. Curtis' headquarters was a mile to the south. Nearby was Colonel Eugene Carr's division; several details from Colonel Grenville Dodge's 4th Iowa regiment were out along the roads felling trees to slow any Confederate night approach. On the bluffs above Sugar Creek, Colonel Jefferson C. Davis' division of Indiana and Illinois regiments was well dug in. West of Davis' position, Sigel's men were building fortifications and emplacing guns, facing southward.

Elkhorn Tavern at Pea Ridge. Drawing from a photo. (B & L)

ALL preparations anticipated an attack from the south. As darkness deepened, a light snow began falling. Four miles away to the southwest, the campfires of the Confederate bivouac began twinkling; by 8 o'clock they were burning in a wide arc.

About 3 o'clock the following morning (March 7) Private Thomas Welch of the 3d Illinois Cavalry was patrolling the road west of Elkhorn Tavern. Snow had stopped falling but the weather was bitter cold, and Private Welch was confident that he would meet neither friend nor foe in that extreme rear area. Then suddenly a party of Rebel cavalry loomed out of the night, and Private Welch was a prisoner. As he was hustled back down the road under guard he could scarcely believe what he saw—company after company of marching Confederate infantry, troops of cavalry, caissons, and numerous artillery pieces (Van Dorn had sixty-five guns against Curtis' fifty). To Welch it seemed that he was passing through the entire army of the C.S.A. Escape was uppermost in his mind, and at the first opportunity he turned into a side road and plunged into the icy undergrowth. As rapidly as he could, Welch made his way back through the woods to Elkhorn Tavern, awakened his commanding officer, and told him what he had seen.

Welch's story reached Curtis' headquarters at 5 o'clock in the morning, about the same time that reports were coming in from Sigel's camp that the enemy was moving in strength along the Bentonville road. By first daylight the entire Federal camp was alerted; the hundreds of Rebel campfires were still smoking but the Confederates had vanished.

THE plan for bypassing the Union army during the night and attacking in the rear was General McCulloch's. Van Dorn approved it, and soon after nightfall of the 6th he started Price's Missourians moving north along the Bentonville detour, an eight-mile road which circled the Federal positions and then entered Telegraph Road, two miles north of Elkhorn Tavern. Ill with a cold, Van Dorn rode in an ambulance with the advance units. He left one division at the bivouac camp to guard the baggage train and keep campfires burning brightly for the benefit of the watchful Yankees.

Around midnight the Confederates were delayed by trees which Colonel Dodge's Iowans had felled across the road. According to plan, Van Dorn should have been astride Telegraph Road, positioned for an attack by daylight, but he was three hours late getting there. Soon after dawn, advance cavalry units were already skirmishing along the Federal flank, and from Curtis' encampments came the sounds of blaring bugles, drums beating the long roll, and the rumble of artillery wheels.

Brig. Gen. Stand Watie, commanding some of the Indian forces who fought with the Confederates at Pea Ridge. (B & L)

AS SOON as Curtis realized that Van Dorn had tricked him, he began turning his army around. "I directed a change of front to the rear," Curtis wrote in his report of the battle, "so as to face the road upon which the enemy was still moving. At the same time I directed the organization of a detachment of cavalry and light artillery, supported by infantry, to open the battle."

It was Sigel's division under Osterhaus that moved out toward the Bentonville road to challenge McCulloch's army. At that time of the morning, McCulloch should have been five miles farther east, massed along Pea Ridge in close communication with Price's army which was beginning to cannonade the Federals near Elkhorn Tavern. This five-mile separation between Price and McCulloch would prove to be crucial before the day ended. Instead of attacking with two coordinated wings, Van Dorn was forced to fight two separate battles, one of them screened from his headquarters by hills and woods and too far away for any unity of direction.

Osterhaus' regiments marched northwestward across fields filled with withered cornstalks, passing around Leetown where yellow hospital flags were already fluttering from the scattered houses of the hamlet. The night's coating of snow was melting rapidly. Along the south edge of a field, Osterhaus deployed infantrymen of the 36th Illinois and 12th Missouri,

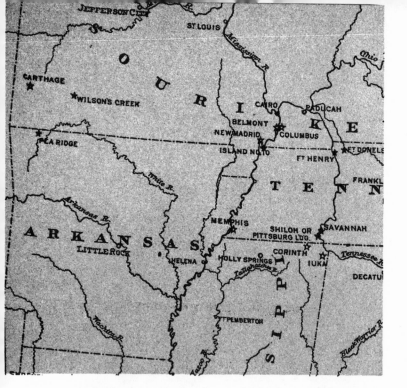

General map of the location of the Battle of Pea Ridge.

supporting them with a battery of the 4th Ohio. With bugles blowing and pennons flying, a squadron of the 3d Iowa Cavalry under Lieutenant Colonel Henry Trimble then crossed the fields and advanced into a brushy wood. Confederate infantry waiting in concealment caught them in short musket range. During the next five minutes a large number of Iowans became casualties, including Trimble with a severe head wound. The survivors broke ranks and retreated.

FOR the next two hours McCulloch's 10,000 Confederates dominated the field. At one time early in the fighting, confused Union artillerymen shelled their own troops, and Sigel was so dismayed by the way the battle was going that he was on the verge of advising Curtis to retreat or surrender.

Around noon a charge by McCulloch's Texans, supported by Pike's Cherokees under Stand Watie, broke through the Federals' forward lines. The Indians attacked with rifles, shotguns, knives, and arrows, and their war whoops were more terrifying than the Texans' Rebel yells. Union cavalrymen went tearing back in retreat, some without hats or arms, riding through the infantrymen with shouts of "Turn back! Turn back!" Stand Watie's Cherokees swept over a battery, killing the gunners, but they were so excited by their success that instead of pressing the Federal retreat into a rout, they milled around the guns. General Pike later described them as "all talking, riding this way and that, and listening to no orders from any one."

Taking advantage of this momentary lull, Sigel unlimbered his rear batteries, and at the first artillery fire the Indians scurried back into the woods as

frightened as the Union cavalrymen had been of their scalping knives. At the same time, Osterhaus sent the 22d Indiana and 36th Illinois Infantry regiments charging across the field to retake the battery.

BY 1:30 McCulloch's advance had been stalled. Pike and Stand Watie had finally restored order among the Cherokees but it was evident that the undisciplined Indians would be of no use in a frontal charge; they wanted to fight individually behind trees and boulders. McCulloch brought up one of his crack infantry regiments, the 16th Arkansas, and sent skirmishers forward. Mounting, he rode out ahead of the Arkansans' advancing lines. When the skirmishers moved into a brushy area, McCulloch went in with them. His black velvet coat and white felt hat made a good target for a squad of infantrymen from the 36th Illinois waiting behind a rail fence. He was struck in the breast and soon expired. Peter Pelican of Aurora, Illinois, fired once, leaped over the fence, and secured the dead general's gold watch before the advancing Arkansans drove him back to cover.

The time was 2 o'clock, a decisive hour in the contest between Curtis and Van Dorn. Carr (at Elkhorn Tavern) and Osterhaus (at Leetown) had both been calling urgently for reinforcements. Curtis decided to send his reserve division under Colonel Jefferson C. Davis to aid Osterhaus. Davis led off with his two Illinois regiments and two batteries of artillery. At this same hour Sigel and Asboth, who had been guarding the Bentonville road flank, started moving toward the Leetown area.

General Price meanwhile had been giving Colonel Carr a severe mauling north of Elkhorn Tavern, and Van Dorn was confident that a coordinated attack by Price and McCulloch would bring a quick victory. He sent messengers racing to McCulloch with orders to attack in full force about 2 o'clock.

McCulloch, however, was dead before the orders reached him. His successor, Colonel James McIntosh of the Arkansas Mounted Rifles, rallied the Confederates and led a charge against Federal infantry concealed in a dense woods. Fifteen minutes later McIntosh was killed, shot from his horse.

LESS than half a mile to the east, Colonel Louis Hébert's Louisianians had become entangled in a thick brushwood and were taking a severe shelling from Davis' batteries. Davis' 59th Illinois was on the edge of this same thicket. "The underbrush was so heavy," Lieutenant Colonel George Currie recorded, "we could not see twenty feet from us." Hébert's men finally surged out, fighting hand-to-hand with the Illinois infantrymen. A few minutes later the 18th Indiana, moving to the front in double-quick time, found the 59th Illinois retiring in disorder. Sure of

victory, Hébert led his men out into the open, only to be flanked and then surrounded by fresh Illinois and Indiana troops. At 2:30 p.m., Colonel Hébert's brigade fell apart and he was captured.

With their leaders gone, the units of Van Dorn's right wing collapsed. Demoralized soldiers retreated in confusion—divisions, regiments, and companies becoming intermixed. Batterymen and cavalrymen along the Bentonville road—most of whom had seen no action—waited impatiently for orders, but none came.

About 3 o'clock General Pike learned of the loss of the army's leaders. He tried to rally the troops near Leetown, but it was too late. He began riding about the rear areas—an odd-looking figure in frontier buckskins—ordering his Indians and other scattered units to move toward the high ground of Pea Ridge and try to make their way to Van Dorn's position near Elkhorn Tavern. When Sigel reached Leetown about 4 o'clock to bring the full power of his artillery to bear on the Confederates, he found no one there to fight.

AROUND Elkhorn Tavern that day, however, it was a different story.

At about the same time that McCulloch's cavalry began their early morning skirmishing with the Federals near Leetown, Price's army of 6,200 men reached the Telegraph Road junction two miles north of Elkhorn Tavern. Very few Union soldiers were in that deep rear area, and the Confederates moved rapidly southward along Telegraph Road, meeting scattered resistance from the 24th Missouri Union Infantry. This regiment had been placed on light guard duty in the rear because its term of service had ended and the men were awaiting orders to be sent home. Two companies of Missouri and Illinois cavalry came to their aid.

In an enveloping movement, Price sent his first

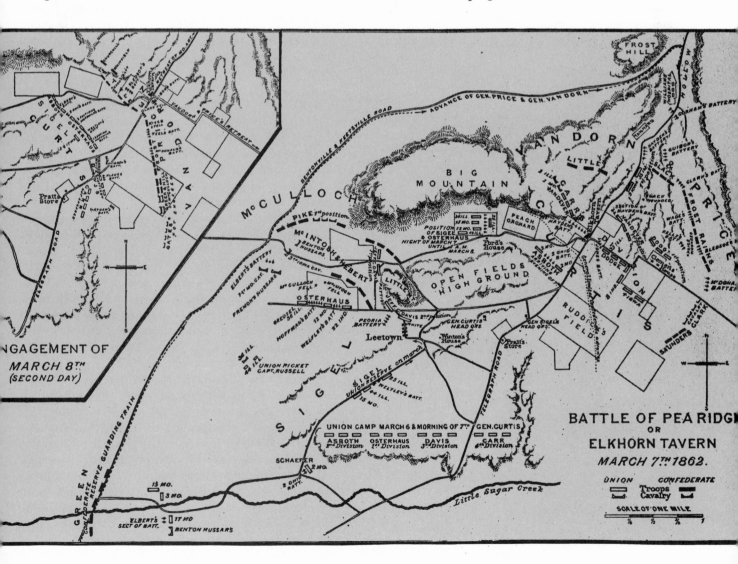

and second brigades down the west side of the road, while he led a third brigade down the east side. A mile north of the tavern, Colonel Elijah Gates led his Missouri Confederate cavalry in a sweeping charge across the fields, fell back before heavy fire, dismounted his men, attacked, and was again driven back.

To meet this thrust at his rear supply area, Curtis chose Colonel Eugene Carr, a born horse soldier with piercing eyes and a jutting black beard. Carr rode hurriedly up to Elkhorn Tavern, ordered his staff to establish division headquarters there, and immediately began forming a battle line. To the east of the road went Colonel Grenville Dodge's brigade; to the west Colonel William Vandever's brigade.

WHEN Carr first saw the advancing masses of Confederates he was amazed at the size of the force that had got in the Union army's rear. He sent an urgent call for reinforcements back to Curtis, and ordered Dodge and Vandever to take defensive positions and hold fast. Union artillery was already emplaced along both sides of the road facing southward; the pieces had scarcely been turned about when the Confederates opened a bombardment.

For thirty minutes the big guns dueled, with Elkhorn Tavern in the midst of the exchange. A New

The Union right under Colonel E. A. Carr at Pratt's store on the second day of the battle. (B & L)

York *Herald* correspondent, who had counted on the relative safety of Carr's division headquarters, reported a shell bursting upon a company of infantry beside the tavern; another fell among horse teams in the rear yard; a solid shot struck the building and passed completely through. Polly Cox, her son, and his wife were not injured; at the first shriek of an overhead shell they had taken refuge in the cellar.

As dense clouds of smoke began covering Pea Ridge, a few reserve companies of infantry and cavalry and a battery of mountain howitzers reached Carr's headquarters. At that stage of the fighting, Curtis dared send no more troops to his right because of McCulloch's fierce assault against his left. "Colonel Carr," Curtis later wrote, "sent me word that he could not hold his position much longer. I could then only reply by sending him the order to 'persevere'."

With almost uncanny accuracy, Price's gunners now began blasting the 3d Iowa Battery from the ridge. A cavalry charge followed up the shelling, but was forced back by Vandever's 9th Iowa Infantry. In a succession of attacks and repulses that continued through the morning, both sides suffered heavy casualties, among them Price's most trusted brigadier, William Slack, mortally wounded. Both Carr and Price also were painfully wounded, but refused to leave the field.

ABOUT 2 o'clock, as though by mutual agreement, the exhausted troops of both armies drew apart for the first lull of the day. During this period Carr, still awaiting reinforcements, consolidated his defense positions, while Van Dorn prepared to mount a massive attack, hoping for a coordinated action from McCulloch's army to the west.

By 3 o'clock the battle was raging furiously again, Price attacking Dodge's 4th Iowa and 35th Illinois with such force that Dodge's left collapsed. When Vandever saw what was happening, he ordered his brigade to shift rightward and close the gap. As Vandever was executing this change of front, Colonel Henry Little's Confederates swarmed out of the brush with wild yells, breaking through Vandever's 9th Iowa, capturing men and guns. "With a shout of triumph," Colonel Little reported, "Rives's and Oates's regiments dashed onward past the Elkhorn Tavern, and we stood on the ground where the enemy had formed in the morning."

Bringing batteries forward, the Confederates quickly enfiladed Dodge's regiments, forcing them back to a rail fence opposite Vandever's hastily re-formed line. "At this time the ammunition of the 4th Iowa was almost entirely given out," Dodge reported, "and I ordered them to fall back, which they did in splendid order in line of battle, the enemy running forward with their batteries and whole force."

AS AN early dusk fell over the smoky battlefield, Captain Henry Guibor unlimbered a Confederate battery directly in front of the tavern and began dueling with Carr's harried gunners, who had fallen back almost to Curtis' headquarters. About 5 o'clock Curtis himself came up with Asboth's division and found Carr still persevering, doggedly holding his line across Telegraph Road almost a mile below the tavern.

Weariness from eleven hours of continuous fighting and loss of blood from three wounds had brought Carr near to collapse. Curtis immediately relieved him, ordered the troops to bivouac in position, and then asked for a report of casualties. The 4th and 9th Iowa regiments had paid heavily for their stubborn resistance. The men of the 24th Missouri, whose terms of service had ended, but who had to bear the first shock of Price's attack, had taken 25 percent casualties.

Elkhorn Tavern, which had served as a Union headquarters in the morning, now became a Confederate headquarters. "My troops," said Sterling Price, "bivouacked upon the ground which they had so nobly won almost exhausted and without food, but fearlessly and anxiously awaiting the renewal of the battle in the morning." The tavern cellar served as a hospital, one of the first patients being Price himself. By the light of a candle, Mrs. Cox cleaned his wounded arm and bandaged it with one of her aprons.

VAN DORN was pleased to learn that Price's troops had captured seven cannon and 200 prisoners, but as the night wore on and the full story of the rout of McCulloch's troops began to come in, he realized that victory on the left had been nullified by defeat on the right. General Pike arrived to report the loss of McCulloch, McIntosh, and Hébert; he had placed Stand Watie's mounted Cherokees on Pea Ridge and was hopeful the Indians would fight better on the morrow. Hours later Van Dorn heard from Colonel Elkanah Greer; the Texas cavalryman had collected remnants of McCulloch's scattered regiments and was awaiting orders. Van Dorn ordered Greer to march his force up to Telegraph Road and prepare for another day of fighting.

Outside the tavern, troops built fires against the night chill. Although orders were issued to extinguish these blazes, many continued to burn long after midnight. From the darkened Federal lines only a short distance away, sounds came clearly on the frosty air. "Their artillery and baggage wagons," noted Colonel Henry Little, "seemed to be continually moving."

General Curtis' artillery and wagons were indeed moving that night—into positions selected by Franz

Maj. Gen. (then Col.) Grenville M. Dodge. (LC)

Sigel, who had been given the responsibility for preparing a massive artillery attack at dawn. Sigel studied campfires along the ridge, estimating the location of Confederate troops, and disposed his guns accordingly. He also ordered his own troops to keep silent and build no fires.

AT MIDNIGHT, Union division commanders and staff officers met in Curtis' tent. Carr, Dodge, and Asboth were wounded and depressed. Only Curtis and Sigel were optimistic. Curtis pointed out that for the first time in the fighting the Union army had four infantry divisions massed for attack; Sigel was confident that his artillery would stop Van Dorn's drive.

In their lines facing Elkhorn Tavern, the Union troops shivered and tried to catch a few winks of sleep. Some angrily discussed the Indians' way of fighting, their barbarous use of scalping knives. They also could hear the sounds of their enemy, "the tread of their sentinels and the low hum of conversation but a few yards away."

Dawn came early on March 8, with a reddish sun in a pale blue sky. Because there had been no wind to drive away the previous day's battle smoke, it still hung in folds over woods and fields. On both sides of the battlefield artillerymen were making last-minute changes in positions. They unlimbered their guns, led horses fifty paces to the rear, and awaited orders.

MOST of the Confederate batteries were in open woods along the base of the ridge, the Federals facing them from a crest of high ground below Elkhorn Tavern. About 7 o'clock a cannon blast from the Confederates opened the second day of fighting. Sigel, who was commanding Curtis' left wing, accepted the challenge with alacrity, and soon had forty guns in action. "A brisk cannonade was kept up for upward of two hours," reported the New York *Herald* correspondent. "The sharp booming of the six-, twelve- and eighteen-pounders followed each other in rapid succession." This was probably the most concentrated artillery duel ever fought west of the Mississippi River; the muffled roar of guns was heard for forty miles across the Ozark hill country.

Sigel's well-placed guns scored hits on the Confederate batteries, and quickly scattered Stand Watie's Cherokees along Pea Ridge. When he was confident that he had his enemy off balance, Sigel ordered the 12th Missouri and the 25th and 44th Illinois to throw forward a strong force of skirmishers. With drums

beating and flags waving, the Federal infantry regiments moved out in perfect alignment. "The rattling of musketry," Sigel later wrote, "the volleys, the hurrahs, did prove very soon that our troops were well at work in the woods, and that they were gaining ground rapidly."

Meanwhile Curtis' right wing had fallen back before the Confederate artillery fire, but as soon as Sigel's regiments began advancing, Curtis ordered Carr and Davis to attack with extended lines, maneuvering so as to get on Van Dorn's left flank. At the same time additional regiments from Osterhaus' and Asboth's divisions joined in the general attack upon the ridge. "The upward movement of the gallant 36th Illinois," Curtis noted, "with its dark-blue line of men and its gleaming bayonets, steadily rose from base to summit, when it dashed forward into the forest, driving and scattering the rebels from these commanding heights. The 12th Missouri, far in advance of the others, rushed into the enemy's lines, bearing off a flag and two pieces of artillery." It was a classical pincers movement, and in a matter of

ROSSER'S CONFEDERATE BRIGADE ON BIG MOUNTAIN.

GUIBOR'S BATTERY.   ELKHORN TAVERN.

CK'S REGIMENTS.   CHURCHILL'S ARKANSAS AND TEXAS TROOPS.   BLEDSOE'S AND GORHAM'S BATTERIES.

← ... Their intention of turning our flanks ... being now clearly evident, we slowly fell back from our advanced position, disputing every inch of ground which we relinquished."

In this last fighting Confederate losses mounted sharply, and included many of the South's most promising young officers. Among them was 19-year-old Churchill Clark, a battery commander, grandson of William Clark the famous Western explorer. While covering the withdrawal, young Clark was decapitated by a round shot.

A soldier of the 36th Illinois who was among the first to reach the top of the ridge described the scene: "The mangled trunks of men lay thickly scattered around, and so close as to require the utmost care to avoid stepping on their cold remains. From each tree or sheltering nook the groans of the wounded arose, while muskets, saddles, horses, blankets, hats and clothes hung in shreds from every bush or in gory masses cumbered the ground. . . . Federal soldiers shared the contents of their canteens with thirsty wounded Confederates. The fierce passions which animated them an hour before, while panting for each other's blood, had subsided, and pity for the maimed supplanted the feelings of hate and fury."

BY NOON all artillery fire had ceased. In the mistaken belief that they were close on the heels of Van Dorn's army, Sigel's infantrymen poured northward up Telegraph Road in pursuit of fleeing Confederates. The main army, however, had slipped away southeastward on the road to Huntsville, with Shelby's cavalry covering the rear.

After the fighting ended, and Colonel Carr was moving his division out to find forage for his horses, he stopped briefly at Elkhorn Tavern. Polly Cox, her son, and daughter-in-law had already departed; twenty-one hours under fire had been enough of war for them. Carr glanced at the ridgepole of the abandoned, shell-torn tavern, then ordered the huge elkhorns brought down as a souvenir of the battle. (Years later the horns were returned and are now in a museum at Garfield, Arkansas.)

Carr's division had suffered more casualties than the other three Federal divisions combined. Total for the Union forces was 1,384. The Confederates lost about the same number, but they lost three good generals and too many line officers who could never be replaced, and they had lost the crucial battle for control of the Missouri border. Missouri was now secure for the Union, and Arkansas was open for eventual Federal occupation.

minutes the Confederates were caught in a concentrated crossfire.

BY 10 O'CLOCK Van Dorn knew that he was beaten. All morning he had been waiting for ammunition wagons from his temporary base camp near Sugar Creek; they had been delayed because of a mix-up in orders and were still a mile from the battle ground when the Federals opened their flanking attacks. Confederate gunners used stones in their cannons when their shot gave out; infantrymen threw away their useless rifles and fired short-range shotguns at advancing Yankees.

Van Dorn started his ambulances moving eastward from Elkhorn Tavern down a side road that led to Huntsville, and for the next half hour the Confederates were fighting to cover a general withdrawal. "The enemy advanced," said Colonel Henry Little who was in the midst of this engagement. "On, on they came, in overwhelming numbers, line after line, but they were met with the same determined courage which this protracted contest had taught them to appreciate.

Guerrilla Warfare on the Border

by James M. McPherson

A good deal more fighting between organized Confederate and Union armies would take place in Missouri and Arkansas during the next three years. A series of small battles from December 1862 to September 1863 would give Union forces tenuous control of Little Rock and much of Arkansas. A Confederate army under Sterling Price launched a counteroffensive through northern Arkansas into Missouri in September 1864. Enjoying some success at first, Price got almost as far as Kansas City before converging Union forces pummeled his army in Oc-

tober and broke it into pieces that drifted southward in retreat to Texas.

Union political control of Missouri remained firm enough to elect a new legislature in 1863 and put in place a new constitution that abolished slavery in January 1865. But Missouri remained plagued through the war by guerrilla warfare that left a legacy of hatred and feuds lasting for generations. The postwar outlaws Frank and Jesse James along with Cole and Jim Younger got their training as Confederate guerrillas during the war. Their robberies of banks

and trains were a continuation of attacks on "Yankee" institutions that had been sanctioned by political purpose during the war and remained legitimate in the eyes of many ex-rebel Missourians after the war. Unionist counter-guerrilla Jayhawkers from Kansas replied in kind to the tactics of rebel guerrillas, leaving a trail of ambushes, raids, murders, and burning farms from one end of Missouri to another but especially along the border with Kansas.

The Missouri guerrillas attracted psychopathic killers to their ranks. One of their most notorious leaders was "Bloody Bill" Anderson, whose band included the James and Younger brothers. On one occasion this band burned a train in Centralia, Missouri, and robbed its passengers. Among the passengers were twenty-four unarmed Union soldiers traveling home on furlough. The guerrillas murdered them in cold blood. Chased out of town by gathering companies of militia, Bloody Bill's band picked up allies from other bands, turned on their pursuers, and killed 124 of them, including the wounded, whom they shot in the head.

Even more infamous than Anderson was William Clarke Quantrill. The son of an Ohio schoolteacher, Quantrill had drifted around the West until the war came along to give full rein to his peculiar talents. Without any particular ties to the South, he chose the Confederacy apparently because in Missouri this allowed him to attack all symbols of authority. From time to time he gathered smaller guerrilla bands under his leadership, including Bloody Bill Anderson's. So successful were Quantrill's raids behind Union lines that the Confederate government commissioned him captain.

In an attempt to deny sanctuary to known guerrillas, the Union commander in western Missouri arrested many of their wives and sisters who had been feeding and sheltering Quantrill's men. On August 14, 1863, fourteen of these women died when the building in Kansas City where they were being held collapsed. Thirsting for revenge, Quantrill mobilized a large band to invade Kansas and attack Lawrence, the hated center of free-soil Jayhawkers since antebellum days. This foray produced the greatest atrocity of the war.

Guerrilla bands, carrying out raids and ambushes and committing arson and murder, were responsible for the worst terrorism of the Civil War. Far left: Confederate supporters Fletcher Taylor, Frank James (wearing a Confederate general's coat), and Jesse James. (State Historical Society of Missouri) Near left: "Bloody Bill" Anderson, a Confederate guerrilla chieftain whose notoriety matched that of the infamous William Clarke Quantrill, the son of an Ohio schoolteacher. (CWTI Collection) Matching the Confederate guerrillas in tactics were the Unionist "Jayhawker" counterinsurgency forces, such as those Kansans led by James Lane, Charles Jennison, and James Montgomery.

The Lawrence Raid
by Dwight E. Stinson

MASSACRE AT LAWRENCE—Artist's concept ("Frank Leslie's" magazine) of the atrocities perpetrated by Quantrill and his guerrillas in Lawrence, Kansas.

LATE IN THE afternoon of Aug. 20, 1863 an excited farmer entered the headquarters of Capt. Joshua A. Pike, 9th Kansas Cavalry, at Aubrey, Kan. Pike was commander of a series of posts strung along the Kansas-Missouri border at 12-mile intervals from Kansas City to Fort Scott. As such, he was inured to frequent alarms caused primarily by the bands of Confederate guerrillas infesting the Missouri portion of the District of the Border. He was also aware that numbers could easily be overestimated by the untrained eye. Hence Pike was not unduly excited when the farmer blurted out that a guerrilla force of 700 men was encamped eight miles east of Aubrey along the Middle Fork of Grand River.

Pike took down the information, thanked the farmer, and set about writing dispatches. Soon a rider headed north to Capt. C. F. Coleman's station at Little Sante Fe and another southward to Pike's commanding officer, Lt. Col. C. S. Clark, at Coldwater Grove. Perhaps because he doubted the story, Pike took no action beyond the requirements of his orders, which were to forward all intelligence to the two stations bracketing his own at Aubrey. He sent no scouts to check the credibility of the report and he sent no alert westward. Pike certainly would have acted differently had he known that there was indeed a strong enemy force present on the border and that in the pockets of many of its members were proscription lists bearing the names of leading citizens of his home town of Lawrence.

The observant farmer *had* overestimated the numbers, but not by much. Camped amidst the concealing brush were almost 500 well-armed and superbly mounted guerrillas comprising one of the largest of such forces assembled during the entire war. Its composition ranged from 104 Confederate recruits under Col. John D. Holt to 50 volunteers from the Grand River area. The rest was made up of experienced guerrilla bands officered by such bushwackers as George Todd, Dave Pool, Bill Anderson, and William Gregg. Only one man could bring together such a body and that man was "Colonel" William C. Quantrill, alias Charley Hart, erstwhile Kansas school-teacher whose skill as a partisan leader was already almost a legend on the border.

QUANTRILL'S men had assembled on August 19 along Blackwater Creek, Missouri, and traversed the 35 miles to their present location slowly, threading their way past Federal patrols and stations. The approach to the border had been relatively easy but the worst was yet to come, for Quantrill's mission was to destroy the city of Lawrence, located 40 miles within Kansas. The reasons for the raid were many but the plan was chiefly born of an overwhelming desire to get back at Abolitionist Kansas for its part in the harshly, sometimes brutally, conducted Federal suppression policy in border Missouri. The raid

WILLIAM C. QUANTRILL—This rare photograph of the notorious partisan was furnished by the State Historical Society of Missouri.

would serve no real military purpose but it would take a great deal of tactical skill to carry it off. Chivalrous warfare did not extend to the border and each man was aware that capture meant instant death.

At 3 p.m., with men and horses well rested, Quantrill moved his column westward. He would cross the state line 1½ miles below the Federal station at Aubrey, proceed into Kansas a few miles, and then wait for sundown. An all-night march would bring him to Lawrence at dawn.

AT SEVEN o'clock that evening another farmer appeared at Pike's headquarters with the ominous news that Quantrill had slipped through the porous Federal border defenses and was in Kansas with 800 men. There was no doubt now that something deadly was afoot. Pike hurried another rider northward to warn the Little Sante Fe post. The message was received by Captain Coleman at 8:15 p.m., only 15 minutes after Pike's first dispatch. As he had with the other, Coleman relayed the new message up to Westport and Kansas City and also sent a rider westward to warn the post at Olathe. Then he raced to Pike's aid with the 80 men of his garrison.

Coleman thundered into Aubrey at 10 p.m. and was astonished to find Pike present and apparently waiting for him. It was incomprehensible to the senior captain that Pike had not sent the second message to Clark at Coldwater Grove, that he had made no attempt to alert the interior towns, and that he had remained at his post while a formidable enemy force penetrated the state unmolested. Coleman suppressed his anger long enough to send a courier to Clark with the new information. Then he ordered Pike to have the 100 troopers of the Aubrey garrison saddle up. By 11 p.m. the two captains were leading their 180 men southward to grope for Quantrill's trail.

Pike's two messages reached District Headquarters at Kansas City at 11:30 p.m. and 12:30 a.m. Brig. Gen. Thomas Ewing, Jr., had left that day for Leavenworth but his chief of staff, Maj. Preston B. Plumb, gathered up 50 men and by 1 a.m. was on the road to Olathe.

QUANTRILL passed through Gardner at 11 p.m., 20 miles ahead of Coleman's pursuing force, which was just leaving Aubrey. He had veered northwest at Spring Hill and was now on a straight course for Lawrence. So far everything was going according to plan. The column was staying well-closed, moving at a good speed, and resisting whatever temptation for plunder the defenseless, prosperous looking farms along the route may have offered. This spoke well for the command capabilities of Colonel Quantrill who, at 27, was leading crack fighting men and nervous recruits on an extremely hazardous mission.

Beyond Gardner, with the target less than 20 miles away, the raiders killed their impressed guides. Farmhouses were visited by the guerrilla vanguard and in some cases male occupants were remorselessly slaughtered to assure that they would not warn the city after the column passed. In spite of these dreadful measures several courageous citizens managed to slip through the net and go speeding off toward Lawrence. None was destined to make it.

In Lawrence itself the townspeople were retiring with nothing more serious on their minds than the discussion at the town meeting that night on the subject of railroad rights-of-way. There was no premonition that wholesale death was approaching over the prairie.

CAPTAIN Coleman came upon the guerrilla trail south of Aubrey and followed it for three miles before losing it. He fumed for two hours while his men struck matches to try to relocate the trace. Successful at last, the pursuers moved on.

Coleman's message reached Clark at Coldwater Grove at 3 a.m. but the reinforcements he had ordered up on receipt of Pike's first warning had not arrived. Figuring that Quantrill's objective was Paola, Clark gamely started in that direction with his 30 available men. He soon learned that the raiders had turned northwest so he altered his course accordingly and rode on into the night.

Major Plumb's detachment from Kansas City reached Olathe at 5 a.m., having already lost 20 of the original 50 men through exhaustion of their mounts. An infantry company was stationed in the town but would be useless in the present emergency. However, Plumb accepted the offered services of Lieut. Cyrus Leland, Jr., an infantry officer on detached duty. Leland was to play an important role later in the day.

As Plumb and Leland trotted out from Olathe, Coleman was entering Gardner, where feverish citizenry informed him that he was six hours behind Quantrill. Coleman paused to send couriers south and west with the word

CAPT. CHARLES F. COLEMAN. (Kansas State Historical Society.)

that the raiders were moving northwestward. Then he plunged on.

But it was already too late to save Lawrence.

THE GUERRILLAS reached the outskirts of the doomed town at about 4:30 a.m. Here Quantrill issued his final orders, sent scouts to Mount Oread, and enclosed the sleeping community with a line of pickets. Then with a wave of the hand he unleashed his men in three columns. Roaring into Lawrence on separate streets, the guerrillas reached the Kansas River at the far end and cut the ferry cable. Then the men fanned out to go about their mission. Half-awake citizens armed themselves and stumbled outside only to be cut down by revolver fusilades. So complete was the surprise that the townspeople who chose to fight had to do it as individuals and thus had no chance at all.

Capt. A. R. Banks, Provost Marshal of Kansas, awoke to find himself and some 60 other guests surrounded in Lawrence's leading hotel, the Eldridge House. There was not a weapon among them. Quantrill himself appeared among the howling crowd of raiders outside and promised the captain and guests quarter if he would surrender instantly. Banks had no choice but to comply. The prisoners were shaken down for valuables and then led up the street to Quantrill's temporary headquarters at the Whitney House. Clearing a path through the menacing partisans was burly George Todd, clad in Banks' blue uniform coat. Quantrill placed a strong guard over the prisoners to prevent their becoming revolver fodder for his more bloodthirsty followers.

On the edge of town a recruit depot was overrun and over 30 white and Negro volunteers shot down. On the main street guerrillas broke into stores, looted safes, scattered goods over the streets, and helped themselves to the contents of the liquor stores. Any Negro or white man of German appearance who chanced to show himself was killed instantly. Others met with fates of varying cruelty determined by the mood of their finders. Fires were set and soon destruction and murder was cloaked in a mantle of thick smoke.

The same treatment was accorded the residential section where the search was on for men known to have participated in jayhawking outrages in Missouri. Sen. James H. Lane who, not without reason, was at the head of the proscription lists, managed to secrete himself in an adjacent cornfield where he witnessed the burning of his house. The mood of the several guerrilla parties varied. In some cases they assisted terrified women in removing furniture before firing a house. In others, men were prevented from leaving and were mercilessly burned alive. The mayor, who took refuge in a well, suffocated.

Quantrill took no part in the actual killing, preferring instead to observe the massacre from the vantage point of the Whitney House, where horror-stricken survivors sought sanctuary in his care. By 9 a.m. Lawrence was an inferno and scouts were signalling the approach of an enemy force. Quantrill decided that his mission was accomplished. Leaving Lieutenant Gregg to round up drunken stragglers, Quantrill and his guerrillas moved out of town to the south, mounted on fresh horses and loaded with plunder. In the streets and flames of Lawrence over 150 citizens—men and boys—lay dead or dying. On the flanks of the main column rode 20-man bushwacker details with instructions to cut a fiery swath through the countryside.

FOUR MILES southeast of Lawrence, Major Plumb finally caught up with the Coleman-Pike column, but smoke billowing on the horizon had long since told the story. Plumb took command of the combined force of

CAPT. JOSHUA A. PIKE—One of the Federal commanders who unsuccessfully pursued the guerrillas. (Kansas State Historical Society.)

some 200 men and began moving overland where fresh smoke indicated that the raiders were heading south. The four-hour stay in Lawrence had closed the gap considerably and in spite of the fatigued condition of the troops there was a good chance of forcing the invaders to fight deep in Kansas.

It was not the troops who made first contact with the guerrillas, however. Senator Lane had taken the trail with an assortment of about 30 farmers and Lawrence residents. Near Brooklyn they put to flight a few raiders who were burning homes in the wake of the main body. Plumb caught up with Lane at about this time and some precious minutes were wasted while the two men argued over which of them should take command of the pursuit. Plumb refused to be browbeaten and the usually fiery lawmaker reluctantly acquiesced.

In a hasty council, to which Captain Coleman was a party, it was decided that Quantrill might be trapped at a ford on East Ottawa Creek. The plan called for Coleman to attack the rear of the enemy column while Plumb raced down the east bank to block the ford. Coleman carried out his orders with a spirited charge which drove in the guerrilla rearguard and forced Quantrill to deploy. Plumb, upon hearing the firing, judged that Coleman was in trouble and doubled back to assist. He arrived only in time to see Coleman's men recoiling from a driving guerrilla counterattack and the enemy moving off to cross the unguarded ford. The miscarried plan expended what little energy remained to the troopers and their mounts after the all-night chase. From that point on they would be able only to follow slowly behind the crowd of over 200 militia and citizens whom Lieutenant Leland was then rapidly organizing into 50-man companies as fast as they reported from the aroused countryside. Taking the point, Leland was soon closer to the rear of the guerrilla column than he was to Plumb's soldiers who, grimly fighting off sleep, clung to their saddle horns as their horses slowly prodded forward.

Meanwhile, far to the east near Gardner, Lieutenant Colonel Clark found he was running 12 hours behind Quantrill. It was 11 a.m. when he wearily faced his 30 men about and began the long trip back toward Paola. He deduced that the guerrillas would leave Kansas by a different route and the most practicable plan seemed to be for him to call out the militia along the way with the hope of locating the raiders and setting up a roadblock to hinder their escape. The chase continued over the prairie through the hot afternoon with the guerrillas bearing in the general direction of Paola.

BY NOW Quantrill was concerned with what might be encountered in front of the column before the quasi-sanctuary of the Missouri line, over 30 miles to the east, was reached. His men were also aware of the danger. Discarded plunder began to mark the line of march as they lightened loads to ease the horses' burdens. Lieutenant Gregg was in command of the guerrilla rearguard and it became a contest between his 60 men and Leland's 200 hard-riding Kansas home guards. When the Kansans got close, Gregg deployed in open order and engaged them until the Federal cavalry came into sight. Then he would gallop off in column leaving the enraged Leland to reorganize his amateur soldiers, less than 50 of whom, the young officer found, were really willing to

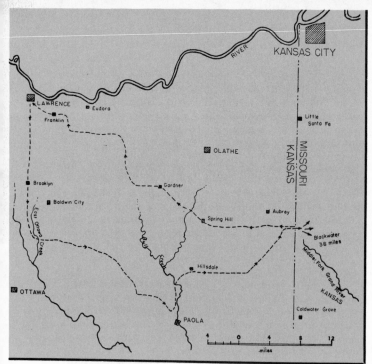

QUANTRILL'S ROUTE—The broken lines and arrows show the route taken by Quantrill's force from the Kansas border to Lawrence and return.

come to grips with the formidable and desperate raiders. Gregg would be able to hold the rear as long as Quantrill could keep the main column away from trouble.

Clark arrived at Paola at 5 p.m. to find the town crowded with armed citizens, militia, and a few troops. He ordered out scouting parties, one of which returned hurriedly to report that Quantrill was five miles away and heading straight for the town. It was dark now but Clark ordered his men to the ford at Bull Creek where they waited tensely for the guerrillas. At length, growing impatient, Clark sent out a patrol which, to the surprise of all concerned, rode into the vanguard of Plumb's pursuit force. What might have been a tragic all-Federal encounter at Bull Creek was thus avoided but the elusive Quantrill had veered north and disappeared into the darkness. Clark listened to the other officers argue about what direction to take and then overruled them all by ordering everybody into Paola for food and rest. Scouts combed the prairie for the trail and at 2 a.m. reported it located. Clark considered the exhausted condition of the men, the chances of running Quantrill down in the dark, and the possibility that the raiders might be intercepted by other troops farther east. It was dawn before he ordered the pursuit to continue.

INTENSE FATIGUE and hunger began to tell on the guerrillas also, but one attempt to bivouac having been thwarted by a wandering militia unit, Quantrill decided to keep the column moving through most of the night. Eastern Kansas by this time was teeming with Federals but the guerrilla chief slipped through the cordon. At daylight he led his column back into Missouri where they had entered almost 40 hours before. The raiders dispersed along the Middle Fork of Grand River, with Quantrill himself leading 200 men north toward Jackson County. On Big Creek near Pleasant Hill he encountered several hundred Missouri troops under Lieut. Col. B. F. Lazear but managed to slip past with a loss of five men.

After this affair, the guerrillas entered the brush country and scattered into small groups. The Lawrence Raid was over despite the fact that hundreds of Federal troops scoured the countryside for weeks. Any known or suspected guerrilla apprehended was killed on the spot.

ON AUGUST 31 General Ewing reported that his patrols had accounted for as many as 100 of the raiders. Undoubtedly his figure was exaggerated. He took steps to assure that the border counties of Missouri would never again be able to subsist the guerrilla bands. The general's Order Number 11 virtually depopulated the counties where the irregulars were known to have civilian support.

But the patrols and Order Number 11 had little effect on Quantrill's activities. Less than six weeks after dispersal the guerrillas reassembled and moved south for the winter. On October 7 Quantrill suddenly appeared at Baxter Springs in southeastern Kansas. In a slashing attack he routed a column under the personal command of the hitherto unbeatable Maj. Gen. James G. Blunt. More than 80 Federal soldiers lost their lives.

APPALLING as Quantrill's atrocities were, his feat of penetrating 40 miles into Kansas and returning with a loss of only 10 men must rank as one of the most prodigious undertakings of the Civil War. Of course, it was not strictly a military operation, as it had no tactical objective, but was a raid for revenge and plunder.

While disclaiming any wish to mitigate or excuse the misdeeds of Quantrill and his men, the writer feels that it is only fair to point out that the most distressing feature of guerrilla warfare is that atrocity breeds atrocity, and that these dreadful acts were not confined to one side. The 9th Kansas Cavalry, of which Clark's, Coleman's, and Pike's commands were a part, was a new unit organized in 1862 from companies which had been in a brigade organized by Lane in 1861, of which Halleck wrote to Stanton:

". . . the Kansas jayhawkers, or robbers, who were organized under the auspices of Senator Lane. They wear the uniform of and it is believed receive pay from the United States. Their principal occupation for the past six months seems to have been the stealing of Negroes, the robbing of houses, and the burning of barns, grain, and forage. The evidence of their crimes is unquestionable. They have not heretofore been under my orders. I will now keep them out of Missouri or have them shot."

The result of all this was a reorganization in which Lane's brigade was broken up and formed into new regiments, one of which was the 9th Kansas Cavalry. In other words, the men who were chasing Quantrill in 1863 were those who had entered Missouri in the fall of 1861 and whose conduct was so bad as to have their units dispersed by the Government.

In 1864 Quantrill was mortally wounded in Kentucky while on his way to Washington in the hope of assassinating President Lincoln. The residue of the loot he had taken in his raids, some $500, was used by his mistress to found a bawdy house.

Delegation of Indians at the White House in Washington, D.C. Prior to the war many tribes from Indian Territory held great councils and sent representatives to Washington to treat with the government. As the Navajo and other tribes would discover after the war, these meetings accomplished little for their people. (National Archives)

The Struggle for the Southwest
by James M. McPherson

The principal Confederate war aim was to sustain the independence of this new nation by defending its territory from invasion. But Confederate strategy was not solely defensive. Before the war the South had tried to neutralize the growing northern majority by acquiring Cuba (where slavery existed) and by expanding southern influence into the Southwest. The latter effort continued by military means during the war.

The Confederate government negotiated treaties of alliance with the five "civilized tribes" of Indians in Indian Territory (present-day Oklahoma). The Cherokees were the largest of these tribes; the others were the Chickasaws, Choctaws, Creeks, and Seminoles. Some of these Indians, especially the Cherokees, owned black slaves and therefore sympathized with the South. They also hoped to achieve greater autonomy within a southern Confederacy than they had enjoyed in the United States—an irony, since it had been southerners who drove them out of their ancestral homeland in the Southeast a generation earlier. Confederate Indian troops fought at Pea Ridge and elsewhere in the border regions of Indian Territory and Arkansas. The Union also recruited Indian troops in this area, and managed to frustrate southern efforts to gain control of Indian territory.

The most spectacular Confederate effort to expand into the Southwest came to grief in 1862, as narrated in the following article. This abortive invasion of New Mexico proved to be the first and last Confederate offensive west of Texas.

Major Charles A.R. Dimon of the 1st U.S. Volunteers, shown posing with local chiefs, commanded the new Fort Rice in the Dakota Territory. (U.S. Army Military Historical Institute)

The New Mexico Campaign

by Broech N. Oder

Early in July 1861, Brigadier General Henry Hopkins Sibley, Confederate States Army and late of the United States Army, received the orders he wanted. A letter, signed by the Adjutant General of the Confederate Army, read:

> In view of your recent service in New Mexico and knowledge of that part of the country and the people, the President has intrusted [sic] you with the important duty of driving the Federal troops from that department.

With his scheme for a New Mexican campaign now a reality, Sibley prepared to leave Richmond and raise a brigade in Texas.

Born in Louisiana in 1816, Henry Sibley graduated from the United States Military Academy in 1838, thirty-first in a class of forty-five. Like his classmates, among whom were Pierre G. T. Beauregard, Irvin McDowell, and William J. Hardee, Sibley served in the Seminole and Indian wars with the United States Dragoons. Before the Civil War, Sibley earned some repute as the inventor of the Sibley tent, a tepee-like structure designed for use on the plains. The outbreak of the Civil War found Sibley stationed in New Mexico with the 1st Dragoons. He soon resigned his commission as major and offered his services to the South, along with a plan for a campaign in the Southwest.

Arriving in Texas about August 15, 1861, with a brigadier general's commission, Sibley established headquarters in San Antonio and began the creation of the three regiments that would comprise his force. One month later, Sibley had over 800 men formed into companies, and by October 4, some 1,100 men had mustered under the Stars and Bars. The prospect of high adventure in New Mexico motivated many Texans to join Sibley, and on November 18, 1861, the mounted men of the Sibley Brigade commenced the dry ride from San Antonio to Fort Bliss, near El Paso.

As his cavalry rode the 500 miles to El Paso, scarlet guidons flapping, Sibley contemplated his plan of action. From his own service in New Mexico, he knew the territory contained a large quantity of United States Army supplies. These supplies could be used to replenish and expand the Confederate force during the campaign, a campaign which, due to the barren terrain, had to be self-sustaining. The conquest of rugged New Mexico would be only the begin-

Texan troops in the Gran Plaza of San Antonio on February 16, 1861, two weeks before Texas formally joined the Confederacy. In mid-August, Brigadier General Henry H. Sibley established his headquarters here. (Harper's Weekly, March 23, 1861)

ning of Sibley's strategy. With New Mexico as a base, Sibley felt confident that he could lead his force west across Arizona, gathering men who "were scattered all over the Western States and Territories . . . anxiously awaiting an opportunity to join the Confederate Army." Once in California "'on to San Francisco' would be the watchword." The occupation of New Mexico, Arizona, and California would not only break new soil for the seed of slavery, but it would give the Confederate States access to California gold and the Pacific Ocean.

To accomplish this task, Sibley had to rely on the 4th, 5th, and 7th Regiments of Texas Mounted Volunteers, as well as on a small battery of artillery. The 3,700 men, whom Sibley loved, proved to be a motley crew, armed with double-barrelled shotguns, bear guns, squirrel rifles, Colt revolvers, and wide-blade Bowie knives. Sibley's favorites were the lancers, armed with ten-foot lances topped by colorful streamers intended to "drink" the enemy's blood. As for the men, they followed in the spirit of most Civil War Texans, regarding Sibley as "being an able and skillful, as well as a zealous and efficient officer."

On December 14, at Fort Bliss, General Sibley assumed command of all Confederate forces in New Mexico and Arizona, designating his force as the Army of New Mexico. Because he knew the people of New Mexico so well, the new "army" commander shrewdly opted to enter the Territory of New Mexico as a liberator rather than a conqueror. His proclamation of December 20, 1861, issued from Fort Bliss, informed New Mexicans:

> Upon the peaceful people of New Mexico, the Confederate States wage no war. To them we come as friends, to reestablish a governmental connection agreeable and advantageous both to them and to us; . . . Your persons, your families and your properties shall be secure and safe.

Sibley firmly believed that the people and soldiers in New Mexico could be induced to join the Confederate side; indeed, as early as June 1861, he wrote a fellow officer: "I am now satisfied of the disaffection of the best of the rank and file in New Mexico." Sibley further lamented that he had not brought his entire command out of New Mexico and feared his Union comrades would consider him a deserter. Well did Sibley know the unhappiness in New Mexico. The Regular Army men had not been paid in over a year, and the New Mexico Volunteers had never been paid. This state of affairs, naturally, hindered the muster of additional volunteer companies. In addition, even the men in Washington came to realize

Confederate Brigadier General Henry Hopkins Sibley, who received permission to make his scheme for a New Mexico campaign a reality. (U.S. Army Military History Institute)

New Mexico was "that recently conquered and imperfectly loyalized region." Apprehensively, the new Union commander of the Department of New Mexico, Brevet Lieutenant Colonel Edward R. S. Canby, wrote:

> The people of the territory . . . are apathetic in disposition and will adopt any measures that may be necessary for the defense of their Territory with great tardiness, looking with greater concern to their private and often petty interests, and delaying or defeating the objects of the Government by their personal or political quarrels.

Sibley further desired to entice native New Mexicans to his side by making overtures to the Mexican states of Chihuahua and Sonora. The general sought sources of supply in these regions, or, if no stores could be secured, at least to receive pledges of neutrality. The prospect of Union troops moving through Mexico to strike at Texas seemed real to Sibley. To be assured of the peaceful mien of Mexico, Sibley dispatched one of his officers, Colonel James Reily, to the governors of Chihuahua and Sonora before leading his army into New Mexico during the first week of January 1862.

The chief executive of Chihuahua, Luis Terrazas, proved to be a masterful diplomat. His equivocal

Union Brevet Lieutenant Colonel Edward R.S. Canby, the new commander of the Department of New Mexico, worried that the territory's people were "apathetic." (CWTI Collection)

replies professed "the most sincere and earnest disposition to cultivate these relations," while also pointing out he could not impugn the neutrality of Mexico. Sibley, the governor continued, had found a "sincere friend . . . of the Confederate States," but Mexican law forbade the selling of supplies to belligerents. The Confederates received the sole absolute assurance that Union troops would not be allowed to cross Mexican soil to reach Texas. The governor of Sonora replied in a similar, albeit less amiable, vein. Ironically, while Sibley fretted over Union violation of Mexico, Federal officials became concerned that Chihuahua might join the Confederacy.

Undeterred by this failure to secure allies, Sibley pushed his men north along the Rio Grande at an unhurried pace. On February 7, 1862, the Army of New Mexico left Fort Thorn, New Mexico Territory, bound for Union-held Fort Craig, some seventy miles to the north. Fort Craig, the only important Union post remaining in southern New Mexico, guarded the lines of communication in that sector. Sibley proposed to take the fort with some 2,600 men, having left garrisons at several strategic points.

On February 16, a Confederate reconnaissance-in-force came within two miles of Fort Craig manned by some 3,800 Union soldiers. Approximately 1,200 of these men belonged to the Regular Army, the remainder being militia and volunteers in varied stages of discipline and organization. The scouting party discovered the fort could not be taken by frontal assault without heavy artillery, so Sibley decided "to cross the Rio Grande to the east bank, turn the fort, and force a battle for the recrossing." By circling above the Union stronghold, Sibley knew he could block the road between Albuquerque and Fort Craig, not only splitting the Union forces in half, but also stopping the flow of men and supplies to southern New Mexico.

The Texans crossed the river about four in the afternoon on February 20. A mounted force from Fort Craig formed for an assault, but after a brief skirmish contented themselves with observation. The Confederates proceeded to establish camp within a mile and a half of Fort Craig. Late into the evening, Sibley planned strategy and tactics for the next day. The 5th Regiment, part of the 7th, and one of the artillery sections would make a "strong threatening demonstration on the fort" while the remainder of the force captured Contadero Ford at Valverde, just north of Fort Craig.

A surprise Union attack (of sorts) almost wrecked the Confederate scheme that night. An enterprising Union officer received permission from Canby to make a "mule attack" on the Confederate camp. Two old mules were loaded with howitzer shells set to explode on a time fuse. A small band of New Mexicans drove the mules toward the Confederate camp, slapped them, and then ran desperately for cover near the Union lines. The horrified men turned to see the faithful mules had not gone on, but had reversed course and dutifully headed back to the Union camp. The New Mexicans tried unsuccessfully to put the mules back on course toward the Texans, but finally ran for their lives, the mules trotting along behind. When the shells erupted, the men had placed enough distance between themselves and the animals to escape injury. Their mission, however, had some success. The tremendous fireball stampeded one hundred Confederate mules. The loss of motive power forced the Confederates to abandon a number of wagons filled with supplies; it was the first of several such incidents that plagued the Confederate effort.

At dawn on February 21, the shrill notes of "Boots and Saddles" pierced the chill of the New Mexican morning. Yet, even before his men arose, Sibley had been up, completing his plan and refining the details. Shortly before eight the main body of Confederates exploded in a tremendous mock assault on Fort

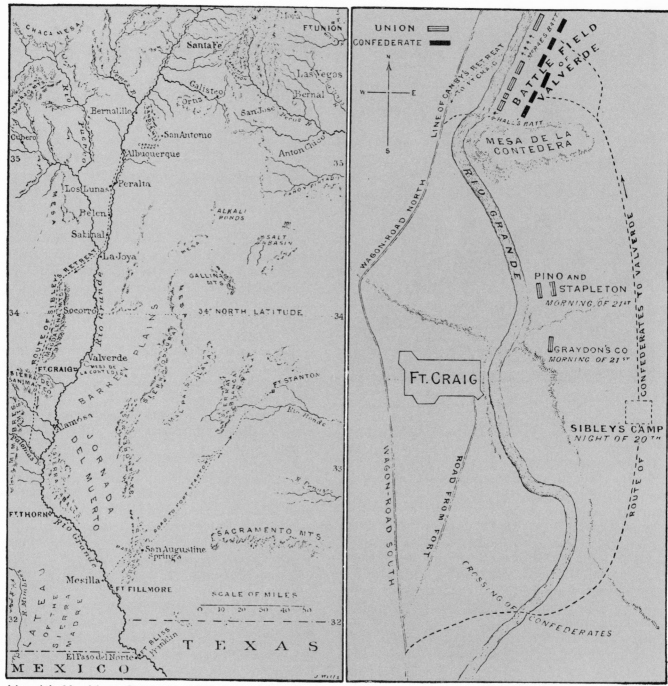

Map of the New Mexico Campaign and Sibley's retreat from Albuquerque. (Battles and Leaders of the Civil War)

Map of the Union-held Fort Craig and, across the river to the north,
Valverde. (Battles and Leaders of the Civil War)

Craig, while the flanking force attempted to slip unnoticed toward Contadero Ford. Colonel Canby,
having graduated only a year behind Sibley at West
Point, anticipated such a maneuver and dispatched
portions of the United States 3d Cavalry to contest
the crossing.

The Texans won the race to the ford, but their
vanguard had scarcely emerged from the river when
the dismounted Federal troopers attacked. The Confederates wheeled a small cannon into position, and
the accurate rain of 6-pound shells kept the Union
men at bay for nearly ninety minutes. The unionists
brought up their own heavier artillery and the "fire
soon became so galling that the enemy was driven
. . . in great disorder and with heavy loss."

At noon, with reinforcements from Fort Craig, the

Union soldiers forced the Confederates to retreat about 800 yards to a series of sand hills on the east side of the Rio Grande. By now, Sibley realized his plan had gone slightly awry: Instead of a surprise action, the skirmish at Valverde had become the main battle, as both sides shifted more and more men from the Fort Craig engagement. Sibley, however, would not see the end of the battle. Having been confined to an ambulance for several days prior to the action, the strain of battle and lack of sleep during the previous night became too much for the general, and he had to turn command over to his senior colonel, Thomas J. Green, at about one in the afternoon.

Desultory shots continued to fly between the two sides as the Confederates re-formed behind the sand hills. Colonel Canby arrived at the field at about 2:30 and devised a simple, yet effective plan for capturing the new Confederate position. With the left flank secured, Canby sought to pivot his right flank upon the center of his line and surprise the Confederates on their own left flank. By 4 o'clock, the men on the Union right, spearheaded by the still-dismounted 3d Cavalry, began to move forward. No sooner had the advance begun when a terrific "cannonading and roar of small arms was heard . . . and immediately a large force of the enemy's cavalry came charging down." The Texan lancers, red guidons flying, attacked with a shout.

The Southerners, too long held at bay by the Union batteries, determined to make a final, furious assault. The mounted Texans bore down upon the Union battery on the right. Desperate artillerists rammed home shot after shot, while the crouching infantry supports, led by Colonel Kit Carson, awaited the shock of the attack. The cannon cut wide swaths through the Texans, and both Regular Army men and New Mexico Volunteers poured rifle fire into the horsemen. Suddenly the Confederates had had enough; they reined in, wheeled, and fled from the carnage, leaving piles of their comrades and horses behind.

The cheering Union men prepared to pursue when, to their horror, they discovered the attack just repulsed was only a diversion. On the Union left, dismounted Confederates scrambled over the top of the sand hills and began the long, 700-yard run to the Union battery on the left. With shotguns, Colts, and Bowie knives, the cursing Texans proved unstoppable in spite of shells smashing into them from six Union cannons. As the Texans drew closer, the New Mexico Volunteers panicked, broke, and ran, leaving only a few Regulars and Colorado Volunteers to face the human wave about to break on the artillery pieces.

With a terrible crash, aggressors and defenders came together in vicious hand-to-hand combat. Shotguns exploded in men's faces, Bowie knives slipped to their marks, and artillery rammers flew wildly. The wounded fell and were trampled under foot as the attack pressed forward.

Weight of numbers forced the Union soldiers into retreat. The gleeful Texans turned the cannon around and fired them at the former owners. The entire Union line, in danger of being enfiladed, bent and then collapsed as retreat became rout. Splashing across the river, the Union soldiers found refuge in Fort Craig. A truce settled on the battlefield as both sides gathered up the dead and wounded.

That night, Sibley and Canby evaluated their respective situations. Canby, in a strong fortification with supplies and men had only to decide whether to renew the battle the next day or to remain in the fort. Given the performance of some of his men, Colonel Canby chose the latter course.

Brigadier General Sibley had further complications. The care of the dead and wounded consumed two days, and the Army of New Mexico had only five days' rations. "In this dilemma the question arose whether to assault the fort in this crippled condition or move rapidly forward up the river were supplies of breadstuffs and meat could be procured." The sight of the thick adobe walls of Fort Craig convinced Sibley that his army had to move north and replenish its supplies.

At Socorro by February 27, 1862, Sibley established a hospital for the sick and wounded and left enough Confederate paper money to purchase medicines. Daily on shorter rations, Sibley worried his men would not reach Albuquerque, but the Texans marched with an eager step, knowing a quarter of a million dollars' worth of Federal provisions awaited them. The Union Army quartermaster in Albuquerque learned of the arrival of 400 Confederates at Belen, thirty-five miles south of Albuquerque, on March 1. With but a token force, the unionists prepared to evacuate:

> I [wrote Captain Herbert Enos, quartermaster] gave the order to fire the property at about six-thirty on the morning of the 2d. instant. The destruction would have been complete had it not been for the great rush of [New] Mexican men, women, and children who had been up the whole night, waiting anxiously for an opportunity to gratify their insatiable desire for plunder.

On March 4 Sibley led his men into Albuquerque, but the destruction or theft of so many supplies again prevented the acquiring of necessary stores. Sibley faced another difficult decision. Should the army remain in Albuquerque or perhaps move on to Santa Fe, the territorial capital? To remain in Albuquerque would only allow more time for the Union forces to gain strength; Sibley soon made the proper decision. He detached a force of about 600 men to Santa Fe "to capture such as might be found there." The remainder of the Army of New Mexico would stay in Albuquerque to delay any possible advances from Canby in the south.

The arrival of the Confederates near Santa Fe prompted a repetition of the earlier scene in Albuquerque. The Union quartermaster burned supplies and fled the territorial capital, along with the government of New Mexico. The Texans captured the town on March 23.

As the news of Valverde, Albuquerque, and Santa Fe reached the East, concern for the Union cause in New Mexico mounted. One of Canby's officers wrote the War Department:

> Since the battle of Valverde . . . the state of affairs . . . has been daily growing from bad to worse. All the militia and a large number of the volunteers (native) who were called into the service of the United States have deserted and taken to the mountains. A general system of robbery and plunder seems to be the order of the day. There is a general panic in the country and people are flying from their homes.

This graphic description, as well as entreaties from Canby and the governor of the territory, motivated a flurry of activity. Major General Henry W. Halleck, commander of the Western Theater, ordered three regiments of infantry and two of cavalry, plus artillery, from Kansas to New Mexico. Halleck, a classmate of Canby's at West Point, wrote: "The Government has shamefully neglected him."

The Union response to the capture of Santa Fe came quickly. Thirteen hundred Regular Army men and Colorado Volunteers marched on Santa Fe from Fort Union. To counter the threat, the Confederates moved east from Santa Fe to intercept. Santa Fe had to be held until General Sibley arrived with the main body.

On March 26, the two forces met in Apache Canyon near Glorieta. With an inferior force, the Confederates deployed across the steep rocky valley and awaited the Union attack. After sharp skirmishing the Confederates fell back, but their opponents did not pursue for fear of an ambush.

The two forces glowered at each other over their guns on the 27th; on the 28th the reinforced Union detachment renewed the battle. The Confederates

again spread across the defile and stood near their artillery; again the Union soldiers took the offensive. For the detachment of Colorado Volunteers, this action would be their first combat. The "Pike's Peakers" sprang to life and flung down their canteens, coats, and haversacks in an effort to speed their assault. The Coloradans, with great shouting, rushed forward, the various companies jostling and elbowing to the fore to earn a full share of the honors. The sharp crack of Confederate firearms reverberated off the walls of the canyon, but the Federals charged onward; the rain of whistling minie balls and buckshot fell without mercy. Soon even the doughty Colorado Volunteers could take no more and the Union line fell back.

Lieutenant Colonel William R. Scurry, commander of the Confederate force, ordered an immediate counterattack to sweep the unionists off the field. The Texan war cry rang out in Apache Canyon as the Confederates scrambled over and through the boulders and scrub. Just as at Valverde, the Texans ran straight at the flaming mouths of Union cannon. Grapeshot and canister gouged bloody holes in the advancing formation, but the undeterred Confederates could not be stopped. They smashed into the Federals and literally cut them to pieces. The Union soldiers broke and ran. The tireless Texans stayed right behind, and "the pursuit was kept up until forced to halt from the extreme exhaustion of the men."

The celebration of the glorious victory halted quickly when word arrived from the Confederate rear areas that the supply train had been captured. A band of Colorado Volunteers had circled behind the main Confederate force and fallen upon the lightly defended wagons. The supplies fell into Union hands, and the sorely pressed Texans lost irreplaceable provisions, including ammunition and blankets. The till-then victorious Confederates returned to camp to find themselves destitute. Realizing how tenuous his position had become, Scurry acted with dispatch and a disgusted Colorado Volunteer noted:

> A flag of truce, which seems their best hold, arrived in camp as soon as we did, requesting an armistice of eighteen hours duration, ostensibly to bury their dead and take care of their wounded; really to gain time to return to Santa Fe which they immediately commenced doing in the greatest confusion.

Indeed, the Confederates began to fall back on Santa Fe. With all their rations captured, the Texans ate the corn wasted by their animals. Two days after the "Gettysburg of the West," the Confederates re-entered Santa Fe.

General Sibley and the remainder of the Confederate force arrived in Santa Fe soon after Scurry, according to the plan. Sibley again had to improvise a new plan to obtain supplies. Before any scheme could be put into effect, however, messengers arrived from the garrison at Albuquerque. Canby, now a general, had appeared outside Albuquerque with 1,200 men, hoping to crush Sibley between two Union forces.

After a swift march back to Albuquerque, Sibley faced his three options. He could stay in Albuquerque and starve; he could attack the now united forces of Canby at worse than one to two odds and probably be defeated; or he could attempt to retreat out of New Mexico.

On April 12, the Confederates evacuated Albuquerque and began to cross to the west bank of the Rio Grande. But only part of the Confederate force succeeded in fording the river, so on the next day the remainder of the Army of New Mexico marched south to Peralta. As the Texans attempted to cross the river here, General Canby and the Union force appeared and began a bombardment. Faced with being defeated in detail, Sibley recrossed to the east bank, and "the day was occupied at Peralta in ineffectual firing on both sides."

After dark, the Confederates returned to the west side of the river, and for the next three days the Confederates marched down the west side of the Rio Grande while Canby's unionists paralleled on the east bank. The forces remained in sighting distance the entire time, but neither exerted an effort to get at the other.

The sandy roads bogged down the wagons and cannon badly on the west side of the river. Fearing a sudden attack, Sibley and his senior officers decided to take a new route, through the mountains. Sibley planned thereby to sweep well to the rear of Fort Craig and emerge on the river below the fort. The Confederates also hoped such a move would mystify their pursuers.

On the night of April 17, the Texans slipped away from their still-burning campfires and entered the mountains, using their mules to carry seven days' rations and pull the artillery. The Confederates abandoned all their wagons at the river.

At first light, the startled General Canby found an empty camp on the opposite side of the river. Correctly surmising the Confederate course, Canby decided to abandon direct pursuit and proceed to Fort Craig.

A member of Sibley's beloved if somewhat motley crew of soldiers. (Lossing's Pictorial Field Book of the Civil War)

The Confederates, however, continued to suffer difficulties. The sun beat the Texans more mercilessly than any Yankees ever had; men's tongues became so swollen with thirst that the men could scarcely curse as they wrestled the artillery pieces through the narrow mountain passes by hand. Water proved so scarce that before the Texans reached home, some of the men cut their own veins or those of their animals to quench the dry thirst with blood.

Finally, after surviving ten days on only a week's rations, a mere 1,700 Confederates staggered out of the mountains and emerged on the Rio Grande well south of Fort Craig. The exhausted Army of New Mexico dragged itself southward into Confederate territory, and by May 4, garrisoned villages along the Rio Grande from Mesilla to El Paso. Confederate arms in New Mexico had been expelled, never to return on such a scale. In terms of other Civil War campaigns, the casualties had been light, barely exceeding 4,000 for both armies. General Sibley's hopes of returning to New Mexico dissipated rapidly when he later learned of the approach of the California Column.

Controversy arose after the Army of New Mexico returned to Texas. While Sibley praised his "brave boys," some of the junior officers and men made remarks that cast aspersions on Sibley's character, intelligence, and sobriety. Some soldiers maintained Sibley had not exercised command, but rather let his subordinates make decisions. Sibley similarly endured comments that stated his expedition had been poorly planned and even more poorly executed. How much of this was true, though, can only be determined through careful consideration of the materials and personalities involved.

Sibley had been ill for several days before the battle of Valverde, yet on the morning of the fight the general took the saddle and directed the Confederate action until well after noon. The strain of command, together with the physical rigors endured over a period of months in the temperature extremes of Texas and New Mexico did not wear easily on a man of Sibley's age (45).

The question of care in the procurement of supplies arose from several sources, chiefly from Captain Trevanion T. Teel, commander of artillery in the Army of New Mexico. Teel felt that Sibley had been too little inclined to worry about only one day at a time. In this respect, Sibley probably did make an error of judgment. Out of earnestness for whatever motives, some leading Texans had assured Sibley he need not worry about supplies, as they would ensure a steady flow of materiels to the Army of New Mexico. Furthermore, Sibley, in his reports, complained bitterly of how his force had not received sufficient support from Richmond. Also, New Mexicans hesitated to accept Confederate paper and scrip as legal tender. Sibley, as the commanding officer, must accept at least some portion of the blame in this respect.

A final charge against Sibley held that the New Mexican invasion had been ill-conceived from the beginning. The hope of conquering the vast region of New Mexico with less than 4,000 men now seems fantastic, all hopes of California aside. Yet, from the view of the entire Confederacy, the invasion had much to gain and practically nothing to lose. A modest investment in men and practically no investment in materiels gave the South an opportunity to win much in the Southwest, albeit the odds of success had never been great. In the context of the Civil War, Sibley had the chance to win stunning victories for the Confederacy and draw off Union men and supplies from the main theaters of the war. Indeed, 6,000 men destined for other Union operations ultimately had received changed orders that routed them to New Mexico.

Had Sibley been successful, his would have been one of the most daring and significant campaigns of the war. As a failure, though, the campaign remains an interesting sidelight of the Civil War. Ironically, the only official recognition received by Sibley and his men came while Canby pursued them down the Rio Grande in April 1862. The Confederate Congress resolved:

> That the thanks of Congress are hereby tendered to Brigadier General H. H. Sibley and to the officers and men under his command, for the complete and brilliant victories achieved over our enemies in New Mexico.

LIFE IN
CIVIL WAR
AMERICA

by Maury Klein

Wartime is by nature abnormal. Even a distant war deranges the routine of life at home. Men leave to fight, and some never return. Episodes of heroism and cowardice, sacrifice and exploitation color the moral landscape in extremes. Civil liberties usually taken for granted are suddenly challenged, even restricted. Nothing in life seems to move in its normal groove so long as the war continues.

Civil war compounds these problems and adds new ones. The conflict is not remote but fought within a nation's own borders. Every casualty is a citizen, every piece of damage a national loss. The struggle pits brother against brother, friend against friend. The carnage of war drenches familiar landscape, leaving scars and wounds that will not heal for generations. It is as if some form of madness has seized the land and wreaks bloody destruction until it drops at last of exhaustion.

Northerners and Southerners faced common problems during four years of madness: how did they cope with the horrors and uncertainties of Civil War?

Life in the North

For most northerners the war was a distant but not remote event. Except for Lee's brief invasions of Maryland in 1862 and Pennsylvania in 1863, some fighting in the western border states, and a few raids, their cities and farms escaped the devastation that blighted large areas of the South. Seldom did the din of combat reach their ears or the menace of invading troops disturb their daily routines. Life went on, not as usual, but at least with a minimum of disruption.

But distance from the battlefield could not protect northerners from the effects of war. The ordeal of sustaining so massive a struggle intruded upon people's lives in countless ways. The most obvious of these was of course the absence of friends and kinfolk in the service. Every town and hamlet watched its young men depart for the front, some to die and others to return home with maimed bodies or broken spirits.

Concern for the safety of loved ones permeated households throughout the North. The slowness with which accurate details and casualty lists reached home after a major battle aggravated their distress. In this way distance from the seat of war bred anxiety as well as security. The pain of loss often found expression in popular culture. Two Civil War composers, George F. Root and Henry Clay Work, depicted it in their songs. One immensely popular tune by Root included the following lyrics, written by Henry Stevenson Washburn:

At our fireside sad and lonely
Often will the bosom swell
At remembrance of the story
How our noble Willie fell;
How he strove to bear our banner
Through the thickest of the fight,
And uphold our country's honor
In the strength of manhood's might,
(Chorus)
We shall meet, but we shall miss him,
There will be one vacant chair;
We will linger to caress him,
When we breathe our evening prayer.

The presence of men in uniform, whether home on leave or forming into newly organized units, served as constant reminders to civilians. Soldiers could be found on the streets of towns and villages everywhere. In a city like Washington they were essential for keeping order; one report declared that without them, "this District would have been simply uninhabitable." Returning wounded also brought home stark evidence of their ordeal in combat. Rare was the town that did not welcome home a veteran minus an arm or leg or worse.

Hospitals filled with wounded had a similar effect. As the city nearest the eastern theatre, Washington endured the greatest crush of incoming casualties. Sick and wounded soldiers overflowed the hospitals into converted rooms in churches, the insane asylum, government buildings like the Patent Office, and even the hallways of the Capitol. At times their number exceeded 50,000, "a population," Walt Whitman observed, "more numerous in itself than the Washington of ten or fifteen years ago." Creaking carts lumbered through the streets every night bearing their cargoes of dead to the cemeteries.

Some towns also housed army camps or prisoner-of-war compounds. Another agent of war, the conscription officer, began appearing after 1862, once the enlistment enthusiasm had passed. These officers became objects of loathing and often violence in many places, as did officers searching for deserters. During 1863 draft riots plunged New York City into turmoil, and in the lower Midwest resistance to the draft led to riots, the murdering of several draft officers, and a string of "outrages, robberies, and incendiary fires."

The conflict had its psychological effects as well. In 1863 the superintendent of the Illinois State Hospital for the Insane argued that the strain of war had brought a "vast invigoration of the American mind . . . national athleticism on a grand scale." But the shocks and dislocations of wartime did not find true reflection in mental institutions, partly because so few of their victims ended up there. A more perceptive judgment came from historian H.C. Hubbart,

Wounded Union soldiers in Carver Hospital, Washington, D.C. (National Archives)

who concluded that "the West and the nation as a whole was torn by war-strain, indecision, party faction and demagogism, anxiety, sacrifice, devotion, suffering, insanity, and death. Democracy was in convulsion."

Apart from its advantage in men and guns, the northern war effort depended upon its superior industrial and agricultural might. In terms of productivity, the war was fought as much at home as on the battlefield, and this struggle enlisted men, women, and children alike. The increased demand for goods, coupled with the drain of manpower for military service, meant that there were fewer people to do more work. Farm and factory responded to this need by increasing their use of machinery to replace human labor and by putting more women and children to work.

The North relied upon its staple crops both to feed its people and army and to produce surpluses that could be sold abroad for badly needed gold. As thousands of men left their farms to fight the war, women, children, and older men took up the field work. As a popular song enjoined:

> Just take your gun and go;
> For Ruth can drive the oxen, John,
> And I can use the hoe!

A missionary in Iowa observed in 1863, "I met more women driving teams on the road and saw more at work in the fields than men." Another wrote from Kansas, "Yesterday I saw the wife of one of our parishioners driving the team in a reaper; her husband is at Vicksburg. With what help she can secure and the assistance of her little children, she is carrying on the farm."

The rapid spread of farm machinery made this possible, a fact that delighted manufacturers who sniffed bonanza profits. Cyrus McCormick consoled a salesman in Illinois, "Don't be so blue over prospects. Remember 20,000 militia have to leave this state . . . and these men will have to come, many or a large share of them, from the farms." McCormick was correct. As the Cincinnati *Gazette* proclaimed in 1862, "A hundred thousand agricultural laborers are gone; how are we to meet the deficiency? We have met it chiefly by labor-saving machinery."

Mowers and reapers were still relatively new machines when the war began. By 1864 mower production exceeded 70,000, or twice the output of 1862, while McCormick alone turned out 6,000 reapers in 1864. These devices saved human labor and could be operated by women and children. Other machines, including the horse rake, new harrows, cultivators, corn planters, steam threshers, and grain drills were

*Workers fill cartridges at the U.S. Arsenal in Watertown, Massachusetts. While Northern industrialists'
profits soared, inflation kept workers poor. (Harper's Weekly, July 20, 1861)*

devised. In 1863 *Scientific American* boasted, "This year the demand for reapers has been so great that manufacturers will not be able to fill their orders. Farming is comparatively child's play to what it was twenty years ago, before mowing, reaping, and other agricultural machines were employed."

The use of machinery increased the scale of agriculture and enabled farmers to bring more land under cultivation, especially in the West. The results were impressive. Northern farmers produced large enough corn, oat, and wheat crops during the war years (including record crops in 1862) to fill domestic needs and still sell huge quantities to England, which experienced three consecutive years of crop failures. Hog and cattle output also increased sharply, and wool production jumped from 60 million pounds in 1860 to 140 million pounds in 1865. During those years the number of sheep in the North doubled, an important gain since wool offered the most common substitute for the cotton supply lost when the South seceded.

If northern farms basked in prosperity, so did its factories and mills. From their bustling, clanging interiors poured a swelling stream of muskets, cannon, equipment, locomotives, rails, wagons, tools, uniforms, shoes, and countless other items. Wartime needs accelerated the development of other industries besides armaments and farm machinery. The sewing machine, little over a decade old in 1860, revolutionized the clothing and shoe industries when harnessed to the demands of war. Men's shirts, which took over fourteen hours to make by hand, could be done in little over an hour. The new McKay sewing machine enabled one man to sew several hundred pairs of shoes a day. Small shops gave way to factories throughout Massachusetts as the industry boomed. "Operatives are pouring in as fast as room can be made for them," reported a Lynn newspaper; "buildings for shoe factories are going up in every direction; the hum of machinery is heard on every hand."

One by-product of this boom was the discovery that uniforms and shoes manufactured in a few basic sizes would fit most men. This standardization simplified production in quantity and after the war spurred the rise of the ready-made clothing industry. Military needs also stimulated the canned food industry, including Gail Borden's canned milk. The need to produce canned foods quickly and in quantity led to improvements in canning techniques and machinery.

As farms and factories responded to the war effort, an aura of prosperity settled across the North. Newspapers and politicians alike waxed eloquent over the nation's material well-being. *The New York Times*

enthused in 1864 that northerners were better housed, clothed, and fed than ever before, "in the midst of the most gigantic civil war . . . yet seen." Wholesale farm prices doubled during the war years while non-agricultural wages rose 43 per cent. Farm land values soared, as did other real estate values. No one doubted the source of this windfall. As one commercial magazine observed of Massachusetts in 1863, "The war has brought into activity many mechanical employments for which there is little occasion in time of peace . . . Wealth has flowed into the State in no stinted measure, despite of war and heavy taxes. In every department of labor the government has been, directly or indirectly, the chief employer and paymaster."

For many northerners, however, this prosperity proved more apparent than real. As usual war brought inflation, which in many cases erased gains in income. Wholesale prices more than doubled while the consumer price index increased from 102 to 177 (1851–1859 = 100). According to one recent calculation, the real wage index actually declined from 102 in January 1861 to 67 in January 1865. *Fincher's Trades Review* declared in 1863 that "Two years ago, a man who received $1.50 per day, could satisfy his wants with that sum just as well, if not better, than he can now with $3.00 per day."

Wage earners suffered most from the ravages of inflation, but attempts to better their position made little headway during the war. Most wartime trade unions began at the local level, primarily in New York, Pennsylvania, and Massachusetts, and boasted some 300 locals with 200,000 members by 1865. City federations, begun in Rochester in March 1863, soon sprang up in most industrial centers. Attempts to revive national trade associations made some gains, but the national organizations were loose bodies with little effective power over their locals. In general the labor movement remained weak during the war.

Unskilled workers, especially women, children, and blacks, endured starvation wages and sweatshop conditions with little hope of improving their lot. In 1861 the government's Philadelphia Armory paid women 17 1/2 cents to make a shirt. Three years later that figure had fallen to 15 cents, despite the rise in prices. By contrast, private contractors were paying only eight cents. To keep wages down employers hired not only women but young boys and, especially, immigrants. They also utilized blacks as strike-breakers and resorted to labor-saving machinery where possible. Strikes proved futile in wartime. The public regarded them as disloyal and the government sometimes responded with troops. On several occasions President Lincoln felt obliged to intervene in an attempt to salve workers' feelings and preserve their loyalty to the war effort.

While workers found prosperity elusive, many businessmen reaped fat profits from wartime opportunities. Alert contractors were quick to take advantage of the government's needs. Some were content to earn legitimate fortunes; others resorted to chicanery to make their killings. Never had the nation created so large an army or required armaments and equipment in such huge quantities. The scale of operations, coupled with the urgency of purchasing so much so quickly, invited corruption of unprecedented dimensions. As early as July 1862 a report to the Secretary of War declared:

> We have found the system under which have been issued numerous orders or contracts for ordnance and ordnance stores . . . strongly marked with improvidence. The amount of these orders or contracts has been ascertained to be largely in excess of the public wants, and the prices fixed by many of them beyond necessity or means . . . It has been impossible for us to protect the Government against lamentable losses in these loose and irregular transactions.

Revelation after revelation rocked the public, prompting the New York *Herald* in June 1864 to denounce the "gross corruption prevailing in nearly every department of the government." Large commissions went to men whose only service was to obtain lucrative government contracts for firms.

On the stock and gold exchanges, speculators thrived on the uncertainties of wartime. Gold and security prices, like public morale, fluctuated with ebb and flow of news from the front. Hordes of speculators, including some women braving ridicule in a traditionally male arena, plunged into the treacherous currents of Wall Street seeking a quick fortune. One crafty manipulator, Daniel Drew, recalled that "Along with ordinary happenings, we fellows in Wall Street had the fortunes of war to speculate about . . . It's good fishing in troubled waters." Another financier put the case more bluntly: "The battle of Bull Run makes the fortune of every man in Wall Street who is not a natural idiot."

Not all northern businessmen were dishonest, and not all made fortunes. But the war created a free-wheeling atmosphere that invited opportunism and abuse.

It is important to remember that not all northerners bothered to fight the war or even tender it active support. Some people lacked strong interest in the conflict and either ignored it as best they could or resented it as an intrusion into their private affairs.

Among this group were men who found the wartime situation a golden opportunity for self-advancement. These ambitious young entrepreneurs used the war years to establish themselves while their peers were absent at the front. Some made fortunes even before the war ended, while others planted the roots of what were to be long and prosperous careers.

Within this group could be found a surprising number of the business titans who were to dominate the economy, and therefore much of American life, during the next half century: Andrew Carnegie, J.P. Morgan, John D. Rockefeller, George F. Baker, Frederick Weyerhauser, Gustavus Swift, Charles A. Pillsbury, George M. Pullman, Mark Hanna, Jay Gould, Marshall Field, John Wanamaker, and Peter Widener, to name but a few. These men, and others like them, ignored the call to arms and devoted themselves to the windfall opportunities bred by wartime conditions. Few of them even tried to enlist, fewer still stayed home because of disability (James J. Hill was one), and several (Carnegie, Gould, Rockefeller, and Philip D. Armour among them) hired substitutes.

In later years some of these men grew defensive about their failure to enter the service. "I was represented in the army," Rockefeller insisted. "I sent more than twenty men, yes, nearly thirty. That is, I made such arrangements for them that they were able to go." The majority, however, seemed content to concentrate on the business at hand. One son of banker Thomas Mellon begged his father for money to speculate in wheat. Writing from Wisconsin, he observed that people "continue growing richer and don't care when the war closes." Mindful of the education offered by prevailing conditions, the elder Mellon flatly forbade another son from enlisting:

> I had hoped my boy was going to make a smart intelligent businessman and was not such a goose as to be *seduced from duty* by the declamations of buncombed speeches. It is only greenhorns who enlist. *You can learn nothing in the army* . . . In time you will come to understand and believe that a man may be a patriot without risking his own life or sacrificing his health. There are plenty of other lives less valuable or ready to serve for the love of serving.

To most of these men wartime opportunities brought financial nest eggs from which huge fortunes later hatched. For them as for many others who advanced their prospects during these years, prosperity was anything but illusory.

Editor William Cullen Bryant, who made New York's Evening Post *the nation's leading paper in the mid-1880s, was a staunch supporter of Northern war efforts. (CWTI Collection)*

Society reflected this mood of prosperity, especially in the cities. As the war dragged on through month after weary month of bloody battles that produced defeat or indecision, northerners grasped eagerly at diversions to dispel the gloom of uncertainty that clouded the future. So frenetic did the pursuit of gaiety and amusement become that public-spirited citizens periodically denounced this apparent indifference to the suffering and hardships endured by soldiers at the front. Even a foreign observer, the correspondent for the London *Times*, expressed his disgust in 1863:

> There is something saddening, indeed revolting, in the high glee, real or affected, with which the people here look upon what ought to be . . . a grievous national calamity. The indulgence in every variety of pleasure, luxury, and extravagence is simply shocking. The jewelers' shops in all these cities have doubled or trebled their trade; the love of fine dresses and ornaments on the part of women amounts to madness. They have the money, well or ill gotten, and must enjoy it. Every fresh bulletin from the battlefield of Chickamauga during my three weeks' stay in Cincinnati brought a long list of the dead and wounded . . . many of whom, of the officers, belonged to the best families in

the place. Yet the signs of mourning were hardly anywhere perceptible; the noisy gayety of the town was not abated one jot.

A New York editor registered the same complaint a year later: "Who at the North would ever think of war, if he had not a friend in the army, or did not read the newspapers? Go into Broadway and we will show you what is meant by the word 'extravagance.'" From Washington a Springfield *Republican* correspondent complained, "At present Washington is mad with gayety, reeling in the whirl of dissipation, before it sits down to repent in the ashes of Lent. There are three or four grand parties a night; theaters, operas, fairs, everything to make its denizens forget that war and sorrow are in the land." Frederick W. Seward, son of the Secretary of State, noted that "Gayety has become as epidemic in Washington as gloom was last winter . . . A year ago the secretary of state was 'heartless' or 'unpatriotic' because he gave dinners; now the only complaint of him is that he don't have dancing."

Most critics agreed that the presence of so many newly made fortunes was to blame for this spectacle of self-indulgence. The editor of the Providence *Journal* chided those "who have made more in a week or in a month than they are accustomed to gain in a year . . . it is such men and women that are in especial danger of rushing into extravagance as unbecoming the state of our country as it is injurious." William Cullen Bryant of the New York *Evening Post* thundered, "Extravagance, luxury, these are the signs of the times; are they not evidence of a state of things unhealthy, feverish . . .? What business have Americans at any time with such vain show . . .? But especially how can they justify it to themselves in this time of war? Some men have gained great fortunes during the past two or three years, but that does not excuse their extravagance."

This rampant gaiety did not infect rural areas, where the workday was always long and sources of amusement few. There life went on much as it had before the war. There were church socials, husking bees, barn dances, and the ever popular county fairs. Some counties found the fair tough going, especially early in the war. An Ohio newspaper lamented in 1861 that the Crawford County fair "was in one particular a success, and in another, a failure. Financially, it was a success, as the attendance was almost as large as usual . . . But the exhibition was a failure. A number of those who have heretofore taken an interest in the institution, were opposed to holding a Fair this season, and . . . threw cold water upon the enterprise."

Methodist camp meeting. Religious revivals in rural areas of both North and South often were camp meetings marked by fervid preaching and public conversions. (CWTI Collection)

Religious revivals or camp meetings, accompanied by picnics and other festivities, sometimes enlivened rural communities for a week or more. Many a small town possessed an "opry" house that never saw an opera but welcomed touring lecturers, dramatic companies, or minstrel shows. Occasionally a traveling circus might wend its way through the countryside, thrilling farm folk with its exotic menagerie of animals and freaks. No event rivaled the celebration of national holidays like the Fourth of July. Families gathered from miles around to enjoy patriotic oratory, fireworks, barbeques, games, and dancing, usually accompanied by generous swigs from jugs of whiskey or hard cider. Sports too had their place. Young men played baseball or competed in foot races, wrestling, and shooting matches.

Rural folk who contented themselves with these pleasures hardly reveled in extravagance or self-indulgence. Even in small towns the standards of gaiety remained modest. In 1862 an English journalist visited Racine, Wisconsin, and concluded that "The amusements of Racine are about as limited as if it stood in our midland counties. Judging from the pos-

ters of ancient date which hung upon the walls, a passing circus, an itinerant exhibition of Ethiopian minstrels, and an occasional concert, were all the entertainments afforded to the inhabitants . . . Society in Racine is still in a primitive stage. Dinner-parties are unknown, and balls are events of great rarity; but tea parties, to which you are invited on the morning of the day, are of constant occurrence."

City life offered far more varied and sophisticated amusements. As always, the upper class set the standards and indulged themselves most freely. Few wartime shortages, interrupted their pleasures. The loss of southern cotton hampered the textile mills and caused a shortage of paper; sorghum and maple sugar were substituted for sugar; and chicory seed replaced coffee; tobacco was in short supply; and high taxes on whiskey drove the poorer classes to drinking more beer. Otherwise, life went on much as before. As Constance McLaughlin Green said of the nation's capital, "For most Washingtonians this bloodiest, bitterest war the United States ever fought changed every-day routines very little."

While soldiers fought and died, the fashionable frolicked. Here: the supper room at the Russian Ball in the New York Academy of Music. (Harper's Weekly, November 21, 1863)

In every city dinners, receptions, and elegant parties occupied fashionable people. Picnics became the rage in New York; then roller-skating made its appearance in 1863 and the city's social denizens seized upon it as a pleasure that they hoped to confine to "the educated and refined classes." Ice skating lightened the tedium of winter, and the first hot breath of summer sent people fleeing to Newport, Saratoga, and other watering holes. There too the tone of life drove more sensitive spirits to despair. A Boston reporter at Saratoga grumbled, "Of fashions here there is no end. Indeed it makes one's heart sick to see the folly which reigns triumphant . . . What the women spend in dress, the men spend in 'liquoring up,' until they can't stand, in horses and in gambling."

Every major city had its lyceums and lecture halls, and in New York grand opera imported from Europe enjoyed a vogue at the Academy of Music. Pianist Louis Moreau Gottschalk drew huge audiences for his concerts, and in every city crowds packed the theatres night after night. Comedies were the staple fare, both in high-tone playhouses such as Wallack's or Niblo's Gardens in New York, and in lower class theatres like those in the Bowery where enthusiastic audiences gathered to yell and whistle, cheer and hiss, munch peanuts and spit tobacco juice. Although the rage for comedy reflected a desire to escape the war for a few hours, dramas based upon recent battles also proved popular. One energetic producer opened a play about Bull Run within a month of the battle, and later engagements were put on the stage by adapting a standard script to each occasion.

Besides theatre, New York offered three different minstrel shows, dance halls, beer gardens, and "The American" on Broadway—an emporium where men only could smoke and drink and enjoy "the feast of reason and the flow of soul." A Broadway veteran recalled that "Ten years ago, girls danced here in a state of nudity; but the authorities have now effectually put down such exhibitions."

P.T. Barnum's American Museum, with its West Indian snakes and fish, whale, hippopotamus, giant and giantess, and other exotica, offered New Yorkers titillation of another kind. Imitators in other cities drew large crowds, and Barnum sent to the rest of the North his traveling circus, the Grand Colossal Museum and Menagerie, with curiosities borrowed from the American Museum and animals gathered from every corner of the world.

Sports also flourished during the war years. Horse racing, once the province of southern and border states, attracted a great following. New tracks opened in Chicago, Boston, and Washington to help form a racing circuit with tracks in St. Louis, Hartford, Louisville, Philadelphia, Saratoga, Paterson, and elsewhere. Prize-fighting, although illegal in most places, created intense interest among the "less refined classes." An epic fight between two noted Irish pugilists, Coburn and McCool, took place only ten days and a hundred miles distant from the battle of Chancellorsville and nearly upstaged that bloody struggle. Amidst a carnival-like atmosphere and heavy wagering, Coburn flattened his rival after 61 rounds of bare-fisted pounding.

Clearly amusements offered a counterpoint to anxiety and uncertainty. But the stark contrasts of gaiety and vulgar prosperity in a time of national tragedy was too much for concerned observers. In 1863 the New York *Herald* threw up its hands in despair and proclaimed, "The world has seen its iron age, its silver age, its golden age and its brazen age. This is the age of shoddy." The term struck a vital nerve and was widely used. In that sense life in the North had set the stage for the excesses that would characterize the postwar Gilded Age.

Yet large numbers of people kept the sorrows of war before them and did what they could to ameliorate their suffering. Women joined relief societies to provide clothing, bandages, and amenities for soldiers, and many served as nurses. More than two hundred hospitals serviced the sick and wounded, sanitary commissions tried to improve conditions in camps, and homes for the disabled were opened. National charities appeared on the scene for the first time in American history, while state and local charities increased their efforts to assist those afflicted by the exigencies of war. Many communities organized fairs, exhibitions, concerts, and other activities to raise money for relief work. Religious organizations sent Bibles, pamphlets, and missionaries to troops in the field. Efforts were made in most towns to care for the families of soldiers either absent or dead. Philanthropists filled some of the gaps left by organizations.

The intense sympathy aroused by the sufferings of war extended to peacetime charities, many of which underwent a resurgence in funds and volunteers during the war years. The "age of shoddy" represented one side of northern life; this widespread expression of sympathy and eagerness to help shoulder the burden reflected quite another. The contrasts were stark and jarring. They amounted to a sort of national schizophrenia. For a people caught up in the largest, bloodiest, and most immediate war in their history, it could not be otherwise.

New Yorkers gather at a fair held by the Sanitary Commission, a philanthropic organization created to coordinate wartime relief and medical care. (Harper's Weekly, April 9, 1864)

Life in the South

The Civil War conferred a unique legacy upon southerners: they became the only Americans ever to lose a war and suffer military occupation by the enemy. As losers of that struggle southerners inevitably underwent different wartime experiences than the winners; but of course there was much more to the story than that. The South differed radically from the North, as a region and as a culture. As Senator Lewis T. Wigfall told English journalist William H. Russell:

> We are a peculiar people, sir! You don't understand us . . . because we are known to you only by Northern writers and Northern papers . . . We are an agricultural people; we are a primitive but a civilized people. We have no cities—we don't want them . . . We have no commercial navy—no navy—we don't want them . . . We want no manufactures: we desire no trading, no mechanical or manufacturing classes. As long as we have our rice, our sugar, our tobacco, and our cotton, we can command wealth to produce all we want from those nations with which we are in amity, and to lay up money besides.

Unfortunately for the South, most of its "peculiarities" worked against it during the war. A population of 9 million (compared to the North's 22 million)

A scene often repeated: At a cemetery in New Orleans, a widow and her daughters, dressed in full mourning, carry flowers and wreaths to adorn the graves of loved ones killed in the war. (Frank Leslie's Illustrated Newspaper, *April 25, 1863*)

included 3.5 million black slaves who would serve as laborers but not as soldiers. As a region it produced less than 10 per cent of the nation's industrial goods. The South lacked not only factories but skilled labor, machinery, foundries, shipping, and a reliable transportation system. Although its culture was far more homogeneous and close-knit than the North's and less ethnically diverse, it was not unified. An exaggerated sense of individualism, which found political expression in the state rights philosophy, undermined the war effort with endless divisions and rancor. Finally, the South was an overwhelmingly rural region, a fact that heightened its people's sense of isolation and uncertainty as the war went on.

The war was fought almost entirely on southern soil. Invading troops, as well as military engagements, caused great destruction and loss of property (including slaves), some violence to civilians, and military occupation. Many southerners avoided this last humiliation by fleeing from advancing Federal troops. Thousands became refugees, trudging toward Texas or some remote corner of the Confederacy alongside wagons laden with their dearest possessions. Those who returned home after the war often found the destruction to their property more severe than that suffered by those who elected to remain behind. Like refugees in every war, they endured great hardships and found little comfort at their journey's end. Kate Stone, who fled with her family to Tyler, Texas, from their Louisiana plantation in 1863, complained bitterly that "The more we see of people, the less we like them, and every refugee we have seen feels the same way. They call us *renegades* in Tyler. It is strange the prejudice that exists all through the state against refugees."

Invading armies did more than cause hardship. They disrupted the South's war effort and transformed difficult problems into insurmountable ones. Portions of the border states, Kentucky, Missouri, Maryland, Tennessee, the Sea Islands off the Florida Gulf coast, and the vital port of New Orleans fell early into Federal hands. The surrender of Vicksburg in 1863 gave the North possession of the Mississippi River and cut the Confederacy in half. As more territory fell into northern hands, problems of supply, transportation, and communication mounted steadily. The invading armies shattered not only the South's ability to wage war but also its morale. Sherman's devastating march through Georgia in 1864 provided the most conspicuous example of this twin effect.

The South's resources for waging a major war were modest at best. Its economy depended upon the sale of staple crops abroad, but the northern blockade cut off that vital market almost entirely in 1862. Agriculture alone could scarcely sustain a nation engaged in modern warfare, and comparatively little industry had developed in the South. Although factories could be found in several towns, few could produce heavy industrial goods or meet the voracious demands of wartime. The South was rich in raw materials but made almost no machine tools, steel, rails, munitions, sewing machines, or other necessities of war. The Tredegar Iron Works in Richmond remained the South's most important industrial plant—and an important reason for defending Richmond at all costs.

An inadequate transportation system complicated the problem of supply. The South's river system ran mostly north-south while the Confederacy's supply lines ran east-west. In 1861 the section possessed about 9,000 miles of railroad (compared with the North's 22,000 miles), most of it lightly built and poorly equipped. The Pennsylvania and Erie railroads alone owned almost as many locomotives as the entire Confederacy, and the South lacked the means to improve or even maintain its system. As Captain F.W.

Sims, the railroad coordinator lamented in February 1865, "not a single bar of railroad iron has been rolled in the Confederacy since the war [began] . . ." That left only horse and wagon, but the South's roads were in terrible shape and the army had first claim on the supply of animals and wagons.

These and other problems forced the South to fight the war on a shoestring, which meant that civilians no less than soldiers had to exert their utmost if the cause was to succeed. More than sacrifice was involved. The overwhelming fact of life in the Confederacy was the perpetual struggle against shortages. Nearly everything was in short supply and grew more so as the war progressed. Shortages caused some problems and compounded others into a vicious circle of privation and improvisation that taxed the ingenuity of southerners, strained their morale, and ultimately doomed their cause.

Most southerners made far greater sacrifices than their northern counterparts, not from superior virtue but because they had no choice. The war intruded

The Tredegar Iron Works in Richmond, Virginia, was the Confederacy's most important industrial plant— and an important reason for the staunch defense of Richmond. (CWTI Collection)

upon their lives to a degree unknown in the North. It compelled them to endure constant privation, intense suffering, and the anguish of personal losses made in the shadow of impending defeat. Their reward was not victory but the destruction of their civilization and its way of life.

The wiser among them recognized early the South's fatal weakness in depending upon outside suppliers "for everything from a hair-pin to a toothpick, and from a cradle to a coffin." But the euphoria of war excitement lulled most southerners into early complacency. "It is perfectly surprising how well we get along without Yankee notions," proclaimed the Charleston *Mercury* two months after the outbreak of hostilities. "It is surprising how little we really needed, or should have bought their jimcrackeries . . . We can supply every want as well as every need at home."

It took only a few more months to prove the folly of that statement. Shortages appeared first as inconveniences and turned quickly into severe hardships. The loss of cities and territory to invading armies aggravated the supply problem, as did the inevitable evils of hoarding and speculation. Loss of the Mississippi River isolated one half of the Confederacy and its productivity from the other. The naval blockade had the most devastating impact of all. Even within secure portions of the Confederacy, the overtaxed transportation system could not cope with the demands thrust upon it. The government's effort to solve the transportation problem deserved the criticism that "no department was worse neglected and mismanaged."

Southern railroads lacked sufficient locomotives, rolling stock, iron rail, and other equipment to service the region adequately in normal times, let alone provide for military and pressing supply needs. Equipment deteriorated under constant use and could not be replaced. Neither Tredegar nor smaller iron works could produce both locomotives and arms, and the latter had priority. Few cars were made, no rails were rolled, and both tools and skilled labor were scarce. Travel in the South became more horrendous than usual and came to a virtual standstill by mid-1864. Nor was travel by road any better. The government conscripted not only men but horses, mules, wagons, and carriages as well. Civilians were usually left the most decrepit animals and vehicles. According to one observer, a Richmond teamster changing horses merely "changed one skeleton for another."

These same shortages plagued industry and agriculture as well. The South's few factories lacked iron, lubricating oils, nails, screws, new parts to replace worn ones, even containers and sacks, and of course skilled labor. Available supplies disappeared quickly,

Drumming up recruits for the Confederate Army—a common scene in the early days of the war. Later, men—as well as horses and wagons—were conscripted. (Harper's Weekly, June 1, 1861)

little more could be produced, the military had first claim on what was produced, and effective substitutes could not always be found. Farms and plantations suffered not only the loss of draft animals but basic tools and implements, harnesses and saddles, rope, barrels, tubs, and kegs, and even such simple items as buckets and troughs.

Despite strenuous efforts to patch up old equipment and find substitute materials, factory and farm production dwindled steadily because of shortages. Even the elements conspired against farmers; droughts, floods, late freezes, and disease crippled food production in parts of the region during the war years. As in the North, women replaced men absent at the front, either running plantations or toiling in the fields of smaller farms. "Measuring corn, weighing shucks, and soaking wheat is a new business for me," wrote the mistress of a small North Carolina plantation in 1862. She had to supervise the planting, harvesting, and storing of crops, raising and slaughtering of hogs, wood cutting, spinning, weaving, and clothes making, as well as care for her two children and her slaves. Some women bore the enormous burden of work and responsibility nobly; others staggered under the load. One Georgia woman, left with a farm and four small children to tend, wrote her husband in 1862, "I am so tired for I never get any rest night or day, and I don't think I will last much longer."

Fires and war damage intensified these shortages. Natural conflagrations, and those touched off by shelling, destroyed vital factories, warehouses, and businesses. The fall of Nashville in 1862 cost the South an important industrial center just as the devastation of the Shenandoah Valley blighted the Confederacy's primary breadbasket. A fire lasting several days destroyed much of Charleston in December 1861, while smaller blazes consumed a Richmond warehouse filled with flour and the Bath Paper Mills in North Carolina. Another fire in 1863 severely damaged the Tredegar Iron Works and Crenshaw Woolen Mills in Richmond. Such losses could not be replaced and caused serious declines in production.

The South ran short of every necessity of life. Perhaps the war's cruelest irony was the spectacle of an agricultural nation unable to feed itself decently. Southern fire eaters had proclaimed cotton to be king, but cotton proved a poor monarch. It could not be eaten, nor could it be sold to obtain provisions.

Although some cities, notably Memphis and New Orleans, developed a lively trade in contraband cotton, the Confederacy was reduced to burning large quantities of cotton to prevent its capture by Union armies. A small Tennessee planter, watching Confederate troops burn his bales, mourned, "It was a sad thing to behold a body of armed men to roll out a man's whole dependence for money and the support of his family before his eyes, and cut it open and stick fire to it and he dare not open his mouth."

With their staple crops cut off from market, southerners shifted more of their land into food production. Yet even that did not alleviate the problem, for several reasons already mentioned: bad weather, lack of labor, tools, and even seed, loss of acreage to enemy armies, and inability to transport food supplies to where they were needed. Many people went hungry, and some were near starvation by the war's end. Areas near the front or in the line of advancing armies suffered worst as foraging troops from both sides picked these regions clean.

Cities also felt acute shortages as the transportation system broke down and neighboring farmers, fearing impressment, withheld their produce. Shortages of feed and salt created an acute lack of meat.

A cotton plantation on the Mississippi. The Confederacy, unable to sell its cotton, burned large quantities to prevent capture by Union armies. (Drawing by W. Walker; Currier & Ives print)

Since the salt problem was never adequately solved, pork and beef could not be preserved in any quantity even where it existed. Fish and fowl ran short as the demand increased while hunters and fishermen scrounged for ammunition and tackle. In desperation, people turned to every available substitute, including mule meat, rats, and occasional household pets.

One resident of Richmond marveled at the city's cleanliness, "everything being so cleanly consumed that no garbage or filth can accumulate." He quoted President Davis as approving the consumption of rats because they were "as good as squirrels." Ladies circulated recipes for them. In besieged Vicksburg they were standard fare; one lady saw them "hanging dressed in the market for sale . . . there is nothing else." Mule meat was more popular but also more expensive. In Savannah a furor arose over some men accused of butchering dogs and selling them as lamb.

Besides the persistent meat and salt problem, southerners ran short of many staples, including most

A Northern artist's imagined scene of the Richmond Bread Riot. Actually, the women took everything but bread in their looting of the stores. (Frank Leslie's Illustrated Newspaper, 1863)

fats: butter, oil, lard, and mayonnaise. The absence of two items, sugar and coffee, drew the loudest complaints. The sugar supply dwindled after the fall of New Orleans in 1862. Sorghum made a passable substitute, and prompted one lady to observe that "a history of the 'Southern Confederacy' would be incomplete without . . . mention of sorghum." No decent substitute for coffee was ever found, although southerners tried chicory, corn, rye, okra seed, peanuts, even sweet potatoes.

Lack of flour caused a shortage of bread, leading to the invention of "Secession Bread" made with rice flour. Fresh fruits and vegetables, condiments, flavorings, vinegar, baking soda, tea, and milk were among other items in short supply. In Richmond and other cities people kept gardens to assure themselves some fresh vegetables. Government clerk J.B. Jones noted of his own lot that "Every inch of ground is in cultivation—even the ash heap is covered all over with tomato vines." Yet in July 1863 Jones confided to his diary, "We are in a half-starving condition. I have lost twenty pounds and my wife and children are emaciated to some extent." By January 1865 he had grown desperate enough to write, "What I fear is starvation."

Everywhere southerners tried to ease the hunger that nagged at them. Young people in Richmond formed the "Starvation Club," which offered nourishment for the spirit if not the body: "money was contributed . . . for the music required for dancing; but all refreshments were strictly forbidden, and the only expense to the generous host . . . was an extra fire in the rear parlor, then not in every-day use, from the scarcity and high price of fuel." But gaiety did not always dispel the demons. In April 1863 a large crowd of women and children rioted for food and looted stores until troops and pleas by President Davis dispersed them. The "Bread Riots" so shocked the government that it asked the Richmond press "to avoid all reference directly or indirectly to the affair."

Clothing, housing, medicine, and household effects of every kind were as scarce as food. The term "substitute" came to tyrannize the lives of southerners. According to one estimate, southern women were compelled to "manufacture or devise a substitute for three-fourths of the articles in common use." Another observed that

If that era of home life had to be characterized by one word, there could be no choice as to the term 'substitute.' . . . There was hardly a tree or a plant that did not in the long run furnish a substitute, being laid under tribute to feed or clothe the people, or to cure their ailments.

Southerners leaving their home. Thousands of Southerners became refugees, fleeing toward Texas or some remote corner of the Confederacy alongside laden wagons. (Library of Congress)

The list ran well beyond trees and plants. When their wardrobes could be patched no longer, women resorted to everything from drapes to carpets. As one bit of doggerel ran, "Let me whisper: this dress, that I now wear for thee,/ Was a curtain of old, in Philadelphee!" The lack of shoes affected civilians almost as much as soldiers; inventive southerners used horsehide, dogskin, deerskin, pigskin, wood, and leather from worn articles and even book bindings. As clothing grew short, women took up spinning, weaving, and knitting with a vengeance. In 1862 one patriotic girl wrote a popular ditty entitled "Homespun Dress" which included these lines:

My homespun dress is plain, I know;
My hat's palmetto, too;
But then it shows what Southern girls
For Southern rights will do.

The shortage of drugs and medicines, especially quinine, caused great hardship in a region susceptible to fever epidemics. By 1864 quinine cost $100 an ounce in Louisiana—when it could be obtained at all. One planter immunized his slaves from smallpox with the vaccination scabs from his own family. In their desperate search for substitutes people turned to Doctors too were hard to find, many having joined

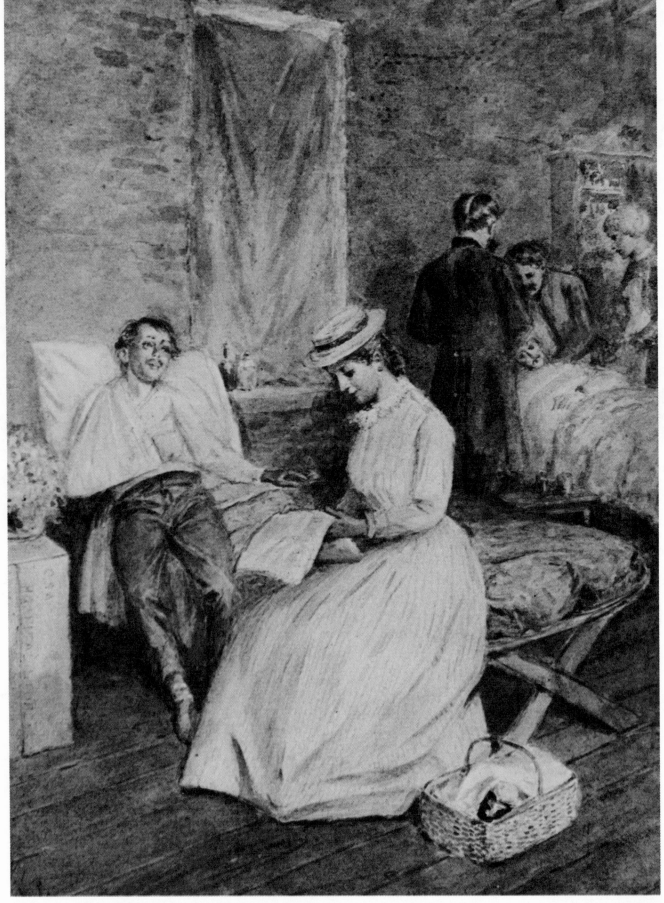

William Ludwell Sheppard's watercolor "In the Hospital, 1861," preserved in the Museum of the Confederacy in Richmond, shows the early wartime spirit of Southern women who volunteered to work with the wounded. The biggest killers of troops were not bullets but sickness and disease.

nostrums of every kind, especially herbs. "The woods . . . were . . . our drug store," declared one southerner. A book entitled *Resources of Southern Fields and Forests*, published in 1863 by Dr. Francis Porcher, became popular, but in the end no reliable substitutes for quinine, morphine, and chloroform were found. the army. As Mary Elizabeth Massey concluded, "Imaginary ills were about all that could have been cured with Confederate medicines."

Ordinary household needs, like candles, matches, utensils, linens, soap, bedding, furnishings, dishware, kettles, oil and gas for lighting, coal and wood for heating, and cutlery, were no less scarce. Lack of paper crippled newspapers and forced them to resort to wallpaper or anything they could obtain. Some editions appeared in every color of the rainbow, while others suspended publication for want of paper or ink. Publishers and magazines also closed down. No item was too small to run short. Needles grew precious and were carefully preserved, as were pins. In April 1863 J.B. Jones noted that "Pins are so scarce and costly, that it is now pretty general practice to stoop down and pick up any found in the street."

The twin evils of inflation and profiteering aggravated the problem of shortages. As always scarcity drove the price of commodities up, especially in cities. Even worse, the value of Confederate money declined as its gold supply vanished and the exigencies of war compelled the government to crank out ever more paper money. In January 1862 it took $120 in Confederate currency to buy $100 in gold. That figure soared to $1,800 in January 1864, $3,400 in January 1865, and $5,500 by the time of Appomattox. By the end of 1863 about $730 million in Confederate notes circulated; during the last two years of war that amount more than doubled.

Skyrocketing prices hurt everyone, especially wage

The folding room of the Currency Bureau. As the South's gold supply vanished and as ever more paper money had to be printed, the value of Confederate money fell. (CWTI Collection)

172

earners and those on fixed salaries. Robert Kean, a government employee, complained in October 1863 that "My salary of $3000 goes about as far as $300 would in ordinary times in purchasing all the articles of household necessity. . . . There is already great suffering among clerks, who get $1500." A few months later J.B. Jones wrote, "With flour at $200 a barrel, meal $20 per bushel and meat from $2 to $5 a pound what income would suffice?" By 1865 flour had gone past $1,000 a barrel, meal $100 a bushel, and bacon $20 a pound. Poor people suffered grievously, but public opinion turned against attempts by workers to strike for higher wages. The government responded by drafting strikers into the army.

Profiteering took its toll, although few businessmen reaped fortunes from government contracts. Clement Eaton explained why: "Government contracts had many disadvantages which deterred businessmen from seeking them. Notably the failure of the government to pay its bills." Yet enough profiteering occurred to prompt General Josiah Gorgas to complain in 1863 that "The sins of the people of Charleston may cause that city to fall; it is full of rotteness, every one being engaged in speculation." A year later a Catholic chaplain in Lee's army confided, "Never had I seen such avariciousness as that displayed throughout my travels, but more particularly in Georgia. Money and negroes appeared to be their gods."

As inflation worsened, many people resorted to barter. In New Orleans a woman swapped her $600 bonnet for five turkeys. Doctors took provisions for treatment and schools for tuition. Newspapers were filled with notices like the following from the Savannah *Republican*:

> I will barter salt from my salt factory for produce on the following terms: salt, 50 pounds per bushel; 4 bushels salt for 5 bushels of corn and peas; 1 bushel salt for 5 pounds of lard or bacon; 2 bushels salt for 7 pounds of sugar; 10 bushels of salt for a barrel of 'super' flour; 2 bushels of salt for 1 pr. of shoes.

One observer declared that in 1864 and 1865 bartering was the "best mode of getting supplies and those . . . [with] things to barter fare well."

The atmosphere of privation pervaded every corner of southern life. Higher education lacked students as well as materials. When no students appeared to begin the fall term at Centenary College in October 1861, the faculty secretary noted, "Students have all gone to war. College suspended: and God help the right." Other colleges, especially men's colleges, either closed down or struggled on despite declining enrollments.

Lower schools had a hard time keeping teachers and getting books and supplies. "I have the military fever very strong," one North Carolina teacher told his superintendent. Where possible women replaced men in the classroom, but several schools simply closed. A North Carolinian reported in 1862, "We have 4 or 5 female teachers in this county but not one male." Those schools remaining open often received new textbooks infused with patriotism. An arithmetic primer published in 1864 contained such problems as, "If one Confederate soldier can whip 7 Yankees, how many soldiers can whip 49 Yankees?" Rural districts suffered most from closing schools, as a Virginian lamented in January 1865:

> I live in a neighborhood where there are many children . . . growing up in ignorance, there having been no school in this part of the district since the winter of 1860 & 61. . . . The few persons able to school their children have sent them out of the district & thereby left it entirely in ignorance.

Amusements and entertainments were also hard to come by, and relied upon improvisation. The prohibition laws adopted by most states to conserve grain put a decided crimp in the pleasures of many people. Substitutes made as poor a showing as they were to make in the 1930's; one diarist complained in January 1862 that the Christmas eggnog was made "of borrowed whiskey with a strong flavor of turpentine." Country folk amused themselves in much the same ways they always had, except that lack of ammunition curtailed hunting and scarcity of horses put a damper on racing. Traveling shows had seldom come to the rural South anyway because of its sparse population. The larger towns received an occasional troupe of minstrels, tumblers, magicians, or solo performers like "Blind Tom," the celebrated black pianist. Many communities put on their own entertainments, often as war benefits. One such show in Uniontown, Alabama, charged for admission "$2 or a pair of socks."

Even the larger cities offered little of the gaiety or glitter found in the North. Theatre struggled to remain afloat despite the turmoil of war. In Montgomery, Alabama, the local theatre ran a full schedule of thirteen shows as late as 1864, while in Richmond two years earlier a newspaper had mourned that "The legitimate Drama has been laid on the shelf." Dinner parties went on despite lack of provisions, and there were occasional concerts, balls, and parties. The social ritual of visiting and the usual parlor entertainments continued, but the war cast its gloom even there. "We all tried to be gay, but our hearts were inwardly sad," recalled Senator Thomas J. Semmes of Louisiana. "There was the usual visiting . . . but the old brilliancy and fire were fast ebbing away."

The bar of the Spotswood Hotel, the hostelry used by Lee and other notables in their Richmond visits. (Harper's Weekly)

Southerners found it difficult to escape into gaiety, especially when, as in Richmond, the horrors of war pressed so near. Constance Cary Harrison recalled the scene in that city after the battle of Seven Pines in 1862:

During the night began the ghastly procession of wounded brought in from the field. Every vehicle the city could produce supplemented the military ambulences. . . . All next day, women with white faces flitted bareheaded through the streets and hospitals looking for their own. Churches and lecture-rooms were thrown open for volunteer ladies sewing and filling the rough beds called for by the surgeons. There was not enough of *anything* to meet the sudden appalling call of many strong men stricken unto death. . . . We tramped down Main Street through the hot sun over burning pavements from one scene of horror to another, bringing up finally at the St. Charles Hotel, a large old building. What a sight met our eyes! Men in every stage of mutilation, lying waiting for the surgeons upon bare boards. . . . Some gave up the weary ghost as we passed them by. All were suffering keenly and needed ordinary attention. . . .

The impression of that day was ineffaceable. It left me permanently convinced that nothing is worth war!

Tragedy and sorrow came in many forms. A brief entry in the diary of Mary Boykin Chesnut offered

View of Washington Monument in Capitol Square, Richmond. Like most rural areas, Southern cities felt acute shortages of food and other necessities. (Battles & Leaders of the Civil War)

one poignant example late in 1863: "Mrs. Rooney Lee is dead. One of her babies died too. She was not twenty-three. He is a prisoner still."

The incessant ordeal of sacrifice and sorrow gradually wore down southern morale. As the bloody conflict dragged on, the bravura and excitement of 1861 gave way to anxiety and then despair. Even southern women, who had done so much to stiffen the backbone of resistance with their determination, began to lose heart. They endured not only work and hardship but mental anguish. One woman who had five sons in the army confessed in 1864, "I lie awake night after night, count each stroke of the clock, dread both night and day, tremble to open a letter." One woman lost all seven of her sons in the war, another lost five, and a third had four sons killed at Gettysburg.

Some bore their pain and continued to support the cause. But by 1864, when shortages had grown acute and northern troops had penetrated deep into the South, many women pleaded with their sons and husbands to desert and come home. The effect of their letters upon army morale was devastating. Even women of high station lost the will to resist. Mary Boykin Chesnut wondered in July 1864, "Is anything worth it—this fearful sacrifice; this awful penalty we pay for war?" Mrs. Roger A. Pryor, an officer's wife, admitted that "I am for a tidal wave of peace—and I am not alone."

Religion helped many people sustain their courage. Although a majority of southerners were not church members in 1860, most of them were Christians. All the denominations and their clergy staunchly supported the Confederate cause, and periodic revivals swept up thousands of soldiers and civilians alike in

As the Civil War neared its end, sometimes the tables turned in Southern society. Here, still-loyal blacks hide their "master" from Union troops. (Library of Congress)

Ruins of the Exchange Bank, Richmond. When the city finally fell to Union troops in April 1865, the entire business district was burned. (Library of Congress)

Ruins in Richmond. Although the Civil War broke the South's economic and political power, many Southerners remained determined to maintain the region's way of life. (CWTI Collection)

dedication to God and to what Governor Pickens of South Carolina called "a holy war." Mary Boykin Chesnut came away from church one Sunday exclaiming, "What a sermon! The preacher stirred my blood. . . . A red hot glow of patriotism spread through me." English correspondent William H. Russell declared that "Southern faith is indomitable." At least one Confederate general thought this religious zeal exerted too blinding an effect upon political and military issues. "I can only account for it," Edward Porter Alexander wrote years later, "in the general religious character of our people. They believed in a God who . . . in the end brought the right to prevail. They *knew* they were right & they were! It was only waiting on God, a little more or less."

One other anxiety preyed upon southern minds during the war. As Mary Boykin Chesnut observed in 1865, "The fidelity of the Negroes is the principal topic everywhere." Recalling the bloodbath in Santo Domingo, southerners were haunted by the spectre of slave insurrections. But on the whole blacks remained peaceful and loyal. In the interior their lives scarcely changed except for slimmer rations and more work. The approach of Federal armies prompted

thousands to flee to liberation, yet a surprising number remained on the old homestead even after freedom. Some took advantage of the men's absence to bargain for extra privileges or slack off from work. Women in charge of plantations could not always keep taut rein on the field hands. As one Texas woman wrote her husband, "I shall say nothing if they stop work entirely . . . [and] will try to feel thankful if they let me alone."

The people of the South lived intimately with war. They had underestimated its horrors and miscalculated their chances of survival. What began as a lark or crusade ended in tragedy and destruction. Wigfall had been right: southerners were a peculiar people. And in choosing to go to war with the North, they paid a terrible price for their peculiarities. By 1865 the Confederacy had become a land of misery, filled with ghosts that would stalk the region for years. While the North celebrated its victory, southerners mourned the death of history. Henry Timrod, the South Carolina poet, left them an epitaph:

Sleep sweetly in your humble graves,
Sleep, martyrs of a fallen cause.

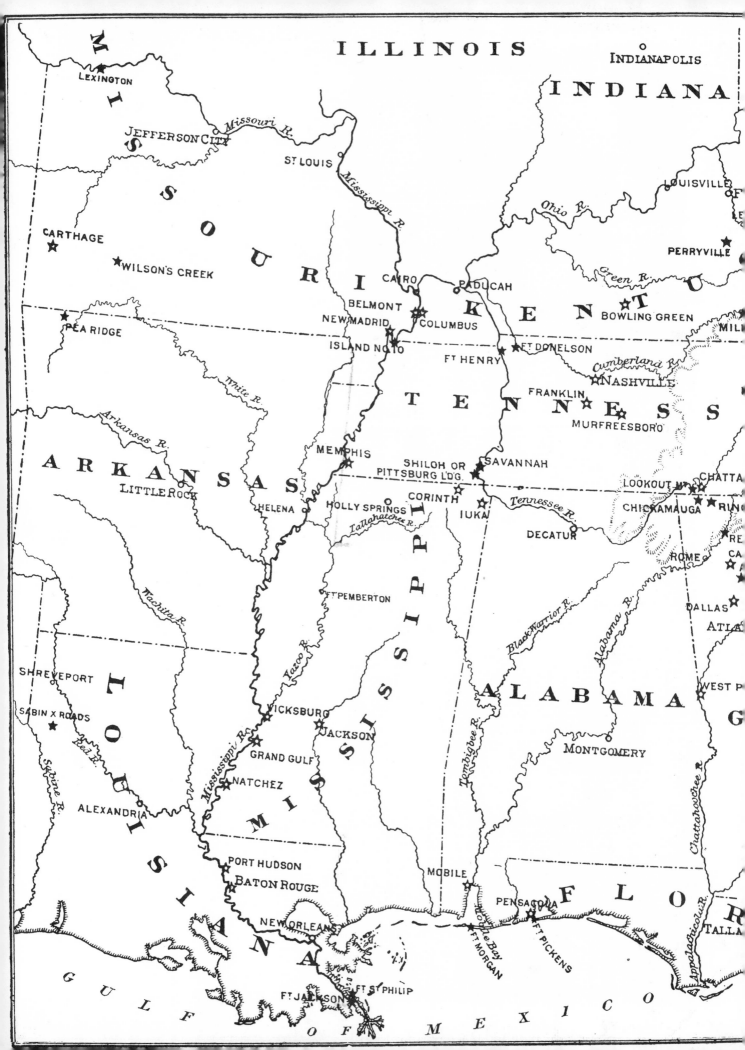